KARL-ERIK SVEIBY has for several years been Professor of Knowledge Management at Hanken Business School, Finland, and Honorary Professor at Griffith Graduate School of Management, Brisbane, and at Macquarie Graduate School of Management, Sydney. He is the author of twelve books on business and management.

TEX SKUTHORPE is a Nhunggabarra man from Nhunggal country in northwestern New South Wales and a painter, educator and custodian of traditional stories. He was awarded Aboriginal Artist of the Year by NAIDOC in 1990/1991 and currently works with young Aboriginal offenders in Kariong correctional centre, New South Wales.

TREADING LIGHTLY

The hidden wisdom of the world's oldest people

**Karl-Erik Sveiby &
Tex Skuthorpe**

ALLEN&UNWIN

Allen & Unwin
83 Alexander Street
Crows Nest NSW 2065
Australia
Phone: (61 2) 8425 0100
Fax: (61 2) 9906 2218
Email: info@allenandunwin.com
Web: www.allenandunwin.com

National Library of Australia
Cataloguing-in-Publication entry:

Sveiby, Karl Erik.
  Treading lightly : the hidden wisdom of the world's oldest people.

  Bibliography.
  Includes index.
  ISBN 1 74114 874 X.

  1. Sustainable development. 2. Aborigines, Australian - Social life
  and customs. I. Skuthorpe, Tex. II. Title.

305.89915

Set in 12/16 pt Filosofia by Bookhouse, Sydney
Printed and bound in Australia by Griffin Press

10 9 8 7 6 5 4 3 2 1

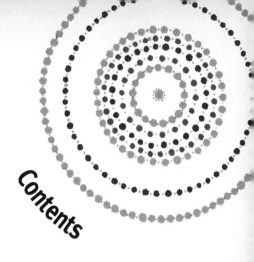

Contents

Nhunggabarra Stories

Paintings by Tex Skuthorpe

See also colour plates in the centre of the book

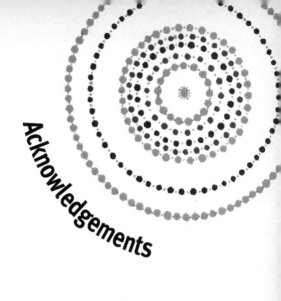

Acknowledgements

We acknowledge with great gratitude our partners in spirit, love and work, Anne Morrill and Dr Kati Laine-Sveiby. Anne, long before we met, had an unshakable belief in the power of the Nhunggabarra concepts for society and today's organisations. It is her knowledge of management and organisations that has allowed her and Tex to bridge the seemingly irreconcilable gap between traditional Aboriginal concepts and business, and to design seminars that managers can relate to. Without her dedication and work this book would not exist.

Kati, with her wealth of knowledge about ethnology and ethnological methods, has been an invaluable, frank and encouraging working partner all the way. She has discussed every idea and concept in the book; her eyes have seen every word, her hand has touched every page.

We are very grateful to Peter and Abigail Dyson, Christer Jacobson and Pat Sullivan, who have been part of the project from the start; they have walked some of the learning tracks with us and their long managerial experience has been valuable to test the validity of the concepts for modern-day organisations and societies. They were also with us during our first walks to the sacred sites, and Pat gave the manuscript a kick in the right direction. Also Tom Lloyd gave valuable ideas at an early stage of the manuscript. Thank you!

The assistance of Dr Philip Clarke, Head of Anthropology at the South Australian Museum, has been greatly appreciated. He put Karl-Erik on the right track at the beginning of the project and he has given detailed and helpful feedback on the manuscript.

We thank Trevor Winne for his help in painting *Vision for a Sustainable Planet*, and Christer Jacobson and Pat Sullivan for permission to reproduce the paintings *Baayami, the Giant Crocodile and the Two Women* and *The Creation*, respectively.

We are particularly indebted to Dr Jared Diamond. His books have been an inspiration and we thank him for his willingness to share his wealth of knowledge on diseases in ancient cultures.

Brother John Giacon and Ian Sim have put a lot of effort into helping us with the spelling of words in the Yuwaalayaay/Yuwaalaraay language. We are grateful to them for their help.

Senior Collection Manager Melanie Raberts, Senior Curator Dr Ron Vanderwal and Collection Manager Simon Greenwood at Museum Victoria have been most helpful. Thank you for your insightful discussions about cylcons and your help with sources.

Special thanks go to the Member for Finland of the European Parliament and presidential candidate Henrik Lax, who has helped us see the relevance of the Nhunggabarra concepts for the European Union. Thanks also go to Professor Andreas Suchanek for the opportunity to bounce ideas about the relevance of Nhunggabarra concepts for modern society.

Thank you Karolina Sveiby and Lotta Jacobson for your enthusiasm and belief in the validity of the ideas for a young generation. Karolina was with us in the very beginning and helped us model our ideas into a book.

Karl-Erik has presented many of the ideas in the book to colleagues and doctoral students at Hanken Business School, who have given useful feedback and many suggestions. We are especially grateful to Professor Jeff Hearn for generously sharing his knowledge on gender issues in society and to Professor Guy Ahonen for his help with sources and his commentaries on intangibles.

Thank you Elizabeth Weiss and Colette Vella at Allen & Unwin for your help and advice on the final draft and to Andrew Bell, who photographed the paintings.

Above all, we are indebted to the Nhunggabarra Ancestors, who kept their wisdom alive for countless generations. Thank you for the Knowledge.

Dear Euluwirri,

You, whose name means Rainbow, you are all colours in one. This is a book not only for you, but for all the young of all the colours on Earth. You are the future custodians of the world, and now is the time to learn from the past.

Sometimes one starts a journey knowing neither its purpose nor its goal. One only knows that one has to go because it touches one's soul. Then the track takes over; it becomes a journey of discovery. This book has been such a journey for me, one that has taken me to unexpected places.

I did not plan to write about the validity for today of the world's longest record for sustainability when I started this journey, or about the world's first model for organising — it was the learning tracks of your Ancestors that led me here.

It has been a humbling experience. The discovery, or rather the re-discovery, of your Ancestors' wisdom filled me with a deep sense of respect — for their knowledge, for the eternal validity of their wisdom and above all for the humanity of their society. The industrialised world is primitive by comparison.

It has been a privilege to work with your great-uncle and an honour to walk the learning tracks of your Ancestors.

Yours,

Karl-Erik Sveiby

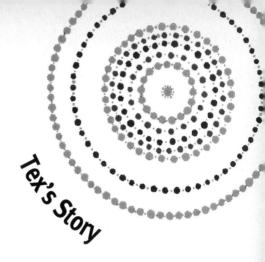

Tex's Story

THE MOST AMAZING JOURNEY OF MY life has been learning about my culture
from the old people. They were so strong in their traditions and belief
and through their teachings they have passed them on to me. I watched
them live the messages in the traditional stories, watched them
demonstrate how to live in a community and how to keep everyone
safe. Colour was not an issue to them – they truly believed everyone
living on their country was meant to be there and, as such, was part
of their community. As I got older I began asking myself, 'How could
they believe in themselves and their traditions, in the face of so much
hardship and disrespect?' They worked to keep everyone safe – not
just the Nhunggabarra people.

I came to learn that everyone in that community had a role: even
though some of the people were from different areas, they were all a
part of that community and their main role was to look after us – the
young people. They lived their belief that their role and responsibility
was to show us how to show respect to ourselves and our beliefs, so
that we could then, and only then, show respect to others and their
beliefs.

I remember two old blokes who showed me what this responsibility
was all about. One, with his sons, would hold regular corroborrees and

dance some of the stories. As he danced he would explain where the story came from, what part of the country it related to and what you could and could not do at that place. The other old bloke would, every afternoon, stand on a mound in the reserve and shout out every kid's name and tell us what laws we had broken that day – first in his language and then in English. When I got home, my granny would tell me the stories again and explain what laws I had broken. But it never felt like a punishment. I always felt it was about teaching me.

No one paid those old men or gave them any recognition for what they were doing – they didn't need it. It was their role.

Seeing this made me want to know more about how they were able to keep the knowledge alive and how they kept it true, how they kept the respect alive. Others were interested in language but my interest, even as a very young boy, was always in our ancestors' knowledge and the strength that those old people got from it.

My own journey of knowledge has continued with the work on this book. Karl-Erik has, from our first meeting, consistently shown respect to the knowledge those old people passed on. He has shown it in so many ways – through listening, through enduring some hardship on our 'journeys', through struggling to pull meaning out of stories, but most of all through showing himself and his beliefs, so that I can understand and show respect to him and his belief.

That is why I am co-writing this book. It is my humble attempt to explain in words and paintings what I have learned from the old people. This is my way of showing respect.

Tex Skuthorpe

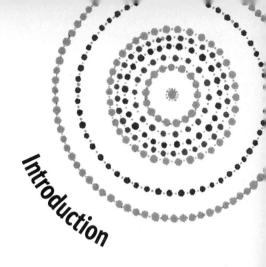

Introduction

THIS BOOK STARTED BACK IN 1999 when Karl-Erik asked Tex: 'What is the word for knowledge in your Aboriginal language?' 'We don't have a word for it,' Tex replied.

He must have felt Karl-Erik's disbelieving look. Struggling to find the words he continued: 'Our land is our knowledge, we walk on the knowledge, we dwell in the knowledge, we live in our thesaurus, we walk in our Bible every day of our lives. Everything is knowledge. We don't need a word for knowledge, I guess. Maybe that's why.'

Tex is a Nhunggabarra man, painter and storyteller from north-western New South Wales in Australia and Karl-Erik is a Swedish professor in knowledge management who currently lives in Finland. This was the first time we met, and Tex's answer was so unexpected and so intriguing that Karl-Erik immediately became interested in learning more about the Nhunggabarra Aboriginal people.

There was in particular one issue that gradually took hold of Karl-Erik and which in the end became the topic of this book: *Australian Aboriginal society's model for sustainability has the longest proven track record on earth.* While societies outside Australia emerged, prospered and went under, Aboriginal society withstood and proved its sustainability over tens of thousands of years of dramatic events, until the

Europeans' arrival in 1788. It is an extraordinary achievement, espe-cially considering that this is something humanity is now struggling with: the way to build a truly sustainable society on this earth.

How did the Aborigines do it? How did they organise for sustain-ability? What type of leadership did it require? They must have had a 'recipe for success'. What was it? Could we reconstruct it?

But how does one reconstruct something that was lost 200 years ago and where practically all sources and written reports are from a younger date? It would be an impossible task were it not for a unique source: the Nhunggabarra stories.

Tex's role is to learn, record and teach the traditional stories that contain the Nhunggabarra Law. He got this role because both his father and his mother were the eldest of their families and because both were law totems. If Tex had not had this specific kinship heritage, he would not have been allowed to co-write this book. The 'story owns the storyteller', not the other way around.

He is also one of the few Aboriginal people in Australia and the only Nhunggabarra person of his generation to have learned the stories in the traditional, 'hard', intellectually challenging way, from the original custodians – his father and his maternal grandmother (who died in 1972 aged 96). This learning allowed him to open up the hidden treasure chest of information contained in each of the stories. This method of interpreting the stories has been a well-kept secret until this day.

Our book is, as far as we know, the first serious attempt to use Aboriginal traditional stories for their original purpose: to convey knowledge from one generation to another, about the world, the law, society and the life and death of people.

A KNOWLEDGE-BASED ECONOMY

A Nhunggabarra law story is like a time capsule. It has travelled through the disturbances of the 19th and 20th centuries virtually untouched. It can thus be a more reliable source about how Aboriginal society was meant to function than many European eyewitness reports. The stories tell of what was once a shared understanding of how to behave as an ideal Nhunggabarra person. This is the value of the law stories for our purpose: they contain the rules that governed Nhunggabarra society, the 'recipe of success' that we reconstruct in this book.

The trouble for all studies of Aboriginal society, especially in the Australian southeast, is that so much of the original knowledge was lost very soon after the Europeans arrived on the continent due to the epidemic diseases unwittingly introduced by the explorers, soldiers and settlers. Maybe half the Aboriginal population of the southeast – some sources suggest even higher casualty numbers – succumbed within a few years of the first settlement.

Apart from the incomprehensible suffering experienced by the people, a large part of their enormously rich, intangible asset base disappeared. The earliest settlers and the first anthropologists did not realise that they were only observing the fragments of collapsed societies that no longer functioned as they once did. And what they saw they could not comprehend, because they could not free themselves from their own cultural blinders. This means that the Aboriginal people were from the first encounter defined from a 'deficiency perspective' – they were lacking technology, lacking agriculture, lacking housing, lacking clothing etc. It was even believed they were lacking leaders.

We have instead approached traditional Aboriginal society from a much more plausible perspective: they knew what they were doing. The combination of the insider, Tex, and the outsider, Karl-Erik, has allowed us gradually, piece by piece, to reconstruct the Nhunggabarra model for sustainability.

The most striking feature of the Nhunggabarra society is their *knowledge-based economy*. Because food and handmade tools were the only production scientists and economists have recognised and have been able to measure, they have long dismissed Aboriginal economy as producing very little of any value. What they have missed is more than half of the Aboriginal economy: the very high production of *intangible value*, such as education, knowledge, art, law, entertainment, medicine, spiritual ceremonies, peacekeeping and social welfare.

The Aboriginals' farming methods were built on intimate knowledge of the ecology of the land, so they were indistinguishable from nature itself. They were treading lightly on earth; consequently, they were long dismissed as 'primitive' both by arriving settlers and by scientists up to our present day. It is only due to the very latest advances in ecological science that their methods are now being recognised. The Aboriginal people created the world's first systematic approach to *ecofarming*. We will explore their intangible economy, ecofarming methods and even *intangible trade* thoroughly in the book.

Karl-Erik gradually realised that the Nhunggabarra principles for organising society were *context-specific leadership* and *knowledge-based organising*. Everyone in society had a leadership role in a specific area of knowledge, and the leader role shifted depending on the context and who, within that context, was the most knowledgeable. This is a highly advanced form of leadership, found primarily in high-performing teams and in knowledge-intensive organisations. It was unknown to the English military commanders who arrived on the Australian continent and its significance has not been understood among other observers until this day.

Together with spiritual principles that emphasised the *interconnectedness* of all and everything, these economic, ecological and social principles were the main ingredients of the Nhunggabarra society's 'recipe' for sustainability.

Focusing on one single community has enabled us to understand and to reconstruct the model as a whole. The focus is our method for research: we are not suggesting that the Nhunggabarra people were uniquely successful or 'better' than other Aboriginal communities. We believe that there is much in this book that is general for many Aboriginal communities across Australia and we have used this belief as a source of inspiration, but we do not try to generalise – that is not our purpose.

ABOUT METHOD AND SOURCES

The 'Further Reading and Research Notes' section of this book contains background material, analytical materials, notes, references and a critique of sources. The notes are organised on a per-chapter basis and we recommend that you keep an eye on them while you read.

The approach in this book is an attempt to 'make sense' of traditional Aboriginal knowledge from an organisation and society perspective. The content and interpretation of the stories form the core, and written sources, interviews and site visits complement the stories. Our 'walkabouts' on the learning tracks of Tex's ancestors in Nhunggal country have been a crucial element. They have added greatly to Karl-Erik's understanding of Nhunggabarra culture and have contributed to several of the key findings in the book.

The analysis is primarily based on qualitative data and the main sources come from oral tradition. For this reason, reliability and validity merit special attention. The methodological approach is to combine the Nhunggabarra stories with as many different sources as possible: written sources, site visits and interviews. Wherever possible, at least three sources have been combined: a story, a written source and a visit to the site in the story. It is a validation method familiar to qualitative researchers and is known as triangulation.

We have also discussed interpretations thoroughly. In situations where the sources are in conflict or when interpretations do not agree, one interpretation has been selected in the main text and the alternatives have been commented upon in the notes. Data with only one source have been flagged in the text.

The process of producing the book has been as follows: Tex concentrated on expressing the stories in a written form with the help of his partner Anne Morrill (many of the stories had never been put to paper before). He simultaneously made the paintings that are found in the book; the painting process also helped him to remember the stories better. Karl-Erik focused on reading the written sources available in the AIATSIS library in Canberra and the state libraries and museums in Sydney, Melbourne, Adelaide and Brisbane.

Tex would tell a story and describe his painting for Karl-Erik. Karl-Erik then went to the written sources to find something that confirmed or rejected the interpretations. Sometimes it was the other way around – Karl-Erik found something in the written sources that might be relevant and Tex confirmed or rejected it, based on the stories and his knowledge of the Nhunggabarra traditions.

This is not a book about the supernatural and spirituality. We are, however, of the belief that in dealing with Aboriginal traditional knowledge one must have an open mind, so Karl-Erik was prepared to test alternative methods for seeking knowledge.

This means that our personal learning tracks have taken us out of our comfort zones. Karl-Erik has felt compelled to test unconventional methods and to travel to places uncommon and sometimes uncomfortable for a scholar in organisation theory and business administration – in both a geographical and a knowledge sense. Tex has had his traditional knowledge tested and questioned by the unforgiving methods of scientific enquiry and he has challenged his fears by climbing Wubi-Wubi Mountain for the first time.

We start the book by describing the Nhunggabarra worldview and their spiritual beliefs from the Time of Creation – the *Burruguu*. In the second chapter we take the reader along one of the *learning tracks*, which combines knowledge of the land and the spiritual world, and here we also describe country, population and language. In chapter three we uncover the Nhunggabarra art of four-level storytelling and in the fourth chapter we describe their learner-driver education system. We display their *ecofarming methods* in the fifth chapter, and in the sixth chapter we discuss leadership, organisation and the unique system for security and welfare: *tuckandee*. We even suggest a new hypothesis: that the Nhunggabarra and their neighbouring communities may have developed *a writing system*. In the seventh chapter we describe the spiritual *Fourth Level* knowledge and our own involuntary touch of it. In chapter eight we bring the reader to present times and compare the state of Nhunggal country today to that of yesterday. Chapter nine summarises our findings in a 'recipe' for *sustainable organisation and leadership*, and validates them. In chapter ten we offer a vision and make some concrete proposals for today's societies.

Tex has been holding the paintbrush, Karl-Erik the pen, so the 'I' in the text is Karl-Erik's voice.

Welcome! In the Nhunggabarra spirit, we thank you for the respect.

Karl-Erik Sveiby   and   *Tex Skuthorpe*
Helsinki, Finland   *Bucketty, NSW, Australia*

1

In the Beginning...

THIS IS WHERE IT ALL BEGAN.

Tex and I are standing at one of the sites of Creation. To me it does not look all that impressive.

STORY | THE RAINBOW SERPENT (PART 1)

The earth gave birth to a snake and it wriggled all over the earth making all the river beds as it went. The snake then asked for the frogs to be born. The frogs were born in sacks of water so the snake tickled them and made them laugh. They laughed so hard that the sacks burst, releasing the water and filling all the river beds. With the coming of water to the land, all the plants, trees, birds and animals were made.

A large mud flat expands in front of us. The mud is dry and hard and sun-cracked. A few small pools filled with fresh water are also visible. It is from them the Rainbow Serpent emerged when the earth gave birth to it.

It is a hot and dry day with a deep blue sky – one of many of these sorts of days in this part of Australia. A buubiyala tree stands in a clump of grass at one of the pools. Tex pulls down a branch with purple berries. They are ripening and their taste is sweet and cool. I venture closer to one of the pools of water, but I have to retreat rapidly when the mud beneath my feet unexpectedly turns soft and threatens to pull me down.

The small pools of water are not as innocent as they look. They are in fact the outlets of a deep underground lake, holes of water penetrating the mud. I suddenly understand why the mud flat is full of the whitened skeletal remains of wild goats. Seeking the precious water, they became stuck in the mud and perished.

The mud between the holes feels strangely wobbly under my feet. Tex jumps up and down and the water in the waterholes ripples. We are standing on water! He explains that the mud is at least five metres thick and covers an underground lake and a system of underground water channels, which are fed by the Culgoa River some 25 kilometres away.

The Rainbow Serpent is gone, but the frogs are still around every-where in the Nhunggal country, although we cannot see them. They sit at least one metre under the surface in their water sacks and breathe through an air canal, waiting for the next flood.

Must be a lonely frog life these days, with laughs few and far between.

BURRUGUU

It is impossible to even attempt to understand Australian Aboriginal people without first appreciating the fundamental difference between Western and Aboriginal thought paradigms. Westerners, raised with a Judaeo-Christian worldview, think of themselves as separate from the natural world in which they live. Aboriginal people considered themselves integrated with and part of the natural world.

The Aboriginal belief system is often referred to as the 'Dreaming' or the 'Dreamtime'. These terms were coined either by Aborigines in an attempt to communicate the content of their spirituality to non-Aboriginal English-speaking people, or by white people in an attempt to find words that capture the Aboriginal worldview. The words are misleading and do not accurately describe the Aboriginal concepts. We will therefore throughout the book use the Nhunggabarra term *Burruguu*, from the Yuwaalaraay language, which means approximately 'time of creation'. The Burruguu was a creative era when the Ancestors travelled the universe. Their travels, their fights, adventures and hunting made imprints on the earth's topography and created the landscape. These ancestral beings possessed superhuman powers, but they were subject to human traits, pleasures, desires and vices; they fought, quarrelled and made mistakes. Aborigines always refer to them as their 'Ancestors'; they were not gods.

When the Ancestors had created the earth they returned to the *Warrambul*, the sky world, where they still live. The earth that the Nhunggabarra walked on was the mirror of the Warrambul, the explicit and tangible expression of their Ancestors' intangible world. Every form thus had both a tangible and an intangible expression. Plants, animals, the soil, even a piece of rock had an intangible counterpart in the sky, just like the people.

For the Nhunggabarra and other Aboriginal people in the north-western part of New South Wales, the most powerful of the Burruguu Ancestors was *Baayami*. The early European settlers and missionaries, eager to find evidence of an Aboriginal 'religion', jumped to the erroneous conclusion that Baayami was the Aboriginal equivalent of the Christian God. The stories, when not distorted by European 'interpretations', however, show that this was not the case. For the Nhunggabarra, Baayami was the first initiated man made by the Creator and he was the 'law maker'. Before the Nhunggabarra people arrived on the scene, he laid out the customs and rules about social relationships to be followed by all the animals.

The Rainbow Serpent story also tells us that there was no difference between an Aboriginal person and an animal. Both were made of the same material as the earth. People and animals were equals, except that the Burruguu animals that had obeyed the law had been turned into people, while the animals that remained in their animal form were the ones that had broken the law.

STORY | THE RAINBOW SERPENT (PART 2)

In the Burruguu one of the laws that the animals learned was about certain places they could not go. Some of the animals broke the law by going to these places and they were turned into hills, mountains and valleys. These animals that broke the law became law totems. In Nhunggal country, the animal that broke the law was the long-neck turtle, and so he is the law totem for the Nhunggabarra people. The animals that did not break the law were turned into Aboriginal people. This is how Aboriginal people got all their different *yurrti* (totems) – from the animals who were rewarded and turned into people.

The Nhunggabarra did not worship any gods – not even nature spirits. Instead, for them every rock and every land form, every plant and every animal had its own consciousness, just as people did. Everything was 'alive'. Hence, every land formation and every creature on earth held hidden meanings. The Ancestors and the connection to the Burruguu were always present in the landscape for the Nhunggabarra people – thus their presence was felt concretely every day when the people walked their country. The Nhunggabarra were at any time able to connect to the spiritual world, either individually or collectively, through a whole range of means. The 'places they could not go' in the Rainbow Serpent story became the sacred sites, sites with a special spiritual connection. They could still be accessed, but only if the people performed the proper ceremonies to respect the law. The sacred sites were generally not visually distinguishable as particularly valuable or remarkable in the landscape.

Spiritual life was much more significant than material life for the Australian Aboriginal people. Instead of putting their surplus energy into squeezing more food out of the land, Aborigines expended it on

The Creation (Rainbow Serpent)

The Rainbow Serpent in the centre of the painting circles the springs, and the frogs sit in their sacks, waiting to be tickled. The animals and leaves symbolise the creation of life with the coming of water. The ant at the top of the painting and the circles of dots represent the birth of insects. The yellow dots among the leaves and frogs symbolise the mission to keep everything alive. The diamonds are one of Nhunggal country's traditional designs, being representative of the designs made by Baayami on the three sacred trees (see chapter two).

intangibles: spiritual, intellectual and artistic activities. They carried their palaces on their backs, their cathedrals were built in their minds and they felt no need to glorify human heroes. It is in the mind and the creativity of the spirit – in the intangible rather than the tangible artefacts – that Aboriginal society stands out.

The sensual lifestyle of the Aborigines, their deeply spiritual communication with the earth and their Ancestors, and their unshakeable belief in ancestral laws created a psychology that was completely disinterested in acquiring and possessing material things. Aboriginal 'high-technology' was largely intellectual and intangible.

Space-time

The Burruguu happened in what those in the West consider to be 'the past'. But for the Nhunggabarra there was no difference between past, present and future. The Burruguu still exists; it is the environment that the Aboriginal people lived in and still live in. Human life and being were as permanent, enduring and unchanging as the world itself. All things had always been the same. Thus people on earth did not create anything new. For the Nhunggabarra, the dynamics and changes that they experienced during their existence on earth were only illusions. An innovation was interpreted as merely the discovery of a feature that had always been there. New rituals and new songs – which, for Westerners, are the products of human creation – were for the Nhunggabarra clearer views of what had always been there.

As the Rainbow Serpent story tells, the Nhunggabarra believed that they had been created together with the landscape, so the past was not an issue. Their language did not even contain a word for time, nor did the Nhunggabarra people before European contact have a concept of time as a straight line. The present-day Western sense of time does not allow us to 'go back' to the past; we can only 'go forward' into the future. The Nhunggabarra and other Aboriginal people, on the other hand, conceived time not as a movement from past to future, but as a continuous channelling of consciousness from an intangible to a tangible and explicit expression. The rock in the landscape was the ongoing tangible expression of the rock's consciousness in the sky world, as it had been since the time of creation. It was the same with people, animals and vegetation. All were both in the sky world and here on earth simultaneously and they had always existed. In this sense the Burruguu was not in the past; it was always present, always 'here'. Western scholars have sometimes tried to understand the Aboriginal concept of time as *past in present*.

The Nhunggabarra also did not make a distinction between time and space in their language. The suffix *–baa* means both 'space of' and 'time of'. A combination of space and time baffles a person with a Western perspective. How could, for instance, the Nhunggabarra invite someone to a gathering to be held in the future if they did not have a concept of time? But they could. The Yolngu-speaking people of the Northern Territory, for example, tell time in terms of synchronicity: an event will happen when all or a sufficient number of conditions are met. Thus when a certain flower blooms in one place it is the appropriate time for harvesting in another; when the flowering of a certain tree occurs then yams are fully mature at a particular place.

It is likely that the Nhunggabarra used a similar method; for them it could have been the right time for the Big Buurra (initiation ceremony) when a certain fish appeared in the Narran River or had reached a minimum fat level.

The Nhunggabarra view of the universe is thus more sophisticated and advanced than it first appears, and is close to quantum physics and the theory of relativity. Time is regarded by quantum physicists as part of a space–time continuum, a concept that the West required an Einstein to discover (in 1905).

MISSION: KEEP ALL ALIVE

To the Nhunggabarra, the role of humanity was to maintain the world created in the Burruguu and to keep everybody and everything alive, including animals, vegetation, every feature of the earth, knowledge, even the Ancestors in the *Warrambul* (the Milky Way). The Nhunggabarra had to continue to tell the stories, and perform the dances and the ceremonies, or else the animals, the earth and the Ancestors would die. If they failed, say, to preserve the emu species on earth, the intangible spirit of the emu would also disappear from the spirit world and, because of the interconnectedness of everything, all the Aboriginal people of the emu totem on earth would also die. This enormous commitment put pressure on each individual and on the Nhunggabarra people as a whole.

Tex: *I remember this old bloke in the 1960s, who continued to perform the dance of the giant emu, a species that has been extinct for 20,000 years. Every year he dressed up and painted himself and performed the dance. He had the role to perform the dance and he was convinced that in doing so, he kept the giant emu alive in the Warrambul.*

The 'old bloke' showed what it was all about. When the Nhunggabarra performed the dances, sang the songs and told the stories it was not trivial entertainment; it was 'work' and a lifetime commitment. It was a mission.

The mission of the Nhunggabarra people was: to sustain the earth (the plants as well as the rocks and the soil), to keep the totems alive (the animals), and, last but not least, to 'sustain the mob' (to keep the Nhunggabarra people alive).

Sustaining the earth

The first European explorers in this region, Charles Sturt (in 1828–29) and Thomas Mitchell (in 1831 and 1835), travelled an Australian landscape untouched by white people. As it turned out they became the last white people to observe Aboriginal people living a traditional life in the region before diseases and settlers disrupted their societies.

This makes their journals invaluable for us when we are trying to understand traditional Aboriginal Australia.

Thomas Mitchell, who passed through Nhunggal country in June 1846, admired the parklands and open woodlands:

> I came to what seemed to me the finest region on earth: plains and downs of rich black mould, on which grew in profusion the panicum laevinode grass [wild millet grass], and which were finely interspersed with lines of wood which grew in the hollows, and marked the courses of streams; columns of smoke showed that the country was too good to be left uninhabited.

Neither the explorers, nor the early settlers who came after them, realised that much of the land and the vegetation they encountered was not natural, but altered by Aboriginal cultivation. The Australian landscape was to a large degree an Aboriginal artefact created by thousands of years of sustaining the earth.

The Aborigines used a wide range of tools for cultivation, both visible and invisible. The most visible and versatile tool in Aboriginal Australia was fire. The Nhunggabarra carried a burning fire stick with them everywhere on their walks, always ready to use. Cooking was only one application for fire. It deterred spirits from approaching camp at night. Smoke was the most popular insect repellent and hot ashes were applied to snake bites by some communities. Fire was used in the manufacture of spears. It provided illumination during moonless nights and a beacon was created by setting fire to a log. Fire was the primary source of warmth during cold nights and a tool in large-scale hunting, both to drive prey towards waiting hunters and for signalling. In some regions (not Nhunggal country) fire burned the dead.

The flat Nhunggal country was perfect for smoke signalling. Smoke signals acted like today's mobile phone: a group could, for instance, indicate the direction of their walk to other groups in the neighbour-hood, and hunters could coordinate their actions when hunting over long distances; the explorers reported that everywhere they travelled they were followed or preceded by smoke signals.

Above all the Aboriginal people burned the land. Fire was their main tool for tending the land: 'fire-stick farming'. Depending on the season, the skies in Nhunggal country were full of smoke from the fires burning off the vegetation. 'All the country beyond the river was in flames...the atmosphere had been so obscured by smoke, that I could never obtain a distinct view of the horizon', the explorer Thomas Mitchell noted in his journal on 23 December 1831.

The Nhunggabarra bushfires were nothing like the wild and uncontrollable fires that threaten human lives and property in the Australia of today. They were carefully managed to avoid killing the animals and the trees; the Aborigines knew how to manipulate fire frequency, intensity and timing to fit the ecosystem. Captain James Cook observed on his first trip to Australia that 'they produce fire with great facility and spread it in a wonderful manner'. Dame Mary Gilmore, the well-known Australian labour rights activist and author, lived not far from Nhunggal country as a child in the 1860s. She described vividly in her memoirs her experience of how expertly the Aborigines handled fire where she grew up. When there was a bushfire in the outback the white settlers would yell out: 'Call in the blacks!' She saw whole stations in full panic when there was a fire; the white men lost their nerves and exhausted themselves in frantic efforts to quench a fire. But as soon as the Aborigines arrived on the scene they would control it with ease.

Thousands of years of burning changed the Australian landscape, both intentionally and unintentionally. The fire-stick farming method that the Nhunggabarra and other Aboriginal people used had the effect of increasing both the amount of food available and the diversity of plants. It allowed certain fire-resistant species to prosper and it enabled the grasses to grow to the benefit of both grazing animals and people. The ash after fire-stick farming acted like manure and encouraged regrowth of eucalypts and of edible plant foods, such as millet grass, bracken roots and shoots. It generated the 'finest region on earth', as described by Thomas Mitchell.

Apart from through the use of fire, the earth was sustained through an invisible and even more important tool – the story. Telling stories kept alive the links between the earth and the animals, the people and the ancestral land in the Warrambul – the Milky Way. Without stories, the knowledge would die and when the knowledge was gone, everything else would die too.

Sustaining the animals

For the Aboriginal people, people and animals were one and the same. Thus, for Tex, who is of the sand goanna totem, it is just as correct to say that he *is* a sand goanna.

The sand goanna clan consisted of (still today) all the sand goanna totem people in Aboriginal Australia. They are all of the same kin. This means that Tex has relatives in every corner of Australia. All he needs to do on his journeys is to ask for the sand goannas and he will be accepted as a son by the oldest sand goanna couple and as a brother by the other sand goanna people.

The Nhunggabarra of all totems had to maintain and improve the habitats of all the plants that the animals fed from. They learned this by observing animal behaviours from a young age. Knowledge and rules of behaviour were also embedded in stories, dances and ceremonies.

It was the people's responsibility to keep this knowledge alive and in this way the animals were kept alive both on earth and in the Warrambul. In particular, they felt responsibility for their own totem animal. Hence, if the sand goanna disappeared from an area the sand goanna people would blame themselves; they would perform cere- monies to try to figure out where they had shown disrespect towards the knowledge and confront themselves with their mistakes.

The people formed a close relationship with their totem animals from a very early age; they often had dreams containing their totem and the sighting of their totem animal would always imply a meaning, which had to be interpreted. Consequently, they were highly motivated to safeguard and keep their totem animal alive – the ultimate threat was that if their animal became extinct then they would die too.

Nhunggabarra people used several methods to sustain and keep animals alive. They kept their fires low-intensity so that larger animals could flee and survive and, after firing, new grass could spring up and feed kangaroos and other herbivores. Some Nhunggabarra stories also outlined the rules for where and how areas were to be – or not to be – protected from hunting and other usage. This would have been the case all over Aboriginal Australia.

There was a dilemma in all this: how did the mission to keep all alive sit alongside the killing and eating of animals? For the Nhunggabarra, it was the same thing as killing and eating a brother or sister. Hunting and eating, particularly big game such as kangaroo and emu, were sacred acts. They had to kill the animals – their brethren – to survive, but they made sure that they only killed a minimum, and that they compensated the spirit of the animal they killed. Before the actual hunt, they performed a ceremony, which made up for the killing – an act of reciprocity. In the ceremony the Aboriginal men internalised the animal so that they *became* the animal in spirit. In this way the spirit life of the animal was extended in the men in exchange for its physical death.

MISSION ACCOMPLISHED – THEN WHAT?

The Nhunggabarra people believed they were created at the same time as the earth and their soul spirits lived forever. They did not believe in reincarnation; they had only one 'turn' in physical form on earth, during which they had a mission to complete. All individuals had their own personal role in their earthly life to help fulfil this mission. When they died their soul spirits left the body and went to the Warrambul, their intangible world in the sky.

No wonder the Nhunggabarra were not afraid of death. After their roles were completed on earth they could look forward to eternal life in the Warrambul, a place that was a mirror image of their Nhunggal country, with the same vegetation and all the animals; they would meet their dead parents and relatives again and they would finally get to see and meet the mythical Ancestors, whom they knew so well from the stories. They did not need a human authority to tell them this; they 'knew' it was true, because they had already visited the sky world in their dreams. There was no hell to fear; they did not believe in hell and so they did not have to fear punishment in the afterlife for sins committed on earth.

The crucial condition for a happy afterlife was that the proper ceremonies were held by the living to help the deceased's spirits to separate from the earth. A Nhunggabarra person had four spirits according to traditional belief: the soul, the totem, the shadow and the dream spirit. These contained the vital essence of a person, and the human body was merely the explicit tangible expression of one's spirits.

The soul was your 'self', the part of you that lives on forever. The totem was 'the animal that is you', both on earth and in the intangible ancestral world. The shadow spirit was active only during your existence on earth and could be sent out to influence other people. The dream spirit was also active only during your existence on earth. It could travel to the Warrambul to meet with the spirits and receive messages from them. These 'spirit travels' usually took place during sleep.

After death, the totem spirit and the shadow spirit were taken care of in ceremonies during the burial of the body. The soul spirit required a lot of support to find its way back to the Ancestors in the Warrambul and it would get lost unless the ceremonies were properly conducted. The successfully guided spirit of a dead person never returned to earth, but it kept in close contact with everything that went on and got in touch frequently with the living by communicating with the living's dream spirits.

The worst scenario a Nhunggabarra person could imagine was for their soul spirit to remain on earth; it was their nearest equivalent of hell. They had met those poor souls in their dream travels; they had heard stories about them, perhaps even seen one of them while awake. Traditionally, the adults would not have been scared by such encounters; these souls were to feel sorry for and to learn from, so the Nhunggabarra could avoid their mistakes.

The Nhunggabarra must of course have been terrified of what they had seen and heard could happen to lost souls and this put a lot of pressure on the relatives of a dead person. As a consequence, the ceremonies for guiding a dead person's soul were quite elaborate and lengthy; they could go for up to two years.

In pre-European times, the Nhunggabarra would have been encouraged from childhood to explore meditative states and to remember what they saw in dreams. They were taught how to behave when they met their Ancestors in the dreams and also how to protect themselves from spirits and the earth-bound ghosts, who would do their best to distort the Nhunggabarra person's travel. When a person woke up from such 'trips' they had had a deeply spiritual and emotional personal experience that reinforced their belief system. They would also often claim to have 'seen' something, sometimes of significance for the Nhunggabarra as a people.

2

The Country is a Story

AUSTRALIANS OF ALL COLOURS LOVE THEIR remarkable country, and no casual visitor returns from a visit to Australian landscapes untouched. It is a land of poetic quality, as encapsulated by Dorothea Mackellar in 1945:

I love a sunburnt country,
A land of sweeping plains,
Of ragged mountain ranges,
Of droughts and flooding rains.
I love her far horizons,
I love her jewel-sea,
Her beauty and her terror —
The wide brown land for me! . . .
An opal-hearted country,
A wilful, lavish land —
All you who have not loved her,
You will not understand —
Though earth holds many splendours
Wherever I may die,
I know to what brown country
My homing thoughts will fly.

The Australia of today is the world's driest inhabited continent; on over 75 per cent of its surface rainfall is exceeded by potential annual evaporation. Levels of Australian rainfall are also among the most varied in the world. In the dry heart a specialised fauna and flora is finetuned to survive the relentless vagaries of flood and drought, abundance and famine.

About 45 million years ago Australia severed its connection with Antarctica and started a journey northwards that still continues by about five centimetres per annum. The journey has been one from a well-watered, green and forested land to an arid, sunburnt country. This island is the youngest continent, yet it is composed of some of the oldest rocks known on earth and it has the longest fossil record of any land. The antiquity is clearly visible in the landscape: wind and water have flattened the land and leached the soil of nutrition.

The changes have been dramatic. Even as late (in geological terms) as 20,000 years ago, Australia looked nothing like it does today. Large proportions of the land the Aborigines of that time saw are now covered by sea; New Guinea was joined to Australia by a land bridge and the island of Tasmania was part of the mainland.

Between 30,000 and 50,000 years ago the climate was cooler and more humid than today.

Then, around 18,000 years ago the climate became warmer and very dry. It was a time when the Aborigines must have been trapped between rising seas and encroaching deserts. Many of them must have lost the land they had been occupying for generations.

Some 10,000 years ago the last remaining land bridge between the mainland and Tasmania became covered by the sea during high tide. Over a period of perhaps a few hundred years the crossings must have become increasingly dangerous and finally the Tasmanian Aborigines became the most isolated group of people on earth. The Papua New Guinea land bridge also disappeared and the exchanges of knowledge and people would have gradually stopped. Australia became cut off from the rest of the world at a time when agriculture began in the Fertile Crescent (present-day Iraq, Syria and Iran) around 11,000 years ago and initiated rapid change there. The peoples of Papua New Guinea began agriculture around 9000 years ago and agriculture later continued to the Pacific islands. But agriculture, and the sedentary life that accompanies it, never crossed the Torres Straits.

Australia's climate has for a long time been heavily influenced by the El Niño/La Niña Southern Oscillation, ENSO, which is a global pattern of oceanic and atmospheric temperature fluctuations. ENSO amplifies fluctuations in both temperatures and rainfall in an irregular and unforeseeable way in approximately ten- to fifteen-year cycles. For example, the township of Bourke, close to Nhunggal country, in the La Niña year of 1950 received 841 millimetres of rain instead of an average 347 millimetres; the following year it received only 217 millimetres. In 1982, which was an El Niño year, Bourke received only 162 millimetres, and in 1983, 552 millimetres.

Water is a rare resource in these regions, but western and northern New South Wales, where the Nhunggabarra lived, had the benefit of more water than their 'own' rain. The region is a low flatland criss-crossed by river beds, which in pre-European times flooded at regular intervals, with water coming from rains further north. Many of the river beds end in swamps and shallow lakes, which dry out between the floods. The settlers both in Queensland and in New South Wales needed the water for irrigation, so they altered the courses of rivers, pumped the water from the river, made weirs and drained the swamps and the lakes. As a consequence, the floods are smaller and more unpredictable these days, swamps have dried out and the micro climate of the region is probably somewhat drier and hotter than it was in pre-European times. The last big flood was in 1974.

The rapid change from drought to flood to drought makes Australia a fire-prone country. Vegetation flourishes extremely rapidly during the wet and then dies in the drought leaving a dry litter that makes large parts of the continent a virtual tinderbox. Australian animals have developed the same 'opportunistic' behaviour; rain immediately starts a breeding response in many animals. For instance, the long-haired rat can breed at a plague-like rate and devour everything in its way. These rats and other small marsupials provide food for predators, which in turn breed in greater numbers. When the rat boom is over, the following year, many of them perish.

The changes in climate were slow, but they must have had profound effects across all Aboriginal Australia on knowledge, economy and customs. Marriage patterns, languages, genetics, stories, the law – all must have been impacted. A people who had once sourced their stone axes from an area that had since become covered by the sea had to find a new source, for example. It is only possible to guess: anthropologists and archaeologists are yet to start even speculating about the effects of climate on the Aboriginal people.

LEARNING TRACKS IN THE LANDSCAPE

The Nhunggabarra were 'the people of Nhunggal country', an area between the Narran and the Bokhara rivers on the border of south Queensland and northwest New South Wales. The word originates from *nhungga*, a tree that is common in the area. It is an evergreen tree with bell-shaped flowers and it was a very important resource for the Nhunggabarra, who used every part of the tree.

The Nhunggabarra people's land is ancient not only in a geological sense. Nhunggal country's sacred places, just as other Australian Aboriginal places of significance, show evidence of tens of thousands of years of continued human and spiritual presence. The mood varies widely; from feel-good sites where you experience a sense of joy, through to sites where the serenity almost forces you to sit down in meditation; to landscapes where you sense that you are being observed; to definite no-go areas where you feel unease in the air and you know that you had better leave, and fast!

The world as we know it – a tangible world with material content – was of little importance to the Nhunggabarra. Instead, they were enthralled by their land's intangible properties. What they saw with their own eyes – the landscape, rock outcrops, plains, mountains and water holes – had been left behind by their Ancestors. The land gave them their food, but the Nhunggabarra were equally interested in its power to invoke the spiritual side of nature. The land was full of symbolic images reminding them about creation, immortality, sacred law and, most significantly, their role within the cosmic process itself. In a very deep sense, the land was a meaningful part of the people just as the people gave symbolic meaning to the land. With story, song and dance they accessed the spiritual power contained in the landscape. You therefore cannot speak of a place in their country without considering its spiritual associations, its *story*.

To the Nhunggabarra, almost every place in Nhunggal country had at least one story connection. The most sacred sites were not necessarily visually significant and they did not generally contain material traces of Nhunggabarra culture. The intangible features were the focal point.

During the course of any one year the people would revisit most of the sacred places and simultaneously recount the stories. The spiritual powers were accessed by performing the sacred ceremonies that were associated with the place while on site.

Links to the spiritual powers were also provided by the corroborees – light and entertaining learning events that would have been performed on almost a daily basis. What better place to retell the stories and perform the dance and songs but around the fire in the evening? Each evening added meaning to the site in the mind of each individual. The build up of daily events and evening performances added also a personal history trail of significant events to the ancestral landscape.

The Nhunggabarra stories linked together to form travel routes, which we have given the name 'learning tracks'. Combined, the learning tracks became a tightly knit, geographically based 'narrative map', which defined for every Nhunggabarra person what 'Nhunggal country' was. One's 'country' then, was the physical manifestation of the underlying stories. Nhunggal country began where the stories began and it ended where the stories ended.

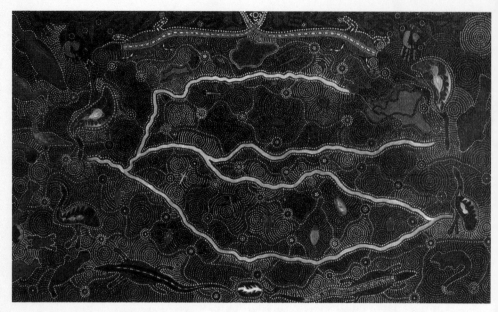

Map Over Nhunggal Country

Provided a person knew the stories and knew how to find the links, they could use the stories as reference sources or a 'map' to find their way across the country. The early explorers and settlers were amazed by the uncanny ability of the Aboriginal people to find their way in the Australian landscape, over very long distances. The explanation for their proficiency is simple: for them their country was a net of learning tracks memorised in body and mind from early childhood.

The Nhunggal country's borders were unmistakable for the educated men and women of the Nhunggabarra and their neighbours, whose stories also linked the borders of their land to those of Nhunggal country. But Nhunggal country's borders were invisible to the uneducated eye or to foreigners, who had travelled far beyond the reach of their own story trail. When a person did not know the stories they would not know the country and could inadvertently intrude upon a sacred place. Journeys outside one's country could thus be dangerous business. Explorer Thomas Mitchell at one point came across a group of Aborigines on the Darling River, who apparently had fled the outbreak of disease in their own country, and he noted that 'this distressed tribe were also strangers in the land, to which they had resorted. Their meekness, as aliens, and utter ignorance of the country they were in, were very unusual in natives, and excited our sympathy, especially when their demeanour was contrasted with the prouder bearing and intelligence of the natives of the plains'.

The custodianship of the land, the story, the songs and the associated ceremonies of a site all went hand in hand and was the highly regarded prerogative of the members of one particular family. Among the Nhunggabarra, custodianship was inherited via the mother's side. This meant that one would often be the custodian of a site in another country. For instance, the Nhunggabarra creation site we visited in chapter one was not in Nhunggal country. Likewise, on Nhunggal land there were sites under the custodianship of persons who originally came from another country. This added to the intricate pattern of interdependencies between the Nhunggabarra and their neighbours.

.

When Tex and I arrive at the two small ponds, they lie tranquil, shaded by big coolabah trees. Native ducks are swimming; there is green grass growing on the edges. It looks like the perfect spot for a family outing; an oasis in the midst of a dry dusty plain hidden only a few hundred metres off the main road. Still, there are no four-wheel drive tracks around the ponds, so people do not come here frequently.

Baayami passed here on his walk from the Angledool Lake to the Coocoran Lake when he created the bullroarer from three sacred trees (see the Big Buurra of Baayami story later in the chapter). The distance from the ponds to the Angledool Lakes is about fifteen kilometres and, according to another story, Baayami's track was visible as a path of white rock.

The Nhunggabarra kept the track clean to allow the white rock surface to glow in the sun, but mud from numerous floods and more than 150 years of debris now cover Baayami's tracks. Tex points to a shallow depression which forms a straight line heading towards Angledool. It shows signs of having been submerged under water during the latest flood. Somewhere under all the debris and mud there should be the white-rock path that Baayami created.

The Learning Track

The white learning track is visible in the middle. It was created when Baayami walked between the two lakes, represented by the two circles of dots. The leaves, the diamond designs and the bullroarers at the top and bottom of the painting symbolise the three sacred trees that were standing along this track. The fish and the cranes represent two other stories which occurred at the Coocoran Lake and at a waterhole near Angledool Lake, respectively. Baayami's track was regularly swept clean by the Nhunggabarra.

Can 'dowsing' help us locate the hidden path? This is a common practice in Sweden for detecting geomagnetic fields and for finding water, and I had become interested in the practice after a family friend showed me 'water divining' with a rod. The right spot to drill for a well at our holiday home was detected by a professional dowser fifteen years ago and the water still flows there today. There exist no references to magnetic fields in the Nhunggabarra stories. However, there is evidence from other sources that archaeological sites are sometimes distinguished by shifts in geomagnetic fields.

I start to walk slowly with my pendulum towards the gravel bed. The pendulum hangs motionless from my hand until I reach the boundary of the gravel bed. There, it first starts to swing back and forth, indicating a negative force field. When I move it into the gravel bed it immediately moves in a clockwise circular swing, indicating a positive field. I begin a slow walk on the gravel bed towards Angledool, and the pendulum keeps its positive swing. When I step across the boundary it immediately turns negative, briefly, and then stops. It seems that I have located a shift in geomagnetic energy here.

The energy shift may indicate the presence of a watercourse or a narrow rock plate under the soil with different magnetic properties than the surrounding rock. Whatever is underneath extends from the ponds in the direction of Angledool, which is the right direction, but I have no intention of continuing my slow walk along fifteen kilometres of dry country with a pendulum in my hand. Also, Tex and I do not have tools for digging, so we have to be satisfied with only the possibility that we have located the physical presence of Baayami's track.

THE NHUNGGABARRA: THE PEOPLE THAT 'DISAPPEARED'

The Nhunggabarra had several neighbouring communities in this area of flood plains and low ridges along the Culgoa, Birrie, Bokhara and Narran rivers and the Big Warrambool watercourse. We use the word 'community' throughout the book rather than 'tribe', which suffers from too many definitions and has even become a derogatory term.

The communities shared a fair measure of common cultural and linguistic background. Each community occupied its own country, with borders defined by the stories, but its members shared similar stories and spiritual views of life with the other communities. The people visited one another's countries more or less freely (provided they knew the proper border crossing ceremonies). They intermarried, got together to perform rituals and they supported each other socially and economically. In many ways the communities formed a type of 'union' or 'confederacy', although without the connotations of a central administration that the words carry. For want of a better word, 'cultural bloc' probably describes their relationships best.

According to Nhunggabarra oral tradition there were 26 communities in the cultural bloc and they populated an area roughly bounded by the Barwon River to the east, the Warrego River to the west, and the Bogan River to the south.

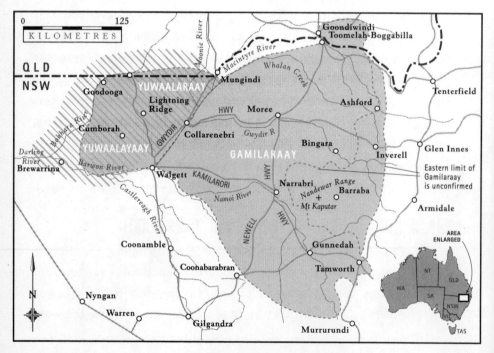

The approximate area of the cultural bloc and languages spoken.

Today the original Nhunggabarra people have disappeared almost entirely from their home country – their language is not known, and not even the name of their country remains, except in the hearts and minds of the custodians. The size of their population at the first arrival of the Europeans in 1788 is not known. How can a people disappear so completely?

Population size

The first population estimates for pre-European Australia were made by anthropologists in the early to mid 1900s. The most commonly cited estimate, made by Radcliffe-Brown in 1930, was a minimum of 251,000 – but more likely 300,000 – people in the whole continent. Recently, both anthropologists and archaeologists have challenged that figure; new archaeological evidence suggests a population in 1788 of one million or even higher.

The economic historian Noel G. Butlin in 1983 also came up with a population estimate of one to one-and-a-half million for all of Australia, based on survival rates of epidemics. Epidemics, unwittingly introduced by the first white colonists, spread with lightning speed ahead of the first explorers and Butlin criticises the early population estimates for not taking these severe effects into account. Disfiguring diseases, such as smallpox and syphilis, were noticeable to some degree, but the common cold was an invisible and equally lethal illness in a population with no immunity to it. Butlin estimates that only 50 to 60 per cent of the population of New South Wales in 1788 was still alive in 1805. He does not estimate the follow-on effects of these deaths on dependents – severe starvation would have increased the death toll even further.

After having examined the little evidence available, our guesstimate is that the 26 communities in the cultural bloc once contained a minimum of 15,000 people in total. An even higher figure is not at all unlikely, considering the fact that anthropologists estimate that the membership of a community in pre-1788 Australia ranged between

100 and 1500 people, averaging around 500 to 600 people. The Nhunggabarra people, occupying the largest area of the communities, may have counted more than 1000.

Whatever size the population once was, one thing seems clear: when the white settlers arrived in Nhunggal country, probably in the 1840s, it was not densely populated. The most likely explanation is that outbreaks of diseases had depopulated it. The first explorer in the area, Charles Sturt, came across victims in many places on the Murrumbidgee River (a tributary of the Murray River system) from an ongoing smallpox epidemic in January 1829 that was '. . . sweeping them off in great numbers', and he noted later on the upper Darling River that '. . . the population at present bears no proportion to the number of huts [and] I am led to believe there has been a sad mortality among them'.

The epidemic seems to have been still active two years later when Thomas Mitchell reported from Wingen in northeast New South Wales on 5 December 1831:

> We reached at length a watercourse called Currungai, and encamped upon its bank, besides . . . [a] tribe, who lay at this place extremely ill, being effected with a virulent kind of smallpox. We found the helpless creatures, stretched on their backs, besides the water, under the shade of the wattle, to avoid the intense heat of the sun.

Three-and-a-half years later the epidemic appears to have passed through the area from east to west and run its course, because on 28 May 1835, Mitchell came across a group of twelve people near Fort Bourke and noted that 'most of them had had the smallpox . . . The disease had almost depopulated the Darling and these people were but the remains of a tribe'. He saw pockmarked Aborigines on several occasions during this journey and observed that 'the population on the Darling seemed to have been much reduced by smallpox, which must have been very virulent . . . and its virulence was indeed apparent in the marks on those who survived'.

We therefore believe that the Nhunggabarra were all but wiped out by diseases even before the white men arrived in the area. Tex's grandmother, born in 1876, always maintained this and although we have not come across confirming evidence from other independent sources, it seems that the most likely cause of the Nhunggabarra people's disappearance was a severe smallpox epidemic that swept through the area some time around 1829–31.

The deaths of possibly something like ten thousand people in a society in a matter of perhaps only a year or two is a human tragedy beyond our imagination and comprehension. Charles Sturt, who came across many victims on his 1828–29 journey, gives a glimpse of the despair that must have gripped the people and the hopelessness they must have felt: 'it appeared that a violent cutaneous disease raged throughout the tribe that was sweeping them off in great numbers'. The *wiringin* (medicine man or 'clever man') pleaded to Sturt's men for help: 'nothing could exceed the anxiety of his explanations, or the mild and soothing tone in which he addressed his people, and it really pained me that I could not assist him in his distress'.

Many of the Nhunggabarra ceremonies died with the people and their mission on earth – to sustain the earth, the animals and the people – could no longer be fulfilled. The enormous losses of knowledge caused confusion internally among the surviving Aboriginal communities as well as widespread misunderstandings between the Aborigines and the Europeans. The misunderstandings started with the first of the white explorers and then continued among the settlers, early researchers and anthropologists, all of whom in Aboriginal Australia encountered a society so different from their own that it was virtually incomprehensible.

All that is available today about the original society in the form of written sources has been largely filtered through the minds of the early white explorers, colonists, ministers and priests and inexperienced anthropologists. The first anthropologists (who at the time were taking tentative steps in what was later to become an academic profession) did not realise that what they saw of Aboriginal culture in New South Wales was but remnants of the once blossoming Aboriginal Australian southeast. A present-day reader of many of these old sources is struck by the prejudice and arrogance that the Europeans of the 19th century displayed. The compassionate, understanding and reflective observers with open minds are few and far between until several decades into the 20th century – but by then it was far too late.

What we do have, though, is a wealth of stories kept alive by a few Nhunggabarra people into the present day. It is this treasure chest that we explore in this book.

Origins

Aborigines in the north have always believed their ancestors came from across the sea; their stories tell about sea travel, and today scientists have come to the same conclusion. Archaeological evidence suggests that numerous waves of people probably arrived on the Australian continent – the first some 50,000 to 60,000 years ago, and at least one other group of people around 4000 years ago, bringing the native dog, the dingo, with them.

To put the timeline in some context: at the time of the Aborigines' arrival in northern Australia the Cro-Magnons (the ancestors of modern European man) were gradually replacing the Neanderthals in Europe. Modern man expanded into northern Europe much later, some 20,000 years ago. North America is assumed to have been settled around 13,000 years ago. Northern Europe was covered with ice until some 10,000 years ago.

The Nhunggabarra had no story about an origin from anywhere other than Nhunggal country. As far as they were concerned they had been there since the time of Creation, the Burruguu. And it is hard to argue against their perspective, because the period the Australian Aborigines have lived in Australia is immense; they have the longest continuous cultural history in the world.

One of the key areas where early human occupation is best documented in Australia is Willandra Lakes in western New South Wales, just south of Nhunggal country. Favourable conditions here have preserved skeletal remains and habitation debris in sediments, so it is possible to trace and accurately date human habitation very far back. Fifty thousand years ago the region was wet and fertile and the Willandra Lakes were full of fresh water and teeming with large fish. The famous 'Mungo man' (actually proven later to be a woman) excavated there was determined to be around 25,000 years old. Red ochre was found on the skeleton, which makes it the oldest evidence of ritual burial in the world.

The excavations at the Willandra Lakes have revealed a high degree of cultural continuity in Aboriginal society from the Pleistocene to the present day and have confirmed that rituals and aesthetic concepts of modern Aboriginal society have their roots in the remote past.

THE NHUNGGABARRA LANGUAGE

The traditional boundaries of the Nhunggabarra language are not known; present-day linguists are not even sure what language they actually spoke. But a general agreement has emerged among the language researchers of the area on an original broad distinction between a northern *Yuwaalaraay* dialect or language and a southern *Yuwaalayaay* version (yes, read again; the difference is only the 'r' and the 'y'!). The language name is a construction by outsiders, derived from an old form for 'no': *yuwaal*. Traditionally, the people would not have used separate names for language and people.

The southern Yuwaalayaay dialect/language is probably the one that most Nhunggabarra spoke. It is, however, unclear whether Yuwaalaraay was a dialect of the eastern neighbouring *Gamilaraay* language or a completely separate language. We do know, though, that the languages were fairly closely related. Today the languages are retained by only a very few individuals.

Although almost all Australian Aboriginal languages are related there existed no shared language in Aboriginal Australia at the time of European arrival. Even where one language covered a very wide area, everyone in that area needed to speak or at least understand many dialects and languages. They also 'spoke' sign languages.

The similarities and differences cause headaches for linguists. Hence, there is no agreed estimate of the number of languages that existed in Australia before the arrival of the Europeans: estimates vary between 150 and 650 languages, with the most commonly accepted number between 250 and 300 distinctly different languages and probably around 500 to 600 dialects. Less than 125 of these languages are still spoken today and only around twenty are learned by children.

Language is a deeply emotional issue for the Australian Aborigines. Given what little else remains of their original culture, language is seen as an irreplaceable part of present Aboriginal identity. A lot of effort is now being invested in relearning languages – this is a demanding task when no one has handed down the rules for constructing sentences, and so much of the languages has been lost. The good news is that – after 50 years of work – a new dictionary combining Gamilaraay, Yuwaalaraay and Yuwaalayaay has seen the light of day. The spelling in the dictionary is based on how the few remaining speakers pronounce the words and we try as much as possible to follow the dictionary's convention for spelling throughout our book. Words that are not in the dictionary have been spelled following the same system as the dictionary. This means that some words are spelled in a different way than the reader may be accustomed to.

STORY | THE BIG BUURRA OF BAAYAMI

Message sticks were placed to tell all the people that there would be a gathering of all people at Gugurruwan.

The old people said that this would be the first time for a buurra. Baayami, who was a great wiringin, said he would take his two sons to the gathering

How the People Got Their Totems (Big Buurra)

The Big Buurra ground is the circle in the centre of the painting, while the U shapes represent the ceremony that took place. The outline figures surrounding it illustrate the people going out speaking 26 different languages and forming their own community. The two large figures portray Nhunggabarra people and the learning we take from the story. The animals surrounding the centre are the different people's law totems.

The figures contained in the three circles at the top of the painting represent all the ceremonies that Nhunggabarra people have. The designs in between are the bullroarer and the three sacred trees.

The figure in the bottom left corner is the old woman who died. The middle circle designs represent the ceremony, where women sit in huts while their sons are taken away. The design in the bottom right circle represents Baayami and the creature he created, who frightened everyone. Between the circles are the boys being carried away.

so that they could begin their learning to become men. As people arrived, each different totem took up different points on the ridge surrounding the clearing where the ceremony was going to be held. Waan (the crows at one spot), the dhamarr (pigeons at another place), maadhaay (the dogs), baayamal (the swans), wubun (the blue-tongued lizards), bhoda (the red kangaroos), dhinawan (the emus), biiwii (the sand goannas) etc. all took different spots.

When everyone was there, nightly corroborees were held with each group decorating themselves and performing the songs and dances that told the story of the totems of their people.

After a while, the wiringins from each group got together and decided they would hold a buurra ceremony. Each day they went out as if they were going hunting but instead they prepared the buurra ground. They cleared a large circle of land; they built earth mounds around the circle and cleared pathways from the bush into the circle, with mounds on each side of the pathways. Each totem built a sculpture of their totem animal in the mounds along the pathway, interspersed with small shrubs turned upside down so that their roots formed a kind of umbrella that decorated the whole pathway.

This preparation had been going on for quite some time when one of the old wiringins walked away as if he were sulking. One of the other wiringins followed him back to his camp and they started fighting. Their fight was so loud that everyone could hear them. All of a sudden, in the middle of the fight, there was a strange new sound. It stopped the two old men from fighting and everyone was afraid. They knew it was the sound of the spirits who had come to the buurra ground to help with the initiation of the young boys into manhood. The old women gathered their children and said 'Gurraymi', meaning buurra spirit. The boys became really frightened and said 'Gayandaay', which also means buurra spirit but men and women must use a different word to describe it. The noise went on all night, so the next day everyone moved inside the buurra circle. In order to move inside the circle, each group had to do a ceremony beforehand.

Before moving, the men left their camps and went into the bush. Then, just before sunset they all walked in a single file out of the bush along the paths they had previously cleared. They walked between the mounds they had built. They each carried a fire stick and a branch of a tree. When they reached the middle of the circle it was the time for the women and young people to leave their old camps and move into the buurra circle. They made new camps inside the circle and held a corroborree for everyone as they had on previous evenings.

However, this evening the corroboree was interrupted by Baayami, the greatest wiringin of all. All through the corroborrees the maadhaay had been laughing and playing among themselves instead of watching, listening and learning about their sacred ceremonies. Doing this had shown great disrespect to the wiringins and their people. Yet again on this night, the maadhaay were talking and laughing. Baayami went over to them and said, 'I am the first wiringin that all people show respect to for my learning. I want you to stop talking and laughing while other people are doing their ceremonies. Because you did not listen to the other wiringins, because you think the wiringins will never make your young boys into men that is why you show disrespect. You will not speak the same way again. You want to be a noisy people who cannot keep quiet when strangers are in the camp and a people who do not understand sacred things? You and all your people will make a noise, but it will not sound like talk or laughter – it will be a noise like howling.'

When the maadhaay tried to say something mocking to Baayami, they found that he was right – they could no longer speak or laugh like men; they could only howl or bark. And as the maadhaay realised what had happened, a great sadness and yearning came into their eyes – which is still there to this day. Everyone who had seen what had happened was in awe of Baayami as he walked back to his people.

That night, another corroborree was held. The women who were related to the boys sang all night and the boys corroborreed for them. At the end of the night the young women were taken into gundhis, made from leaves and grass, which surrounded the buurra ground. The old women stayed on to show the boys their respect for the journey that the boys were about to take from boyhood to manhood. Each man lifted a boy onto his shoulders and did a short corroborree, to show that the boys were in good hands during their journey. So the women paid their final respect to them as boys. Then the women joined the younger women in the surrounding gundhis. When all the women were out of sight, some of the men pulled the gundhi down so the women could not see the direction the boys would take.

As soon as the boys had left, each with their teacher, the women could come out of their gundhis. The men were not allowed to tell them where the boys had gone or how long they would be away.

The women saw the boys some months later at the little buurra ground, which was made out of grass rather than earth. The boys came with their teachers, some with a front tooth missing or with ceremonial marks on their body. When the women had shown respect to the boys and had seen that their sons were all right, the boys and their teachers left together as a group. They spent six to eight months together and then they separated again — one boy with his teacher — and went in different directions. Again, the women did not see this happening.

After the boys had left, the women packed up and moved to the little buurra ground that is made out of earth. After a while, Millindulunubba came into their camp saying that she had been left to carry and look after all her children on her own. She went looking for much-needed water for her children but at every water hole she found only mud. Her children cried because they were so thirsty. Then, one by one, each of her children lay down and died from lack of water, which everyone had drunk before she reached there. A woman went to her with a wirri of water but she would not drink it because she did not want to live when all her children were dead. When she lay down to die, the woman poured the water over her mouth. Millindulunubba got up and said, 'Because of your hurry to get here and your selfishness in wanting to know that your children were all right, you forgot to look after my children.' She pointed and waved her hands, saying, 'Because of this, you will stay here forever — turn into trees, turn into trees.' And everyone close to her was turned into trees and they are all still there, standing around the edges of the buurra ground. The she-oak tree carries spirits who mourn the death of Aboriginal people and who can be heard when the wind moves through the leaves.

All the people in the background were also changed – they were turned into the totems that they were known by. So, the barking maadhaay were turned into dogs, the baayamal into swans, the waan into crows, the dhamarr into pigeons, the wubun into blue-tongued lizards, the dhinawans into emus, the bhoda into kangaroos and so on, each with their own language and customs.

When the boys and their teachers arrived at this little buurra ground made of earth, there was no one to be seen. They waited and waited but finally Baayami said that something must have happened to prevent them from coming. He said that they should all go to a far country to start again and to continue their initiation. Baayami travelled with his dog to Noondoo, where his dog left him, went into the scrub and gave birth to a litter of puppies, the likes of which had never been seen before. They had the bodies of dogs but the heads of bigibila, the echidna. And Nhunggabarra people believed that if they saw one of these yiyamunarri, or long tooth, they would be killed by it. Not even Baayami dared to go near his dog's litter. So Baayami now lives alone on one of the Noondoo ridges.

This long story explains how the cultural bloc of communities was formed: at a big gathering, the first buurra on this ground. It was from here that all the totem animals went out to form their own communities. The story gives a few of the names by which the communities traditionally may have known each other. It tells why each totem group got their own language – to stop the men from arguing!

We get an explanation of the background of the initiation ceremonies and why the men – not the women – had to go through the long education and to live with the other communities. It was to stop the men from fighting with each other. The story also warned the men that they had to prepare themselves properly before they conducted the ceremony, and that they had to undergo tests. It tells how the young men went out on their first learning experience.

The story also describes the first initiation ceremony and prescribes in detail how the ground was to be prepared and how the ceremonies were to be conducted.

The sound in the story came from the first bullroarer that Baayami made. The bullroarer is a flat wooden stick some twenty centimetres long, with a hole in each end. A string is tied to one of the holes. The other hole creates a buzzing sound when you hold the wooden stick by the string and swing it around your head. Baayami did not create the bullroarer out of concern for his people. He wanted to create something to inspire awe, but he got carried away by his ego, and he let loose forces that he could not control.

The spirit, which wandered away into the bush and did not return, has haunted buurra grounds ever since. This is why the bullroarer was used at the beginning of the buurras. The bullroarer makes a formidable and frightening sound, which mimics Baayami's voice and scares away the fearsome spirit that he provoked.

Baayami carved the bullroarer from three different trees, which then became sacred: mabu the beefwood, goolabah the coolabah tree, and nhungga the kurrajong tree. The Nhunggabarra could use parts of these trees — such as the sap, bark and seeds — but they were not allowed to kill the trees or any animals sheltering in them or under them, or to take the seeds of the Nhungga tree out of their country.

The three sacred trees were still standing when the first explorers arrived, but they were cut down later. The explorer Thomas Mitchell is blamed for the act according to an oral tradition still alive in the area. However, at least one tree remained until the 1890s.

KNOWLEDGE FAIR: THE BIG BUURRA

Our drive to the Big Buurra ground at Gugurruwan has taken us a few kilometres off-road across the flatlands, and although the area is fenced in by paddocks it is teeming with wildlife. Kangaroos and emus run in all directions in front of our four-wheel drive. They navigate the fences with ease; as long as they are not barbed wires, the animals jump over or straight through them.

I am surprised by the enormous size of the site. The buurra ground consists of a flat, vast, circular area, at least 400 metres across. Only sparse vegetation covers it and a few small younger trees. The outer periphery of the circle is marked by higher, very old trees. Are the poor women who turned into trees in the story still standing here? I hope not; there has not been much in terms of entertainment for them in the last 200 years.

We cross the buurra ground and reach the Narran River and stop where it curves in a gentle bend touching the periphery of the buurra ring. The river bed is quite dry now, with water only in a few muddy pools between long stretches of rocky bottom.

The stones of a weir are visible downstream. The weir was constructed in the mid 1800s by the first settlers. As building material they used the stones of the fish traps that the Nhunggabarra people had built here. Only a few of the original fish-trap stones remain in place today; Tex explains that once they covered more than ten kilometres of the river in intricate patterns. They secured a minimum supply of fish even in times when the river was not flooding.

The people of all the communities in the cultural bloc came together at the Big Buurra ground to enact the Big Buurra of Baayami story. The Big Buurra took place only after large floods, which would have occurred every two or three years. When the time came the people first cleaned and prepared the ground, marked the three inner circles and created one learning track per community and law totem; pathways leading into the centre as wiggly spokes in a wheel. The story describes how the communities then decorated the tracks with big mud sculptures of all the totem animals. The totem groups were responsible for their own sculptures and decorations, as well as their own totem's stories and dances. Each totem group then performed their totem stories for all the others, and exhibited their sculptures and decorations, and when all the communities had completed their performances, they followed the learning tracks into the centre of the buurra ground for the final ceremony.

One might call it a 'knowledge fair', because the main purpose of the Big Buurra was to give each totem group an experience of who the others were as people, how they were all connected. Including preparation time, the whole ceremony lasted between three and four months and was filled with dance, performances, art exhibitions, stories, ceremonies and drama.

All people in all the communities took part in the Big Buurra. Every man, woman and child was present and each had a role to fill in the re-enactment of the story. I try to imagine what it would have been like to be taking active part in an event lasting for so long. It must have been so emotionally and spiritually charged, and it would have defined and clarified for everyone what it was to be a member of the community and how all the communities were linked together. The persistence of anecdotes about the Big Buurra to this day shows that the events left everybody with an everlasting memory.

I try to visualise a mass crowd of people filling the ground and the neighbourhood. How could maybe as many as 15,000 Aborigines once have gathered here? The buurra ground could have easily contained that many people, but how could the people have sustained themselves on this land where a few lanky cattle are now rummaging the parched earth to find the handfuls of grass still around?

One must remember that the country looked distinctly different in pre-European times. The Narran River carried much more water and was considerably deeper. No property owners upstream pumped the water away, and the river's clear water would have been teeming with fish and unhindered by weirs. The surrounding land benefited from fairly regular floods twice a year, which meant there was edible vegetation for both people and animals. The deep waterholes in the river, which during the droughts once kept its water and sustained fish populations, are now filled with silt from the nearby farm land.

When the ceremonies were over, the people left the ground, the mud sculptures and the pathways were washed away by the next rain and soon nothing tangible remained to remind a casual visitor of the events that had taken place here. For a few exciting months the Big Buurra had been life itself. Life was for living, life was in the moment; in a couple of years the moment would return. Just as was custom everywhere in Aboriginal Australia, the value of such a gathering was in the intangible experiences of the participants in the buurra, not in the tangible artefacts created.

When the first European settlers arrived in the 1840s the Big Buurra was held only in memory by the few old people who had survived the diseases that preceded the European settlers. The stones of the fish traps were used to build the wall of the weir and the plain became a grazing paddock for cattle. None of the white people ever saw a Nhunggabarra mud sculpture – an art form peculiar to northwest New South Wales which has now vanished and of which very little information is known today.

The Big Buurra, however, is still well-known among the communities in the area to this day and each of the communities has its own story about the ceremony and how they came to be as a people. The fact that the Big Buurra ground is situated on Nhunggal country gave the Nhunggabarra a special responsibility for the site on behalf of all the other communities. They had to keep the Big Buurra story alive between the ceremonies and allow access to the site for those who required it.

3

The Knowledge is in the Story

HOW DOES A NON-LITERATE SOCIETY BUILD and retain knowledge? To us living in literate societies it seems incomprehensible that knowledge can be stored and conveyed from one generation to another without writing, without libraries full of books and without (these days) databases.

One of the answers is *storytelling*, an art that the Aboriginal people had developed to masterful level. Long dismissed as children's stories or 'myths' by Westerners, Australian Aboriginal stories have only recently begun to be taken seriously for what they are: the longest continuous record of historic events and spirituality in the world.

The stories linked the people, the animals and the land to the spiritual world and covered every aspect of Nhunggabarra knowledge. To every medicinal plant belonged a story about how and where it was used. The spear maker's 'manual' was a story traded from father to son. His son had to learn the story behind every part of the spear; each barb, the glue, every shape would have had a story about where it came from and how.

The stories about the events and animals that gave Aboriginal people their law, spiritual belief system, behavioural codes etc. were traded orally from generation to generation. Through participation in the ceremonies that were linked to the stories, the Aboriginal people could connect directly with the Ancestors, the spirits and the Burruguu. The stories also functioned as 'maps' for finding the way in the landscape and they defined the country's borders. For the Aboriginal people, the earth was a mass store of knowledge and – for those with the 'key' – the stories still tap directly into this store.

Aboriginal stories sometimes record events that occurred a very long time ago, which suggests the stories have survived for tens of thousands of years. About 5000 years ago a shower of meteorites collided with Australia at a site some 145 kilometres southwest of Alice Springs in an area now called the Henbury meteorite crater. The Aborigines living in the area saw the impact and refer to it in one of their stories as *sun walk, fire devil rocks*.

A story originating from the Blue Mountains, near Sydney, tells of the time *when the earth blew up*, which almost certainly describes the volcanic eruption of Mount Wilson several thousand years ago.

Aboriginal storytelling was a dramatic art. In a live situation there is no medium that distances the teller and the listener. The storyteller supplemented the story with visual effects and could use their whole body in the telling. We must imagine the stories to have been enriched with hand and body movements, a variety of facial expressions, changes in volume and pitch of voice, and any individual antics that a gifted storyteller could come up with. In this sense the stories were subjective: one cannot be sure that a story was told in exactly the same way today as it was 100 years ago.

A Nhunggabarra story was not intended as an accurate never-changing historical document – 'history' was an alien concept. What was crucial was how and where the stories were linked to the land, the Burruguu and the law. The stories had to be understood by the contemporary people, so the language had to be adapted to follow the changes in language and habits. But at the same time, the stories had a high level of stability and continuity over thousands of years. And all of the stories contained hidden levels of meaning, accessible only for those with the 'keys'.

THE KEY TO THE ARCHIVES: THE FOUR LEVELS

The stories and their hidden meanings constituted the Nhunggabarra peoples' archives, law book, educational textbooks, country maps and Bible – in short the whole framework for generating and maintaining the knowledge base of the people. This crucial point tends to be disregarded or missed altogether by story collectors, historians and anthropologists. The 'keys' to this knowledge base were only held by those who went through the traditional education. Therefore, most stories that were collected by white people were never understood beyond a superficial level.

A Nhunggabarra person, undergoing the traditional education, would gradually learn more and more meanings. Not everybody would learn them all; how many meanings one learned depended on one's role. Those of us living in a Western culture can today best understand a Nhunggabarra story in terms of *four levels of meaning* – this is how Tex's father explained the construction to him during his education. Traditionally, the Nhunggabarra would not have talked about the stories and their meanings in this formal way; they would just have learned the meanings, one after another.

STORY | THE CRANE AND THE CROW

Garraagaa, the crane, was a great fisherman. He could catch many fish by hunting them out, with his feet, from underneath the logs in the creek. One day, when he had a great many fish on the bank of the creek, Waan, the crow, who was white at that time, came up and asked the crane to give him some fish.

The crane told the crow to wait until the fish were cooked but the crow was hungry and impatient. He kept bothering the crane, who told him to wait. Eventually the crane turned his back. The crow sneaked up, and was just about to steal a fish when the crane saw him, seized a fish and hit the crow right across the eyes with it. The crow was blinded for a few minutes.

The Crane and the Crow

The painting shows the white crow at the bottom with the crane and all the fish he caught. In the centre is the fish bone, which changed the crane's voice forever. At the top of the painting is the black crow with his white eye. The cross-hatching down the centre represents the river.

He fell on the burned black grass around the fire and rolled over and over in his pain. When he got up, his eyes were white and the rest of him black, as crows have been ever since.

The crow was determined to have his revenge. He waited for his chance and one day saw the crane fast asleep on his back with his mouth wide open. He crept quietly up to him and stuck a fish bone right across the root of the crane's tongue.

The crane woke up and when he opened his mouth to yawn he felt like he was choking. He tried to get the bone out of his throat and, in the effort, he made a strange scraping noise – 'gah-rah-gah, gah-rah-gah'. But the fish bone could not be moved, and still the only noise a crane can make is 'gah-rah-gah' – the name by which he is known.

The Nhunggabarra story: General structure

The Crane and the Crow story is constructed according to a general pattern valid for most Nhunggabarra stories. It is set in the Burruguu, a distant past when there was no difference between animals and people. It tells about animals interacting with each other, in this case an altercation between two common birds. Both birds are totem animals – that is, they are two Aboriginal people. For Westerners this is incomprehensible. Westerners can understand Aesop's fables because the animals are not people, they only act as people. But in the Nhunggabarra stories the animals act like animals and they also are people. The only difference between a person of the crow totem and the bird in The Crane and Crow story is that the crow (animal) was one of those who broke the law at the time of creation. Therefore it was punished and had to remain in animal form. The crow (person) was, on the other hand, rewarded for having obeyed the law.

The story explains natural events and features of the landscape and offers explanations for the existence of natural phenomena. The 'river' is the Narran River.

The story could be simply told or accompanied by a dance (performed by a different person than the storyteller). If the story was sacred (this one was not), it would also be an essential element of a ceremony.

Meaning of the first level

This simple story would have been one of the first a child heard. Its first level is the text itself and it explained natural features and animal behaviours. This level answers some of the fundamental questions that little children living in a natural environment probably pestered their parents with: why does the crow have black feathers and white eyes? Answer: The crow used to be all white, but then he turned black, except for the eyes. Why is the bird with long legs called *Garraagaa* (the Nhunggabarra name for crane)? Answer: Because his voice was choked by a fish bone.

The event described is not uncommon in the real world – a crow stealing food from another animal. This is a valuable feature – the story can come alive. A child could experience it in reality by watching the crane and the crow living out the story in nature. The natural environment thus reinforces the learning on a daily basis.

Typically, the first level is also exciting and entertaining. The story builds from a slow start to become more and more dramatic, and it finishes off on a dramatic high. This construction tells us that it was meant to be told in dramatic form and that it was well-suited to be accompanied by dance.

Meaning of the second level

The second level of meaning concerns the relationships between the people within the community. The second level meaning does not come straight from the story and *it was never told explicitly*. You had to extract the meaning as part of your education and you had to have some pre-knowledge about the law to be able to do this. This level therefore remained hidden for non-initiated people. Some of the second-level lessons to be learned from the story are as follows.

Do not impose your view on others. Instead of giving the raw fish to the crow, the crane tries to force the crow to cook it first. The crane is the expert fisherman so he believes he has the right to impose his views on others. It is an attempt to use his power of superior knowledge to influence the crow's behaviour. Instead he should have shown respect by letting the crow eat his fish.

To impose a view on another person is an abuse of power. There are an infinite number of truths and what is true for one person is not necessarily true for another. This is a central concept of Nhunggabarra law and it survives in much of general Australian Aboriginal thinking today.

Western minds are uncomfortable with such differences. The existence of many versions of a story or an event means that none is true. For Aboriginal people, the existence of many versions means that they are all true — it is only a matter of viewpoint. An example is the Creation story. The Nhunggabarra and the Muruwari had their own creation stories, and so had all the other communities in the cultural bloc. The creation stories would have had one common element — the Rainbow Serpent — but they would have relayed different versions of creation. Still they were all true.

Share the knowledge. The crane does not share his knowledge about fishing. This is wrong: as the expert he should have shared the knowledge in order to enable the crow to independently feed himself. A core value among the Nhunggabarra was that individual expertise must never be used for individual benefit. There are two reasons for this. If the crane keeps his knowledge to himself it will make the crow dependent; the crow will become powerless and the crane will hold a power monopoly.

The other reason is that if knowledge were individually owned and not shared it would disappear when the owner died; the Aboriginal people would not be able to feed themselves and they would die too. This was why knowledge belonged to everybody and the land.

Knowledge was not for keeping; it was for sharing, but only when the recipient was ready to accept the responsibility.

With knowledge comes responsibility. An expert is expected to fulfil a role for the whole community, not for oneself. As the expert fisherman, the crane should have been fishing for the whole community (represented by the crow), but he fulfilled the role only for himself and his own individual benefit.

Everybody in the Nhunggabarra community had a major role to fulfil on behalf of the whole community.

Split the roles. The crane performs three roles in the story: catching, cooking and dividing the catch. This is wrong. Work must be split up to prevent someone from taking ownership of a whole chain of knowledge.

The roles connected with fishing (net-making, trapping, catching, cooking), hunting (tracking, spearing, collecting and cooking), storytelling and many other activities were split among different people.

The European settlers were perplexed by this custom. They could not understand why the successful hunter had no power over the division of his game and could well end up with no meat at all.

Role-splitting accomplished three things: it involved more people in key activities, it forced people to work together in teams, and it reduced the risk that someone would have a monopoly on knowledge. For example, stories had four custodians; all four would know the whole story, but each was allowed to teach only their own part. Each hunter would hold all the knowledge about an animal and its related ecosystem, and each would be able to perform all four roles, but each was allowed to perform only their own role.

If you break the law you carry the shame. The crow's eyes became white so everybody could see the shame the crow carries with him for breaking the law. The crane carries his shame in his voice.

Meaning of the third level

The third level concerns the relationship between your own community and the larger environment – that is, the earth and other Aboriginal communities. Again, the third level does not come straight from the story and it is never told explicitly. You have to pull out the meaning yourself and you have to hold some pre-knowledge about the law.

Do not stay in one place. The crane exploits the fish in the river by fishing more than he needs to. If he continues in this way the crane will deplete the stock of fish. This explains why people have to move camp. If you move camp according to the seasons the resources will be at their prime at each place and you will find food with less effort. If, on the other hand, you become sedentary, you will give the breeding stock no time to recover, and you will very rapidly deplete the resources in this one place.

Another benefit of nomadic life is that if you stay in one place you will start changing the appearance of the country and then you will break the links between land and story and start to lose your knowledge (which is contained in the land). This in its turn will endanger the whole mission to keep all alive.

Do not deplete the breeding stock. The Narran River goes dry at regular intervals, leaving only disconnected waterholes. If the crane stayed in one of the waterholes during the dry season, he would kill all the breeding stock in that waterhole and extinguish the whole species. This would endanger all the bigger fish, which depend on the same small fish on which the crane was feeding. The big fish were more valuable for the Nhunggabarra, so by depleting one piece of the food chain, you deplete the whole chain.

The third level in this way teaches a holistic perspective. The Aborigines were very careful to maintain the breeding stock of both animals and plants. Their careful maintenance of the whole ecology, 'eco-farming', enabled the Nhunggabarra to sustain a large population.

Behave with responsibility towards other communities. The crane was behaving as if he owned the river and the fish, but he did not. He should not have been fishing more than he needed to.

By depleting one part of the food chain the crane was endangering totems further downstream – the species that depended on the smaller fish. The river flows into a lake, so if you live in a society where people behaved like the crane, the animals and the birds in the lake would be affected by the loss of one species in the food chain.

The river and the lake represent two different communities, so this value also describes the relationship with other communities; each community depends on responsible behaviour by the others.

Punish only your own. The story ends with the crane choking on the fish bone that the crow had pushed into his throat. This was the crane's punishment for breaking the law. However, the crow did not have the right to punish the crane. No one except your own people has the right to punish you. A Nhunggabarra person could only be punished by a Nhunggabarra person. So therefore the crow was also punished.

This particular law stopped revenge behaviour. A pay-back or vendetta custom did not exist in the cultural bloc of the Nhunggabarra and their neighbours, and it is unlikely that it existed anywhere in Aboriginal Australia in pre-European times, because it would have gone against the heart of Aboriginal law in general. Reports of blood feuds from other areas describe events that occurred after the disintegration of Aboriginal society.

Meaning of the fourth level

Many, but not all, stories had a fourth level. The fourth level taught spiritual action and psychic skills; it was more doing than talking and listening. The fourth level included practice, ceremonies and experiences, which gave access to the special esoteric knowledge hidden in the story. The fourth level of the stories was only taught by wiringins to wiringins-in-training, and proficiency could only be achieved through hard training and long experience. This was the only way to sustain the sacred laws.

The wiringin would also have been taught how to interpret the Crane and Crow story symbols, so he could help interpret the dreams that he and others in the community experienced.

Tex does not possess the fourth level skills of any story, but he can tell what would have been some of the fourth level skills that were elements of the Crane and Crow story.

Travel in spirit. The story tells that people could learn how to travel 'in spirit'. Travelling 'in spirit' was an accepted form of travel in traditional Aboriginal society. People would sometimes travel in their dreams, while asleep. On waking up they might describe a vision they had seen while asleep; a dead Ancestor, a totem animal or another place. Such dreams were considered of high value and could be the object of much interpretation and discussion in the community.

Wiringins learned how to use this form of travel in a conscious way, to send their spirits to travel and to visit the Ancestors in the Warrambul, other communities and even other countries. These skills were a tightly guarded secret so they have disappeared into oblivion, together with the wiringins. Very little remains in terms of trustworthy written accounts by eyewitnesses, because the early anthropologists tended to dismiss them as superstition and the missionaries actively discouraged the practice.

Watch out for spirits in your sleep. The Nhunggabarra believed that when you sleep on your back, your body is open to all sorts of spirits to enter through your mouth, particularly if you keep your mouth open. Hence you should sleep on your belly. A piece of simple practical advice. Snorers beware!

Changing your appearance. The story tells how the crow changed appearance; it shows that some people can assume the shape of other animals and change appearance at will if they know how to do it. The wiringins reputedly had the ability to change their appearance and body form. They learned this during their initiation into the profession and used it for the benefit of their community.

THE STORY LEARNING PROCESS

The Nhunggabarra people heard and saw all story performances many times, except the most sacred ones, and would be able to recount them from memory. However, the meanings were never told explicitly by those who knew them. People would gain access to the meanings only through hard intellectual work.

Learning the stories by deduction of the meanings was a key element in the Nhunggabarra education system. The young men and women had to pull out the meanings all by themselves, with minute prompts from the old people. This process of deconstruction and reconstruction was a true intellectual challenge. Tex, as one of very few present-day Aborigines in the region to have received at least some of the traditional education, was put through the wringers by his father and some of the old people.

Tex: *My father gave me the first story to pull out the meaning of. It took me three months of hard work to figure it out. The old people used to retell a story I had heard as a kid in Goodooga and asked if I knew the meaning of it. 'No,' I said. 'Then pull the meaning out of it!' they said. 'Look for clues in the story itself and the place it belongs to.'*

When I came back and told them what I had come up with they just said, 'Yes,' and showed no more interest, so I figured out that there must be more to it. And so it went on. They never pushed me; it was my choice to come back or to leave it.

I only knew that I had figured out all the meanings when they gave me another story. It was hard — sometimes it could take a whole year — but I

The Four-level Art of Storytelling

The figures in the centre and the core circle represent the first level, during which the children learn from the women.

The next circle is the second level, where the men prepare the boys for the walk out to the other communities. The pink represents the children and the footprints the first ceremony of initiation and the community coming to see them off.

The third circle is when the boys walk out to the other communities to experience first-hand their stories, ceremonies and languages. The circles of dots represent the communities and the U-shapes are all the different ways of communicating. The three yellow circles and the U-shapes inside are people teaching the boys the knowledge of how to keep all alive. The pink dots represent the young boys. The spirits they will meet during their journey are the figures along the edges and the bags they carry with them are at the bottom. The leaves represent all the things they are not allowed to kill; they have to rely on the different communities to keep them alive. The black footprints in the pink represent their return to their own community.

Those few men and women of the law totems, who have shown special abilities from childhood onwards, are now taught the fourth level; the section outside the third circle. They are taught individually to become wiringins. They learn how to change into their yurrtis – the four big figures in the corners of the painting – and they are given a second yurrti, represented by the snakes around the circle. The big black figures tell how they use their shadow sprits and dream spirits to travel both to the Warrambul and to places on earth. The bags contain the tools they use for their ceremonies, such as the white crystals at the top of the painting.

enjoyed the challenge and it was something different to do. This 'education' went on for twenty years and I am still learning.

Tex put me and his partner Anne to the test one night at our base camp: 'Now you pull out the meaning!' Although I knew a fair bit about the Nhunggabarra by then and also, in principle, how the four levels function, the task proved excruciatingly difficult. The only thing I could come up with, without prompting, was that the crane displayed greedy behaviour; should it not share more voluntarily? 'Hmm', said Tex. 'There is more to it!'

As a test I later did an experiment. I gave twenty doctoral students and professors at a research seminar in Helsinki the Crane and the Crow story and asked them to interpret it. Very little was volunteered. And they did not agree with the meanings described above. They could not, for instance, understand why the crane was to blame for anything at all. All it did was to use the skill it had! A mother of two agreed absolutely with the crane; it must surely be more appropriate to cook the fish first, before eating it. This little experiment illustrates how difficult it is for people without any background in the culture to interpret the stories, and why the European settlers, who did not have the proper 'key', never were able to open the Nhunggabarra 'archives'.

The young Nhunggabarra men and women in the old days were socialised in only one culture and may have found the task slightly easier than Tex. The Western culture that dominates the life of modern-day Aboriginal people makes the interpretation hard for them also.

The ability to pull out meanings depends on the context and it is also accumulative; the more background knowledge you have and the more of the law you have already learned, the more you can pull out. Story learning was therefore both a socialisation process and a coming-of-age process, with in-built examinations, that continued from initiation through your whole life. When you had exhausted the meanings of one story you had cleared that level and you would use that story as background knowledge for the next story. The process therefore also confirmed and strengthened your identification with your culture.

The four-level model also meant that all stories could be told freely to the whole community; the four levels and the education process ensured that each person understood the story on the level that fitted their individual level of development. Children would understand the first level and have their curiosity satisfied, while the older people could reflect on the higher levels of meaning. And everybody, young and old, would enjoy the drama and the excitement of the performance.*

SUSTAINING THE STORY – CUSTODIANSHIP AND TUCKANDEE

Stories are vulnerable compared to documents in one respect: oral tradition cannot guarantee word-by-word accuracy.

On the one hand, verbatim accuracy over the generations was not a goal in itself for the Nhunggabarra. Long-term flexibility was more important – the words in the stories had to change to reflect changing times and changes in language. On the other hand it was crucial to maintain consistency of content.

An intriguing question therefore is: How did the Nhunggabarra keep the stories alive with such consistency over such a long time

---

* This is the first time that all the meanings of the Crane and the Crow story have been revealed and published in written form. This is something that was never intended traditionally. The Nhunggabarra stories are not simple and uncomplicated – they are integrated in everything and were part of what it meant to live life as a Nhunggabarra person. We are mindful that we are interfering with this concept and also defeating the purpose of learner-driven education according to Nhunggabarra tradition. We are potentially pre-empting the learning that new generations of Nhunggabarra boys and girls would gain from pulling out the meanings themselves.

We have weighed the pros and cons carefully and come to the conclusion that we will publish the full interpretation of only the Crane and the Crow story. The interpretation of the other stories in this book are given only to the degree that it is relevant for the purpose it is being used.

without written records? The answer is that they had devised quite an elaborate system, which guaranteed survival even when disaster struck.

A story was always linked to learning tracks, parts of the land itself and often also to animals, none of which changed fast. The physical features of the land thus functioned as mnemonics. In some cases, the story was also accompanied by an illustration, a piece of rock art or a carved tree. This supported the storyteller's memory. Also, the story was generally accompanied by a dance and a song, which would provide further reminders for a forgetful storyteller.

But mnemonics alone could not secure the essential substance of a story against deceitful or accidental change. The task of making sure that the story, dance or ceremony was traded to the next generation in its original form was the role of the custodians.

Every story had four custodians, who each were responsible for maintaining one specific part of the story. The four custodians were the teachers, the ones who were given the role of teaching everybody in the community the first level of meaning of a story. They also had to ensure that the tradition of the story was kept alive, so they would also be the teachers of the second and third levels to all young people during their education.

All the custodians would know all three levels; they would also have visited and learned all about every site of relevance for the story and they would gladly tell the whole story. However, when the purpose was education, custodians were allowed to tell only the part of the story they had the role of looking after. In this way the consistency of the story was secured: the pieces of the story had to fit together and the other custodians could immediately tell if one of the pieces no longer fit their pieces. This rule applied also to Tex when he learned the stories. He had to go to four different old people to learn the complete story.

What if one of the custodians died before they'd had time to hand over the custodianship? In such an event the *tuckandee* stepped in. Each Nhunggabarra person had a remote 'brother' or 'sister' who lived in another community – a tuckandee – who had learned the story too. In the case of someone dying before their part of the story had been handed over, the tuckandee would teach the story to the children of the story custodian. The custodianship would then be passed on to the new custodian. In the language of today, the tuckandee provided a live 'back-up copy'. The tuckandee was a Nhunggabarra safety-net institution covering all aspects of education.

The storytelling model of the Australian Aborigines proved its resilience over eons of time and was able to remain consistent during eras which saw flooding and fires, the sea levels rise and fall. Where would the stories have been today had they relied on written records? What type of vaults could have ensured the survival of the documents and the books? Would a society built on written records have endured this long?

OWNER VERSUS CUSTODIAN

Ownership of traditional Aboriginal land, 'land rights', has been an issue in Australia for well over three decades. We do not enter that debate, but we must point out that the land in Nhunggal country was not individually 'owned' in the Western sense. The Nhunggabarra could not sell or barter their land. They could not buy more land, and they did not 'own' the land they were occupying.

The reverse probably describes the concept better: the 'country owned the people'. Tex belongs to Nhunggal country, so does the grass, the kangaroos and the fish. Tex does not own it; he looks after it. He and his fellow Nhunggabarra have a responsibility to take care of their land and to keep it alive for future generations. The term *custodian*, therefore, is closer to the Nhunggabarra concept of ownership and this is why we use this term throughout the book.

The concept of land ownership that today is dominant in Australia and elsewhere allows the owner – within certain limits – to do whatever they want with the land. If the owner neglects it, no one else would dream of tending to it. Nhunggabarra custodianship, instead, meant there was an obligation for the community to care for all land within its borders; it was unthinkable to neglect land or to leave it untended. A property boundary today in many countries also functions to exclude: it defines a right to prevent other people's access. For the Nhunggabarra, however, a 'boundary was to cross'; it did not exist for excluding non-owners. Instead, the boundaries of their country defined where their responsibilities and their stories and knowledge began and ended.

Custodianship and access to sacred sites were determined by one's descent from shared Ancestors. All Nhunggabarra men and women were members of such land-owning or land-controlling descent groups or 'clans'. The members of a clan consisted of people from many different countries, and the custodians of a site, therefore, were just as likely to be found outside the country it was situated. The Nhunggabarra were matrilineal – that is, the rights were inherited by a child from the mother. Clan membership also determined to some degree which ceremonies to perform. The role as custodian of a particular story was determined by your totem and your order of birth.

The custodian rule applied to almost all goods – tangible as well as intangible. The Nhunggabarra had very few personal possessions – a spear, perhaps, or cooking utensils.

The crane in the Crane and Crow story illustrates the concept of custodianship. The crane had made himself the owner of the fishing know-how in a Western sense by keeping it and not sharing it with the crow. He had made it his 'intellectual property'. Had the crane behaved like a Nhunggabarra custodian he would have felt a responsibility to share his know-how. Knowledge could not be individually owned, and there was no difference between land and knowledge – both were assets that belonged to the country and the community as a whole. Knowledge was to be shared, but with care because it required responsibility. It was crucial to maintain the integrity of the knowledge.

This is why we say that the *story owned the storyteller*. The custodian had the role to both protect the integrity of the story and to allow access to it.

The Nhunggabarra individuals gradually became the custodians of a considerable asset base: the land that they inherited from the mother, the knowledge that formed part of the land, the knowledge about the valuable plants and the behaviour of animals, and the meanings of the stories and the ceremonies which had to be learned to fulfil the obligations in the mission. Finally, via the totem system, the young Nhunggabarra were born into a vast but close network of kin that covered every country in their cultural bloc over many peoples and a very wide geographical area. Because kinship determined the initial behaviour between strangers, a person could, if in need, count upon a larger network of kin all over the Australian continent.

The Nhunggabarra person over the years, therefore, became quite wealthy in terms of intangible assets. But they never accumulated much tangible and financial wealth.

Learning the Story: the Education System

4

CHILDREN LEARNED NOT BY FORMAL EDUCATION, but by actually participating in life itself, by doing. And, since both physical and spiritual environments were created simultaneously in the Burruguu, children learned both the physical and spiritual at the same time. Stories, songs and dances had a physical connection to country, animals and vegetation, as well as a spiritual connection to the Burruguu.

The Aboriginal way of life required the development of a highly refined perception, great physical strength and purity of mind. Spiritual awareness and spiritual capabilities were therefore taught from an early age. Sleep was one of the entrances into the Burruguu. The Nhunggabarra stories are silent on this topic, but other sources describe how Aboriginal children were educated in how to develop awareness during sleep and how to enter meditative and even hypnotic states.

The children learned tricks they could use in hunting and fishing – a skilful click of the tongue enticed crabs from their holes in the river mud; a snake-like hiss could drive a bandicoot from a hollow log. In particular, parents encouraged children to learn all about the behaviour of their totem animals as the way to learn about themselves.

The children also learned about what was edible and how to find and prepare it. They were taught how and where to find water during all seasons. Gradually, the Nhunggabarra person learned everything worth knowing about the land. The education made the Nhunggabarra adults completely self-sufficient in terms of food all year round, as long as they kept to their own country.

The learning process was kept alive well into the 1960s by the Nhunggabarra old people. Tex, one of the lucky Nhunggabarra children not to have been taken from his parents and adopted away by the authorities of the time (such children were known as the 'stolen generation'), was encouraged in his childhood to observe the behaviour of his totem, the sand goanna. He spent months observing the animal – watching its home, its habits, what it needed to survive and how it helped other species to survive.

He also learned that through his *yurrti* (totem) he is related to all those animals, insects, birds and plants which live on the sand hill of the sand goanna. He is even related to the winds, which come to tell the goanna when to bury itself in the earth and when to be reborn again.

Tex was one of the last to go through this traditional form of education. It started when he was very young.

Tex: *I grew up with the old people, who knew a lot. They took us to the sites, made drawings on the ground; we camped and they told us the stories, but some teenagers used to poke fun at them and they influenced the take-up among the younger children.*

The Nhunggabarra were decimated and scattered by then; many no longer lived on their ancestral country and most did not see the reason to learn the 'old ways'. Tex learned most of the stories from his grandmother Violet, who died in 1972. She was born in 1876 and provided a link to the time before white settlement.

When Tex told what he had found out about the life of the sand goanna to the old people, they encouraged him with hints to investigate further. What Tex was able to conclude from his studies he had to translate back to himself – only he could determine what the messages were. He was never given test questions or a quiz. It was his own individual journey of learning – no one imposed an opinion and the old people never gave him a 'right' or 'wrong' mark.

The same process was applied when he later learned the meanings of the law stories in this book. He had to figure them out himself, with only minute hints. Only when he was given a new story to decipher did he know that he had exhausted the potential meanings. When he learned the meaning of his first story he had no idea of 'the process' – he just kept going out of interest and curiosity. In doing so, he displayed his commitment, his respect for the knowledge and his complete trust in the old people, and this allowed them to lead him further and further.

STORY | THE CREATION OF NARRAN LAKE

Baayami's two helpers, Nullawa and Ganhanbili, were preparing food at Coorigal Springs, while Baayami was away collecting honey. They had spent all day collecting yams, frogs and the like, and were very hot. Although they knew that their law forbade them from swimming in the springs, they became tempted and jumped in. As soon as they had entered the springs they were seized and swallowed by two giant crocodiles, two garriyas.

The garriyas dived into two holes in the side of the spring which were entrances to an underground watercourse leading to the Narran River. The garriyas travelled along, following the course as it wound across the country and surfaced at various points to form deep waterholes. And as the garriyas travelled they took all the water with them, so each time they surfaced at a waterhole, they would drain it and continue on.

When Baayami returned to the campsite at Coorigal Springs, he could not find Nullawa and Ganhanbili and he saw the two holes in the side of the spring and knew they had been taken by the two garriyas. So Baayami followed the two garriyas, tracking them by following the now dry watercourse. When he came to a big waterhole called Bullanbillya, which was now

Baayami, the Giant Crocodiles and the Two Women

The two crocodiles represent the two garriyas who, at Coorigal Springs, swallowed the women (shown inside the crocodiles). The linked circles of dots on either side of the painting represent Coorigal Springs and Narran Lake, with the route taken by the crocodiles linking them.

The ants in the painting represent the meat ants' nest that Baayami put the women on so they could be cleaned of the slime from the crocodiles.

dry, he could see the winding course the garriyas had taken and knew that if he travelled directly from one dry waterhole to the next he would catch up with them.

Baayami caught up with the two garriyas at the waterhole at the end of the Narran River, which was still wet. He fought and killed the two garriyas – one with a spear and one by a blow to the head – and as they were dying the two garriyas writhed in the mud, forming great hollows in the ground which the water they had brought with them quickly filled.

Baayami then cut open the two garriyas and pulled Nullawa and Ganhanbili from their stomachs. He laid the two women on a meat ants' nest and soon the ants had cleaned them by eating all the green slime from their bodies. As they were being cleaned, Nullawa and Ganhanbili came back to life.

The story tells about the first time humans broke the law. The women could not resist the temptation to bathe in the pond and were punished for their act. Baayami also broke the law by killing the two crocodiles. He killed two lives to save two. He then used innocent ants to clean the slime. The ants turned white as punishment for taking part in the crime.

To compensate for their disobedience the women must lose their children and to compensate for Baayami's crime the men have to go through initiation. A boy starts his initiation as an ignorant and innocent child. When he has accomplished the initiation walk he is a man, and his mother must mourn the loss of her child. The first test of the initiation is to show that he can resist temptation.

THE INITIATION SITE AT COORIGAL SPRINGS

The first thing Tex wants to show at the initiation site is the small pond in the story. The pond, now dry, is some twenty metres in diameter and surrounded by scattered dry bush scrub on a red-tinged dirt plain. It is hot; there is not the slightest breeze. I understand very

Journey of Knowledge

The star in the middle of the painting symbolises that the Nhunggabarra boy was sent out to find new knowledge, with each point of the star indicating the direction to one of the communities, which are represented by circles of dots. The little pouch in the centre was carried around the back of the boy's neck as protection on his journey.

The four sand goannas represent the learning that came from animals and the fact that Nhunggabarra law comes in fours. The kangaroo and emu at the bottom of the painting represent two of the law totems, and also indicate which gender should be killed and how they should be cut up and distributed among the community. The leaves represent Nhunggal country and the U shapes contained in the two top and two bottom circles represent the different ways of showing respect to different communities. The 'hat'-like symbol and U shapes in the upper-right circle represents all the Nhunggabarra ceremonies.

The kangaroo bottom left is 'x-ray' painted to show that the valuable knowledge is deep within. The leaves are gum tree leaves. The red dragonfly (top centre) is part of the initiation for girls. From her they learned the cycle of life. The symbols in the upper-left circle represent the three women performing the greeting ceremony, with the digging stick and the plant that was used as a woman's headdress.

well why it must have been a temptation for the young women to cool down in the pond.

I can see the spot where the crocodiles in the story attacked and consumed the two women. The crocodiles then dragged them into a small opening somewhere. And indeed, a hole leading into the ground is clearly visible at the bottom of the dry pond between two small rocks. The opening leads into the underground channel that is connected to the Narran River far away. This is the way the crocodiles dragged the helpers. In the wet seasons before European arrival the channel filled the pond with water. These days there is rarely water here. Silt from pig farming in the area clogged the hole and the channel many years ago.

K. Langloh Parker, who lived in the area in the late 1800s, describes in her memoirs how the initiation ground was still prepared up to the 1870s or 1880s:

They cleared a big circle, round which they put a bank of earth, and from the circle was cleared a path leading to a thick scrub; along this path were low earthen embankments, and the trees on both sides had the bark stripped off, and carved on them the various totems and multiplex totems of the tribes. Such carvings were also put on the trees round the Bunbul, or little Boorah ring, where the branches were also in some instances lopped, and the trunks carved and painted to represent figures of men, amongst whom were supposed to be the sons of Byamee's wives.

The stretch between the first small circle of the buurra ground and the second larger circle was marked by two rows of stones forming a path, a couple of metres wide. It led from the first small circle, which one – forgive the pun – could call the 'dress circle', because this was the place where the boys assembled and dressed up for the initiation ceremony. The dress circle is now invisible, covered by scrub.

The carved trees are long gone, but parts of the old track are still visible, and Tex and I follow the remains of the stone rows towards the second, much larger circular area. This is where Tex's ancestors and the other young boys would have come, walking between rows of their relatives and the invited communities standing on both sides of the track behind the stones.

There once were maybe more than 1000 people here – screaming, laughing, making jokes and crying out the names of the boys with the intention of distracting them and making them look up. This was the first test – if they fell for the temptation or displayed any emotion they would be punished.

The boys would walk past the pond and reach the big buurra circle where the men waited in the centre. The boys assembled around the men for the final ceremony. The buurra circle is a fairly large area, some 80 metres in diameter, and it is, surprisingly, still a completely open space with only sparse burr vegetation. It is as if we were standing on a tightly packed dirt floor, recently cleaned.

I decide to test the geomagnetic fields with my pendulum, so I walk to the centre of the big circle. The pendulum swings quite fast in a circular motion clockwise, indicating positive energy – a 'plus pole'. I slowly walk to the edge of the circle towards the track, and at the boundary the pendulum shifts to a swing indicating negative energy – a 'minus pole'. The shift is distinct and occurs within only a few centimetres of movement. There are quite noticeable geomagnetic force fields in play here and the old buurra circle seems to be aligned with them.

One no longer knows what ceremonies took place in the big circle, but the old people told Tex that after the ceremonies the young men were sent out into the bush and into the night, to find the ways to their next goal: one of the neighbouring communities where they would spend the next year or so. They were not allowed to carry food and water and not permitted to kill anything. This tested their ability to trust that they would be looked after if they showed respect. The boys would be secretly monitored at a distance by the men to make sure they were safe.

Back at the initiation site the people packed up their gear and departed, too. The seeds of the millet grass, which had been the staple food during their stay, had been all but consumed. They only left the millstones behind. Next year, at the time of the harvest, they would return to the same site and pick up their millstones where they had left them.

Tex pokes the ground with a stick and unearths a small round dish, some twenty centimetres in diameter. It is one half of a millstone, polished from hours after hours of women's grinding seeds to flour. When I look further, I see remains of more millstones, one after another: there are hundreds of them. Tex explains that the millstones continue along an expanse more than twenty kilometres long!

There once existed a couple of rock paintings at this site. They were destroyed by white people in the early 1950s and no traces remain. Tex never saw them, but the old people told him as a young boy that one of the paintings featured a big crocodile and three human figures. The three humans would have been Baayami and the two women.

Fossils of two now extinct giant riverine crocodile species have been found at Cuddie Springs, about 300 kilometres south of Coorigal Springs, together with human artefacts. (This is where Ganhanbili from the Creation of the Narran Lake story went after she had been saved from the crocodiles by Baayami.) The fossils are estimated to be between 20,000 and 38,000 years old, so the last giant crocodile may have swum in the Narran River some 20,000 years ago.

THE JOURNEY OF KNOWLEDGE

The most overwhelming experience a Nhunggabarra man would ever have was his first initiation ceremony. It was the gate through which he had to pass to become a man. At the age of around twelve he would, together with his contemporaries, embark on a long learning journey that would forever change him.

The young Nhunggabarra man left the initiation site and was now on his journey to the first of the other communities in his area. It would take fourteen to sixteen years before he returned to his own country. His most valuable belonging was a little pouch around the back of his neck. It had been given to him during the first initiation ceremony. It protected him on his journey and told people that he was on his learning walk, so they would take responsibility to teach him all their knowledge – their language, their law, their land and their beliefs. But he was never to open the pouch. If he did, he broke the trust and the pouch would lose its protection.

The young man understood some of the language of each community, because his early teaching was from the women who had married into his community. He could therefore show respect when he went into each different community. But he still had much to learn, including the fact that communication is more than words; people also show respect in the way they speak. To show respect he would, for instance, not look the members of one particular community in the face when he talked (this is still a common Aboriginal habit).

It was essential to know the whole of everything and he learned that the valuable knowledge is hidden within and cannot be seen – only with patience will it be revealed. Surface knowledge has only limited value.

When the young man left a community they would give him something sacred from their belief to respect and keep in his pouch.

When the man finally returned to his home community, he still had to perform three more ceremonies, taking up to six months in total, before he was considered an adult man with the ability to take on his role for his community. And now he could finally marry.

During his initiation he had visited all communities in his area and learned from them. He had lived with them, learned to communicate with them, hunted with them and learned all the knowledge that was essential to them and their country. Above all he had learned to respect the knowledge of all people and he now had the responsibility to use that knowledge wisely and equally for the benefit of his community as well as all the other communities.

The women were considered to mature into responsible adults at a much younger age. Hence the women did not need to travel widely to learn. The girls learned about the neighbouring habits from the women in the community. Because the women married and went to live with men in other communities, knowledge from all the surrounding groups was brought into each community. One of the ceremonies for girls was to be taken to a nearby waterhole. There they stayed for up to three months observing the red dragonfly. From the dragonfly they learned the cycle of life. They also learned many languages from the women, who were from all the other communities in the cultural bloc.

THE CORROBOREE: LEARNING BY ENJOYMENT

Under normal circumstances the Nhunggabarra would have been occupied with singing and dancing or storytelling or taking part in corroborees more or less every evening. Corroborees were organised events or performances held in camp, which could last up to a day and a night.

At the corroborees the traditional stories were told and the traditional songs and dances were performed. Although the corroborees were enjoyable and much appreciated by the Nhunggabarra people, their purpose was rarely solely for entertainment. Their primary functions were to teach the young, to regulate social harmony and to connect with the spirit world. This was generally overlooked by white observers.

Depending on a person's age and experience they would learn on different levels. The uninitiated children were warned about the sites mentioned in the stories and the younger men and women who still were undergoing their process of initiation would be expected to make efforts to pull out the meaning of the stories, the songs and the dances.

Song and dance also contributed to the social harmony of the group and for the community member, song and dance were the major means to connect with the spirit world.

The settler E.M. Curr brings us one of the earliest witness reports from a corroboree performed some time during the early 1840s in Victoria (this particular dance was never performed in Nhunggal country):

This was the first time my brother and I witnessed a corroboree. The Blacks themselves, as yet uninfluenced by civilization, and wrapped up in their own customs, were in a highly excited state, and thoroughly in the humour; the night, though fine, was dark; not a breath of air was stirring; so that the whole of the surroundings were precisely what suited the performance.

The extraordinary energy displayed by the dancers; their singular attitude; the quivering thigh; the poised spear; the whitened shield borne in the left hand; the peculiar thur, thur, thur, which their lips emitted in unison with the measured tramp of their feet; their ghastly countenances; the sinister manner in which the apparition had noise-lessly stolen from the surrounding darkness into the flaming foreground, and executed — now in open order, now in a compact body, to the sound of wild voices, and the clash of savage arms — their can-can diabolique, made up a picture thrilling from its novelty, its threatening character, and its entire strangeness.

Then, when the tumult grew hotter, and heavier the tramp of naked feet, and the voices of the women trembling with emotion waxed shriller and shriller, these wild warriors, worked up apparently to uncontrollable fury, with heaving chest and glaring eyes, their heads turned to their left shoulder, and their savage eyes fixed on my brother and myself; suddenly as one man threw back their right arms and brought their right shoulders forward, as if to plant in our breasts their spears which now converged on us — the display seemed to have passed from the theatrical to the real.

The idea that all was over with us, and an intense longing for my pistols, flashed through my brain. But before I could attempt to move, the climax had been reached, and the performers, dropping their spear-points to the ground, burst into one simultaneous yell, which made the old woods ring again, and then hurried at once out of sight, a laughing mob, into the forest's gloom. Was that yell, fancy suggested, the farewell cry to pleasant earth of a rabble-rout of fiends hurrying back to subterranean prisons in obedience to some mysterious power?

Corroborees must be distinguished from ceremonies, which were undertaken to contact and use the spiritual powers for fulfilling the mission of keeping all alive. Ceremonies were 'serious work' and sacred. They could be spectacular too, but they were never performed as entertainment.

5

Knowledge Economy

WE DO NOT KNOW FOR SURE how the Australian Aborigines lived before the arrival of the Europeans disrupted their production system and changed the land. Were they suffering or doing well? There are no eyewitness reports from the time before 1788. However, the few written accounts that have survived from the early days paint a picture of abundance when the first Europeans arrived, at least in the southeast.

The first accounts of the abundance of the inland arrived in the British settlement in Sydney in 1817. They were from the first white explorer in the interior of New South Wales, John Oxley, who enthusiastically reported on the 'finest open country, or rather park, imaginable', and on the river and lagoons that 'abound with fish'. 'One man caught 18 large fish in less than one hour, [weighing] 15–30 pounds each.'

Sir John Edward Eyre, an explorer with experience from many different areas of Australia, wrote in 1845:

Throughout the greater portion of New Holland, where there do not happen to be European settlers, and invariably when fresh water can be permanently procured upon the surface, the native experiences no difficulty whatever in procuring food in abundance all the year around.

And he observed in one of the rivers that 'the number [of fish] procured...in a few hours is incredible'.

Eyre's observations were echoed by other explorers of the time. Sir George Grey observed in 1846: 'I can only state that I have always found the greatest abundance in their huts. Generally speaking, the natives live well.' And he continues:

> ...it rarely happens in any season of the year when a description of the country does not yield both animal and vegetable food...many are not only procurable in abundance, but in such a vast quantities at the proper seasons, as to afford for a considerable length of time an ample means of subsistence to many hunter natives congregated at one place.

Grey also made another most interesting observation: 'In ordinary seasons they can obtain *in two or three hours a sufficient supply of food* for the day' (author's emphasis).

Eyre confirms Grey's observations: 'In almost every part of the continent which I have visited, where the presence of Europeans, or their stock, has not limited, or destroyed their original means of subsistence, I have found a native could usually, *in three or four hours, procure as much food as would last for the day*, and that without fatigue or labour' (author's emphasis).

Both early explorers and later studies have produced similar evidence: the procurement and preparation of food for Australian Aboriginal people living in the southeast was an everyday activity taking with an average of between two and five hours per person per day. There were seasonal fluctuations but, except during extreme droughts, it was not hard work.

This raises the question: what did they do with the rest of their time? The European settlers and explorers could not detect any activity they recognised as proper work. Their conclusion was inevitable: they did 'nothing'. The Aboriginal people were considered indolent or even lazy.

Grey noticed in 1846 that, although they could procure their food in a few hours if they wanted, 'their usual custom is to roam indolently from spot to spot, lazily collecting it as they wander along'.

In fertile southeastern Australia, where many areas produced a supply of fish so abundant and easily procured that 'a few minutes fishing would provide enough to feed the whole tribe', one squatter on the Victorian scene of the 1840s, wondered 'how savage people managed to pass their time before my party came and taught them to smoke'.

The anthropologist R.B. Smith in 1878 said that the Aboriginals of Victoria 'are lazy travellers. They have no motive to induce them to hasten their movements. It is generally late in the morning before they start on a journey, and there are many interruptions by the way'.

The anthropologist Herbert Basedow, writing in 1925, took it as the general custom of the Aboriginal that 'when his affairs are working harmoniously, gains secured and water available, the Aboriginal makes his life as easy as possible; and he might to the outsider even appear lazy'.

The notion of Aboriginal idleness was an image that stuck and it prevails to our day.

In 1974, American anthropologist Marshall Sahlins published *Stone Age Economics: The Original Affluent Society* in the wake of John Kenneth Galbraith's influential *The Affluent Society*. Galbraith had in his 1969 book argued against US private companies and their ever greater production of consumer goods to satisfy trivial consumer needs. A better quality of life would be achieved, he argued, if resources were used to improve the educational system, healthcare, recreational resources and social services – intangibles.

Sahlins showed that hunter–gatherers had for thousands of years before the agricultural revolution developed an economy that may have been poor in a material sense, but which allowed people to live a fairly easy and pleasant life. Food procurement was not a struggle and life was not physically demanding. Many of his examples were from Australian Aboriginal hunter–gatherers.

Still, Sahlins and other anthropologists struggled to explain why the Aboriginal people chose to maintain a low standard of living rather than following the standard route to 'civilisation' according to anthropological theory. A simplified version of this theory goes as follows: An abundance of food causes the population to increase, which forces people to produce more food, start farming and live a more sedentary life in villages, which develop into towns, then cities and finally nations. As soon as the society starts producing a surplus, some of it is grabbed by a few individuals and a hierarchical society with an upper class is developed.

This evolutionary development from one 'stage' to another is one of the cornerstone theories of anthropology and it has been used to explain development in all societies. According to the theory, the Aborigines had by 1788 not even reached the 'early farming stage' that started in the Fertile Crescent around 11,000 years earlier, and in Papua New Guinea some 9000 years ago, and in the Americas around 5500 years earlier.

But there is something wrong with the theory when it is applied to Aboriginal Australia. If there was an abundance of food, why was the population not growing fast? Why was the apparent surplus not usurped by chiefs and priests as had happened in the Americas, Asia and Eurasia?

To Sahlins it was a mystery that the Australian Aborigines seemed to *underuse* their objective economic possibilities'. And his verdict on present-day Australian hunter–gatherers was unforgiving: 'The failure of Arnhem Landers to "build culture" is not strictly from want of time, it is from idle hands.'

Anthropologists today agree that those few Australian Aborigines still living a hunter–gatherer life do not take a lot of time to procure their daily nutritional intake; they rest quite frequently and they only spend part of the daylight hours searching for and preparing food. Rhys Jones calculates that three types of women's work in Arnhem Land – collecting shellfish, digging for yams, and collecting and processing cycad fruits – yielded roughly 4,000 to 6,500 kilojoules per hour. Given that the body requires an average energy intake of around 8,300 to 10,000 kilojoules per day, this means that a woman could feed herself with two hours of work.

One must of course be very careful when inferring from the lifestyle of present-day Australian hunter–gatherers (who can buy some of their supplies in the village shop) how pre-settlement Aboriginal people lived their life. Even so, the behaviour of the Aboriginal hunter–gatherers does seem at odds with Western theories of economic life to this very day.

In 1993, in *Economics and the Dreamtime: A Hypothetical History*, the economic historian Noel G. Butlin made the first serious attempt to describe pre-contact Australian Aboriginal society from an economic perspective. He found that Australian Aborigines had indeed all the functions of a 'rational economy'. There was a supply and demand for goods and services; they traded goods and the trade seemed to follow the theory of comparative advantages; they achieved some economies of scale; there was a clear division of labour, particularly between men and women; and they had a system for judicial order, a form of ownership and land property rights. Butlin did not imply that the Aborigines acted 'rationally' according to standard economic theory. But he argued that, regardless of overt motivation, the 'outcomes were more or less consistent with this concept of rationality'.

Butlin was the first scholar to apply modern economic theory to Aboriginal society. He argued that one could not, as Sahlins had, regard Aboriginal economic life as separate from social behaviour. Aboriginal production was much more than food and goods – they produced intangibles such as information, education, diplomacy, and services such as feuds, entertainment and ceremonies for death and marriage. The community also had to maintain order in the society, spend time on decision making, agree on communal efforts etc.

Butlin's conclusion was that the Australian Aborigines were not 'underusing' their resources at all; the economy functioned rationally to cater for a high demand for services (intangibles) rather than material goods (tangibles).

A simple calculation shows the possible extent of intangibles production in an Aboriginal economy. Sleep probably required eight hours, which left sixteen hours of 'production time' per day. As we saw above, food procurement normally required two to five hours per day, while production of personal tools, shelters etc. was probably not high, say one to three hours per day. This left between eight and thirteen hours per day for intangibles production. Or to state it differently: between 50 and 80 per cent of an Aboriginal economy may have been devoted to the production of intangibles.

TRADE IS TRUST

It is easy to pass by the two small inconspicuous shallow holes dug into a rocky outcrop. One of the holes is around fifteen centimetres deep and five centimetres wide, the other is smaller. The rocky outcrop is situated on a low ridge just on the old border of Nhunggal country, about 100 metres from the Narran River. The ridge is sufficiently elevated to keep dry during the highest floods.

This is one of the trading places once used by the Nhunggabarra to exchange goods with their neighbours. The Nhunggabarra selected items from their country that they had a surplus of and brought it to the trading place. There they placed a message stick in one of the holes and left. The neighbouring people passing by would see the message stick and leave items of their choice at the trading place. Both trading parties had to accept all the items, even if they did not need them; to leave anything would have shown disrespect. What they did not need they would in their turn trade with people further away. In this way a vast trading network was maintained across all of Aboriginal Australia. The trade was entirely based on trust and no one would steal the goods left for trade. To do so would be to break the law by showing disrespect and would immediately stop the trade.

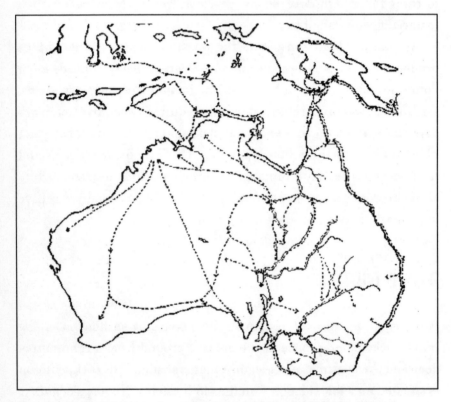

The seven trunk trade routes in pre-European Australia. (McCarthy 138–40)

The first Europeans found many paths or tracks in the landscape. The visibility of those tracks suggested that they were frequently used. It took a long time before the Europeans realised that a whole network of trade routes linked all parts of Australia long before the Europeans arrived.

In the 1930s the anthropologist McCarthy identified seven different trunk trade routes traversing the whole continent, along which people travelled astounding distances, something they must have done for a considerable time before European contact. The trunk trading functioned as sections in a chain: each community was responsible for the trade link over their land. The Aborigines in one section of the chain might not have needed the good themselves; all they knew was that an article came from 'far away north' and was going 'far away south'.

A big-volume trade item was axe stone, which moved 600 to 700 kilometres from a quarry in South Australia. Pearl shell travelled further than any other object; from the Western Australian coast to the Great Australian Bight, a trip of 1600 kilometres. There was also a roaring trade in the native tobacco, *pituri (Duboisia hopwoodii)*, a plant with narcotic qualities, which grows in Nhunggal country. Pituri has been shown to have travelled as far as 800 to 900 kilometres from its source.

Trade was based on physical exchange of goods, also known as barter trade, and the goal was to exchange goods of equal value. No money was involved.

Economists identify two disadvantages with barter trade compared to money transactions. One is that it depends on the 'mutual coincidence of needs'. Before any transaction can be undertaken, the needs of one person must mirror the needs of another person. So, if you have a surplus of stone axes and need spear points, you must find someone who has a surplus of spear points and needs more stone axes. To overcome this problem, intermediaries in medieval Europe would store and warehouse huge volumes of commodities – a very risky business, which they had to cover by increasing prices. The other disadvantage with a barter compared to a money transaction is that the price of goods is harder to fix.

The Baaluu and Muuboop story shows that the Nhunggabarra were well aware of the problems with barter trade. Their model for tangible goods, where 'buyers' and 'sellers' never met eye-to-eye and where you had to accept the whole package of goods, was a shrewd solution. Instead of trade in tangible goods being risky and a potential source of conflict it became a trust-building mechanism – community to community rather than individual to individual.

The Nhunggabarra goods trade was always based on barter, and the exchange values in pre-European times were not set according to market principles. There have been several observations of market-based trading in Aboriginal communities, but these are confined to areas around Cape York, which were under the influence of Indonesians. Auctions conducted by Aboriginal people were even observed by the Europeans, but this was most likely in response to European trading principles.

STORY | BAALUU AND MUUBOOP

Muuboop, the owl, had been camping away by himself for a long time. While alone he had made a great number of barrans (boomerangs), bundis (clubs), muruns (spears), coolamons (dishes) and possum rugs. He had taken great care to carve the hunting tools with the teeth of possums, and paint the inside of the rugs with coloured designs. He had sewn the rugs with the sinews of the possum, threaded into a needle made of a little bone taken from the leg of an emu. As Muuboop looked at his work he was proud of all he had done.

One night Baaluu, the moon, came to Muuboop's camp and asked to borrow one of his rugs. 'No, I never lend my rugs,' replied Muuboop. So Baaluu demanded to be given a rug. 'No, I also never give my rugs,' replied Muuboop.

'So, give me some of your hunting tools,' insisted Baaluu. Muuboop again replied that he never gave or lent anything he had made. Baaluu argued that the night was very cold and again asked to borrow a rug. Muuboop replied, 'I have spoken. Go away. I never lend or give anything I have made.'

Saying no more, Baaluu left. He cut some bark and made a gundhi (hut) for himself. When it was finished and he was safely inside it, down came the rain in torrents. And it rained without ceasing until the whole country was flooded. Muuboop was drowned and his hunting tools floated about and broke apart, and his rugs rotted in the water.

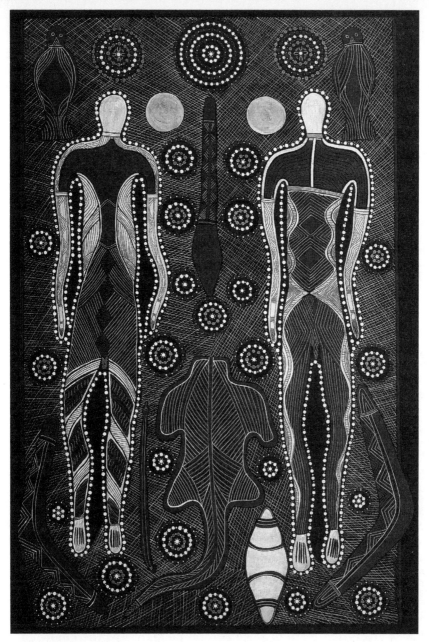

Baaluu and Muuboop

The figure on the right represents Muuboop and the other figure, Baaluu. The possum skin and tools depict all the things Muuboop had made that Baaluu wanted to borrow. The cross hatching throughout the painting represents the rain Baaluu made which rotted all the tools and skins. The circles of dots represent the 26 communities which have this story and the U shapes contained in the two top circles show how the story was kept alive through respect.

This story gives the reason why trade was developed. It tells about the risks and futility in stockpiling tangible goods. Not only will it cause envy among people, losing it all is a big risk. If Muuboop had given some of the goods he did not need to Baaluu, he would have avoided the moon's envy and he would have been given something in return that he might have had more use for. Because Muuboop persisted with his behaviour he suffered the consequences.

The story also explains the logic for the Nhunggabarra trading model. By leaving the goods in a neutral trading place they avoided arguments about the value and they also avoided entirely the risk inherent in warehousing goods.

TRADE IN INTANGIBLES

It is relatively easy for a researcher to follow the trade in material goods by following the artefacts traded. But, typical to a Western mindset, tangible trade has tended to be focused on. But did the Aboriginal people regard trade only in terms of the economic, tangible value of goods? The minimalist design of the goods' trading process, stripped of all face-to-face contact, suggests that the Nhunggabarra were not investing much time in it.

The first to realise that trade in tangible goods was perhaps a side issue for the Aborigines was the anthropologist W.E. Stanner. In a study of the process of giving he remarked: 'It is the *gift*, rather than what is given that matters.' The central element was the enjoyment inherent in the process of giving. The preparation for a visit to relatives, the journey, the ritual, the formalities to be observed, the niceties of etiquette etc. were enjoyable elements of life. The fact that some artefacts were exchanged was the tangible proof that the process had taken place with mutual appreciation, but it was not the main reason for the 'trade'.

The Nhunggabarra were keen to exchange dances, songs and ceremonies and probably invested considerable time in this type of trade. A settler tells:

Three tribes of blacks were assembled here last night...There were 40 men in one of these tribes; they were going to the [neighbouring tribe] to learn a new song that had been invented by some of their country people there. For an object of this kind they often travel great distances.

In the mid 1800s a group of some twenty Aborigines hunted down and killed a newly arrived settler's herd of sheep – an easy new 'game' that had arrived with the white people. The settler gathered a posse, who chased and killed many of the Aborigines. The fellows of the murdered people developed a new dance about the dangers of killing the white man's animals. This dance travelled as a message also to Nhunggal country.

Songs and dances travelled far and wide in Aboriginal Australia. They were passed on, including the accompanying dance performances, from community to community, often without translation. The songs and dances could travel fast too; a ceremonial dance appeared at the Great Australian Bight only 25 years after it was first 'exchanged' in northwestern Queensland over 1600 kilometres to the north – this is considered fast in anthropological terms. If the exchange had been of a new stone tool, the archaeological record would seem to show the appearance of the tool simultaneously in the whole area. Early European observers were impressed by the speed of communication and spread of information in Aboriginal Australia, and one witness concluded that news of any importance would spread throughout the Australian continent in a matter of months. Thomas Mitchell came across a group of Aborigines on the Gwydir River, southeast of Nhunggal country, in January 1831, where no white man had set foot before. They exclaimed 'white-fella' when they saw him and his party; Mitchell concluded that the word must have travelled before his physical arrival.

The major trade routes that crisscrossed the continent show that Aboriginal communities were part of a vast and complex social and economic network; they were not isolated groups. Trade in intangibles supports a conclusion that the Australian Aboriginal people had developed an economy where production, apart from food, primarily fulfilled an intangible demand.

ECOFARMING

When Thomas Mitchell travelled the country close to the Darling River south of Nhunggal country in June 1835, he came across something he could not understand:

> the grass had been pulled to very great extent, and piled in hay-ricks so that the aspect of the desert was softened into the agreeable semblance of a hay-field. The grass had evidently been thus laid up by the native, but for what purpose we could not imagine. At first I thought the heaps were only the remains of encampments, as the aborigines sometimes sleep on a little dry grass; but when we found the ricks, or haycocks, extending for miles, we were quite at a loss to understand why they had been made. All the grass was of one kind, the new species of Panicum... and not a spike of it was left in the soil over the whole of the ground.

While still pondering about what the Aborigines might use the 'hay-ricks' for, Mitchell, with the white man's arrogant ignorance, let his cattle and bullocks loose to feed, and then noted happily in his journal that 'they were very fond of this hay'! Perhaps he would have behaved differently had he realised that the 'hay' was cereal intended for human consumption and that it was in the process of being harvested.

Mitchell had come across one of the ecological farming methods designed by the Aborigines. The 'hay-ricks' were a method for harvesting cereal, perfectly designed to generate maximum nutritional value from the wild millet grass with minimum effort.

One of the problems with wild cereals is that individual grasses tend to ripen at different times, which makes the harvesting and threshing of large quantities very difficult. The solution to this problem developed by the farmers living in the first villages of the Fertile Crescent was to select the best seeds for planting the next crop and, because they were sedentary, they gradually changed the grain genetically and it became 'domesticated'.

The Australian Aborigines developed a different method. The millet grows in the summer and the seeds ripen from December to March. They harvested the grass in the short time-window when the seed was full but the grass still green. The grass was then stacked. When the seeds were ripe and dry, they all fell off in one place and could be easily harvested. The seeds were then milled into flour using seed-grinding stones.

This method neither changed the nature of the wild cereal, nor the soil's ecology; it was an ingenious ecological solution to the problem. The same method was probably used all over northwest New South Wales, including Nhunggal country, where the wild millet grass once grew in abundance. The Nhunggabarra built on the natural habitat, but they did not change it — this would have killed animals and vegetation and been against their mission to keep all alive.

The Aboriginal approach to farming was to learn how nature worked and then 'help it on the way' with minimum energy effort. They knew, for example, that parsnip yams, left in the ground with their tendrils still attached, grew into new yams, so the people made a deliberate practice of replanting them. True agriculture would have produced a higher yam yield per plant, but it would have involved the labour of tilling the ground and irrigation, and it would have changed the soil, all of which the Aboriginal people were keen to avoid.

They knew that fruit trees grow from the seeds of its fruit, so they deliberately spat out fruit tree seeds into the debris of fish remains in refuse heaps at the edge of the camp, which were ideal environments for tree growth. These habits were so consistent that archaeologists use stands of fruit trees as indications of old campsites.

The author Mary Gilmore describes in her memoirs how, after having extinguished an accidental fire lit by a settler, the Aborigines went through the whole area, examining the state of the bushes and trees, testing the seed pods and capsules of bushes and planting seeds in the ashes. Caring – not exploiting. We might say that the Nhunggabarra model was 'knowledge-based ecofarming' – to learn and adapt, but not to change.

Fire was the most important ecofarming tool. As present-day wild bushfires prove, Australian bush land is naturally fire-prone. The Aborigines managed the fire so that it supported, rather than harmed, the animals, and the land and the wheres and hows for this fire management were contained in the law stories – for example, the Crane and Crow story – handed down by Baayami.

Fire was used to expose or capture a harvest and to generate or regenerate pastures for grazing animals. Again, the Aborigines displayed how they fulfilled their mission to keep all alive; the grass fields provided food for the animals, increased their numbers and also made them easier to prey on.

Scientists today are largely in agreement that the Aboriginal methods had achieved an ecological balance on the Australian continent as a whole. For example, Tim Flannery, the Principal Research scientist at the Australian Museum and author of *The Future Eaters*, believes that the Aborigines had gradually finetuned their fire-stick farming methods over the last 35,000 years.

The Nhunggabarra were one of the custodians of the fish traps in the Darling River at Brewarrina. Parts of a once very elaborate system of fish traps still remain. The fish traps comprise a convoluted series of stone weirs and pens, constructed from river cobbles. They were designed to trap the fish at various levels of flooding, and their construction reveals that Aborigines understood very well both the hydrology of the river and the behaviour of the fish. (A Nhunggabarra

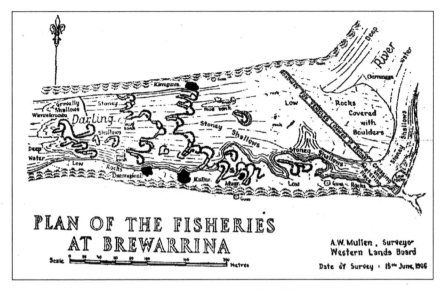

PLAN OF THE FISHERIES
AT BREWARRINA

A.W. Mullen , Surveyor
Western Lands Board
Date of Survey · 15ᵗʰ June, 1906

Map of the fish traps at Brewarrina. (Brewarrina Historic Society)

story credits Baayami and his two sons with the construction, so we leave the question of their origin open.)

The fish went upriver to breed, when the river was flooding. They passed the traps and when the water started receding, the older and bigger fish sensed the danger and escaped over the walls of the traps. The younger fish, with less experience and now free from larger predators, waited until the water had dropped further and thus got caught in the traps. In dry seasons, teams of Aborigines walked the river, beating the water so that the fish fled into the traps. The traps also functioned as a 'live larder', storing fresh fish.

The operation of the fish traps suggests that the Aboriginal people may have known something that has now been shown scientifically: that the biggest fish are the most valuable for sustaining the population. Until only recently it was believed that all larvae have the same odds of survival. Not so. Not only do big female fish produce larger quantities of eggs, larvae from bigger fish are bigger, grow much faster and have a much higher survival rate than those spawned by smaller fish.

The fish traps constituted an ecological system for catching the maximum number of fish with the minimum effort, while at the same time sustaining the stock. The fish traps proved their effectiveness every year as they supported annual gatherings of more than 5000 people.

This ecological farming created an abundance of food in the rivers and the floodplains that we find hard to believe today. Mary Gilmore recollected that the Murrumbidgee River in her childhood days in the 1860s still teemed with fish and freshwater lobsters, some of them so large that one lobster was enough for a meal for her family's two adults and two children. This was the result of long-term supply management: leaving the breeding adults, protecting the young, monitoring the supply. When, a few years later, the fish and lobsters had disappeared. Mary Gilmore's father explained that 'when the blacks went, the fish went'. The Aboriginal ecofarming methods made maximum use of the animals' natural behaviours and changed their natural habitats as little as possible. The results looked like nature itself and most of the settlers never understood that the fish traps were indeed 'farms'.

.

Did the diet of the Nhunggabarra make them healthier than the European settlers and, further, even healthier than Westerners today? There is archaeological evidence that hunter–gatherers in general were lean, fit and free of coronary heart disease. Their physical fitness was due to their active lifestyle and their diet, which consisted mainly of natural and unprocessed food. Compared to the modern Western diet, it contained more fruits, vegetables, nuts, lean protein, polyunsaturated and monounsaturated fats, and omega-3 fatty acids. Their diet also contained little saturated fats, no trans-fatty acids (industrially manipulated oils), and no refined grains and sugars.

The animal meats of the Nhunggabarra, in contrast to present-day meats, were rich in omega-3 fatty acids. This was because the plants and grasses that the animals fed on were rich in omega-3 fatty acids; domesticated animals of today are fed on lower-nutrient corn and grain. The average Western diet today, combined with our sedentary lifestyle, is seen as the prime cause for the rapid rise in obesity, high blood pressure, diabetes and coronary heart disease.

THE LIVE LARDER

The Nhunggabarra did not store food in large containers, and they did not use any conservation technique, such as smoking or salting. This has been interpreted from a Western perspective as a lack of technology – in other words, a deficiency. For example, archaeologist Ian Keen writes in 2004: 'The limited storage, and more or less immediate consumption, of foods meant that food species had to be available in the field all year round.' Keen implicitly echoes the conventional wisdom among scholars of many professions: the Aborigines were so ill-equipped that they had to survive on a daily piecemeal hand-to-mouth basis.

It is only with recent advances in ecological science that a realisation closer to the probable truth is emerging: the Aborigines did not develop European-style storage and conservation methods because their own methods were superior.

Mary Gilmore's father once got the surprise of his life. He was about to fill his billy (or teapot) at a little waterhole and there he found a fish big enough to make him a meal. This probably was some time before the 1850s. What he saw was an example of Aboriginal 'live larder' technology: in pre-European times, fish, eels and lobsters were trapped and stored alive in waterholes and ponds along the watercourse of every river by the Aborigines.

A simple log felled and positioned at precisely the right spot in a creek acted as a barrier against predators for small fish. The Aborigines placed fresh saplings and small branches by the log every year so small fish could congregate there, creating safe havens or 'voluntary' natural coves.

True to Aboriginal style, the live larders made maximum use of the natural environment and were indistinguishable from nature itself. When Mitchell came across what most likely was one of the safe havens for fish on the Darling River in December 1831 he only perceived 'two large trees [that] had fallen across the stream, from opposite banks...interwoven with rubbish', which he ordered to be cleared to give free passage. In the years to come the settlers that followed in his trails continued to clear the streams and, in doing so, they also cleared the streams from the abundance of fish.

The Aborigines also preserved yams in the ground by controlled harvesting, or planting on offshore islands to extend their distribution and to ensure a reserve supply. Deliberate fire-stick farming created grazing pastures in the woodlands for animals, which therefore naturally congregated there; waterholes with permanent water were kept as a last refuge for humans and animals. Mary Gilmore describes Aboriginal sanctuaries where hunting was completely forbidden and areas where hunting was not allowed two seasons in succession. The Gugu-Yulandji people in north Queensland still preserve a tradition of 'story places', where hunting is not allowed. The white settlers regarded the safe havens and sanctuaries as land, which by chance had a plentiful wildlife; within a few years this wildlife was gone.

·

The European granary storage method was developed as a consequence of European climate and farming methods. The land provided only one harvest of grain per year and it had to be stored over the winter season until the next harvest. Conservation techniques were developed for the same reason; to keep hunger away during the lean winter seasons.

By contrast, Nhunggal country provided a multitude of food all year round (albeit of seasonally varying quality and taste), and the Nhung-gabarra's ecofarming methods and live larder technology secured a constant, safe supply of fresh food. The Australian climate made the live larder superior to the 'dead' granary. It was low maintenance: live animals looked after themselves. It was safe: human thieves were not a problem in Aboriginal Australia, but animals, insects and mould were. It kept food fresh: the early European settlers discovered, often to their peril, that the Australian combination of high temperatures and pronounced seasonal rainfall made food storage difficult everywhere, particularly in tropical northern Australia. Even with smoking and salting techniques, they often found that game they killed went bad within a matter of hours.

Smoking for conservation of meat would have been easy to develop for a people so adept at using fire and smoke as the Australian Aborigines. However, they chose not to. The same is probably valid for salt, which was available in many parts of Australia and was used as a flavour enhancer. Why would the Aborigines, who knew the medicinal effects of every plant and the features of every rock and soil in their country, not have understood that salt could be used for conservation?

There must have been a reason for not developing these conservation and storage techniques and the simplest explanation is the most likely: *their methods secured food species available in the field all year round which enabled more or less immediate consumption of foods and required only limited storage*. And when they needed storage, they preferred storing their food live. They knew what we know today: that fresh food tastes best and also contains the most nutrients.

WHY DID THE ABORIGINAL POPULATION NOT GROW?

Archaeological records point towards a very slow growth in Aboriginal population, with only a slight 'intensification' during the 5000 years preceding settlement. In any case, population growth must have been quite slow and well in balance with productivity increases and resources available, otherwise the continent would have suffered from major ecological problems. This raises the question: if the Aboriginal people enjoyed a relative abundance of food at least in the southeast, how did they avoid an explosive growth in population?

We do not know the answer to this. Historically, scholars have tended to explain the low rate of population growth in Aboriginal Australia as being a result of 'natural' causes, such as high child mortality, wars and famine.

But there are several indicators of a more conscious population growth management. We know, for example, that Aboriginal women traditionally breastfed their babies for up to five years, a practice called lactational amenorrhea that is known to reduce fertility. There also exist several medicinal plants known among Aborigines for their contraceptive effects, and we must assume that they would have been used.

For the purpose of this book it is not necessary to know the exact details of the methods used for population regulation. What is important for us is to acknowledge that Australian Aborigines probably applied conscious regulatory practices to check their population growth.

WHY DID THE NHUNGGABARRA NOT DEVELOP AGRICULTURE?

Agriculture and sedentary life constituted a pivotal point in the development of societies. Agriculture dramatically sped up natural erosion and increased pressure on ecologies, and with sedentary living arrived hierarchical organisation in all areas of society. Agricultural societies 'developed' into chiefdoms and kingdoms ruled by kings and priests. Almost every people on earth, including the hunter–gatherers in Papua New Guinea, followed this path and became residential farmers. It is hence crucial to ascertain why the Australian Aborigines never developed agriculture.

Why did the harvesters of wild cereal not become cultivators? Why was the dingo accepted and domesticated, but no other animal? Why was pottery never adopted in Australia? Domesticated animals, such as the pig, and pottery existed in Papua New Guinea at the time of the last land bridge. The Aborigines had all the 'pre-adaptations' generally considered necessary for agriculture; they had the milling technology, the seeds and the storage methods. They also had suitable soil in some parts of the continent.

These days scholars dismiss conservatism as the reason, because the Aborigines quickly adopted many other elements imported from overseas, such as outrigger canoes, wooden sculpture, fish hooks, complex netting techniques and various art designs and myths. On the contrary – early white witnesses describe the Aborigines they met as keen and curious about European tools, eagerly testing them to establish their functionality.

Agriculture and hunter–gathering are alternative and competing strategies. The fact is that at least one Aboriginal people, the Bagundji, tested cereal cultivation, but they seem to have concluded, after a long period of experimentation, that their existing eco-methods ensured a better return on labour. There is some evidence that also other Aboriginal societies tested agriculture, but we do not know for sure.

As we have already established, the Aborigines did cultivate the land; they had developed a sophisticated array of highly specialised techniques for ecological farming. The most likely explanation for lack of agriculture, therefore, is that the alternative Aboriginal methods allowed a sufficient level of affluence. This is argued by both the archaeologist Josephine Flood and an expert in Aboriginal food, Philip Clarke. The return from the Aborigines' highly efficient 'ecofarming methods' was probably so great that agriculture was not worth the additional effort.

But if 'ecofarming methods' were so efficient, why did they not generate more of a surplus? Jared Diamond (1997) suggests at least three limiting factors: one was a lack of cereal grasses with large seeds. The wild predecessors of modern-day wheat and barley in the Fertile Crescent still look remarkably similar to the domesticated versions. The hunter–gatherers in the Fertile Crescent were able to harvest nearly a tonne of high-protein seeds per hectare, yielding 50 kilojoules for only one kilojoule of work – an extraordinary energy leverage. Prehistoric Australia had many grasses, but the seeds were all very small, so they were labour intensive to harvest. One was the wild millet that grew in Nhunggal country.

The other limiting factor was a lack of animal candidates for domestication on the continent. None of the 'big five' domesticated animals – sheep (West Asia), goat (West Asia), cow (Eurasia), pig (Eurasia) or horse (Russia) – were available to the Aborigines. Of a total of 114 wild terrestrial herbivorous species – 'the candidates for domestication' – only one (the red kangaroo) existed in Australia in prehistoric times.

Diamond's conclusion is that the reason some peoples, among them the Australian Aborigines, did not develop agriculture was due to the lack of suitable plants and animals to domesticate.

There is a third factor working against agriculture in Australia: the climate. Not only is it dry, it is also unpredictable. Unlike the European farmers, who could rely on a predictable annual seasonal pattern, the Australian Aborigines had to cope with fluctuations in both temperatures and rainfall which were both irregular and unforeseeable.

The climate is still the worst enemy of farming in Australia. For this reason, Western-style agriculture has a very poor environmental track record on the continent and has largely failed to show sustainability compared with Aboriginal methods. Our conclusion is, therefore, that the Australian Aborigines had a very good reason for not starting agriculture – *it would not have worked!*

The fact that some Aboriginal people, after testing it, decided to abolish cereal cultivation, may even point towards careful consideration and conscious decisions *not* to become sedentary and develop agriculture. If so, these decisions could well be the most impressive leadership accomplishment of Aboriginal society. It probably saved prehistoric Aboriginal societies from environmental disaster and collapse.

Leadership: All Have a Role

6

ON 29 JANUARY 1788, THREE DAYS after the ships of the First Fleet had reached Sydney Cove, the captain of the Marines, Watkin Tench, and some colonists came upon a group of a dozen Aborigines, who were walking along the beach.

The Aborigines were probably members of the Cadigal band, who occupied the territory near what was later to become the first British settlement in Australia. They were well-nourished; they were healthier and in better physical condition than any of the seamen on board the British ships — a group of proud and well-educated men in full command of their territory. The Aborigines must also have been in good psychic health, because they stood their ground although what they saw would have been unbelievable: a 'huge winged monster' appearing out of nowhere and a group of aliens descending on their country.

The British, however, only perceived the Aborigines as a group of 'indians', 'naked as at the moment of their birth' as Tench records in his journal. At first the two parties stayed apart, but then Tench approached them with a small European child by his hand to show a friendly attitude:

...I advanced with him [the child] towards them, at the same time baring his bosom and showing the whiteness of the skin. On the clothes being removed they gave a loud exclamation and one of the party, an old man with a long beard, hideously ugly, came close to us...The Indian, with great gentleness, laid his hand on the child's hat and afterwards felt his clothes, muttering to himself all the while.

Tench and his officers searched for indications of habitation, but they saw no houses, not even huts. And they saw no tangible signs of governance that they could recognise. There were none of the majestic buildings they were used to seeing their own leaders surround themselves with, no royal palaces gleaming of gold and no churches with soaring towers.

And where were their leaders? What was definitely incomprehensible for the officers of His Majesty's Royal Navy was that they did not see anything that distinguished chiefs from subordinates, nor any behaviour that would suggest that there were leaders among the group. Tench writes in his journal:

It would be trespassing on the reader's indulgence were I to impose on him an account of any civil regulations, or ordinances, which may possibly exist among this people. I declare to him, that I know not of any, and that excepting a little tributary respect which the younger part appear to pay those more advanced in years, *I never could observe any degrees of subordination among them* [author's emphasis].

When Europeans met Aboriginal people in the early days of colonisation, they would invariably ask to be shown to the 'king' or 'chief'. Both were alien concepts for the Aboriginal people, who, confused, sometimes would bring the Europeans to the wiringin, sometimes to the oldest person around. The British colonial governments could not cope with a people who neither recognised chiefs with positional powers nor political leaders, and during the 1800s they instituted a system of appointed 'chiefs', who were given brass plaques as a token of their 'distinction'.

The Australian Aborigines had in fact more leaders than the European colonists could imagine; everyone Watkin Tench met on the beach that first day had a leadership role. That is why he could not distinguish a difference.

STORY | THE SOUTHERN CROSS

In the Burruguu (the Creation) there were two men and a woman, who came from the red country and who had been shown which plants they could eat to stay alive. They lived on these plants for a long time, but then a big drought came and it was difficult to find the plants.

They became very hungry and one day one of the men said he would kill a wallaby so they could eat. The other man said they should not kill an animal because they did not know the law of that yurrti (totem). But they were so hungry that the first man did kill the wallaby, and he and the woman ate some of it.

They kept offering it to the other man but, even though he was starving and almost dead, he refused to eat meat because he did not know the law about killing and eating a totem. So he walked away over the sandhills, across the pebbly ridges and across the river on the far side of the Gulabaa plain until he came to a big white gum tree. The woman and the other man followed him and tried to get him to eat but they could not catch up with him. They saw him lie down under the gum tree and die there.

When the spirit, Yaawii, saw that the man would not break his law, he lifted the man and put him in the hollow of the gum tree. Yaawii then lifted the gum tree out of the ground and placed it in the southern sky. As he was lifting the tree into the sky, two yellow-crested white cockatoos, muyaay, flew after it screeching, because their roosting place was in the tree.

After a little while the tree gradually disappeared and all that could be seen were the eyes of Yaawii, the spirit, and the eyes of the first man to die

– these formed Yarraan, the Southern Cross. The two cockatoos still fly after the gum tree trying to reach their home – they are now known as the pointers for the Southern Cross.

And even now the she-oaks sigh and sway, and the gum trees cry tears of blood – which form a gum – to mourn for the first death of Aboriginal people.

The story describes the importance of paying respect to the law, both one's own law and that of other countries. Because the man would rather die than accidentally break the law, he was duly rewarded by the spiritual powers.

The first level of the story describes how the Southern Cross was created, and how one finds it with the help of the two pointer stars. The story also tells why the gum tree bleeds a red resin and why the she-oak makes its distinct swishing sound in the wind. On the second level the story describes the first death and the law about burial (the dead Nhunggabarra were rolled in bark and put in a gum tree). It gives a third level reason why a law about not killing the totem was required. There is also a fourth level element; the spirits that take the people to the Warrambul.

THE LAW

Nhunggabarra law was a code of moral and social behaviour. It regulated life in the community and between communities and was contained in the second and third levels of the stories. Its authority was unquestionable given the fact that it was passed on to the animals by Baayami at *Burruguu*, the time of creation. The law hence provided a moral authority outside the individual and beyond human creation.

The ancestral beings in the stories often make mistakes and behave badly, and they always suffer the consequences for their behaviours. The proper behaviours – the rules – are seldom stated explicitly; they have to be inferred and learned in the passage of initiation.

The Flower of Law

The centre of the painting shows the Big Buurra ceremony, where the 26 groups went out speaking different languages, and around this is the Rainbow Serpent. These are the core and the origin which all 26 communities shared, although the stories may be told differently in each community.

The bottom of the painting shows the turtle – the animal that broke the law in the Big Buurra story and, hence, gave Nhunggabarra people their laws. The sand goanna and the emu at the top of the painting represent two of the three totems that look after and teach the laws.

The leaves represent Nhunggal country and the cross hatching represents the links and connections between the communities – like a cobweb that ties everyone together.

Traditionally, children were brought up to accept a range of core rules, through socialisation, without questioning them. With growing knowledge came more responsibility, so there was considerable variation allowed in adherence to the rules. Permissiveness and doting were the themes of childhood. Aborigines are still remarkable for 'spoiling' their children compared to Western standards. For boys the loose reins were abruptly tightened at the age of around twelve, during their initiation. The treatment of girls, too, became less indulgent. However, only fully adult men and women – for men after their return from their long educational journey at around the age of 30 to 35, for women after their first child – were expected to know the entire content of the law and would be punished for breaking it.

Gradually, they were also taught to value difference in rules and to respect rules from a young age. Individual idiosyncrasies and different behaviours were accepted as long as they did not step over the permitted borders. This meant that all the communities had a range of generally accepted behaviours that were above questioning.

The ideal Nhunggabarra person

The image that emerges from the stories is that the ideal Nhunggabarra person was someone who shared generously, unselfishly and without hesitation; an active provider of care for children, for the old and the in-laws; a person who fulfilled kinship obligations without question. They showed compassion for others and respected integrity. The ideal Nhunggabarra person was unassuming and non-aggressive, someone who took responsibility for actions towards both one's own people and for other communities.

The law stories tell us the shared understanding of what it meant to be a 'proper' Nhunggabarra person. This is the ideal, of course, and they do not tell how the Nhunggabarra actually behaved before the white people arrived. There must have existed non-ideal behaviour and non-ideal people, from naughty children to ego-driven adults and individuals committing serious offences like adultery, kidnapping and murder. It is not possible to know how common such offences were, but what matters for our purpose is the 'normal' behaviour.

The behavioural code was imprinted upon a child even before they could walk. An example is a Nhunggabarra nursery rhyme cited by K. Langloh Parker in 1905, which drives home the value of generosity from a very early age:

Oonahgnai Birrahlee,
Oonahgnoo Birrahlee,
Oonahgnoo Birrahlee,
Oonabmillangoo Birrahlee,
Gunnoognoo oonah Birrahlee.

Give to me, Baby,
Give to her, Baby,
Give to him, Baby,
Give to one, Baby,
Give to all, Baby.

The telling and retelling of stories made sure that every adult knew the norm; therefore, offending adults would have known that they were behaving outside the norm. The few reliable independent eyewitness accounts preserved from the early days of white settlement tell a story of people who lived by their laws. 'They were a finer people than the whites; they not only had better laws, but they lived up to them,' a white man who had lived with the Aborigines over long periods in the mid 1800s told Mary Gilmore.

Sanctions

Aboriginal law all over Australia was not a law in the Western sense: it was not upheld by formal courts. But crimes against the law were recognised as offences and carried penalties. However, even after coming of age the offender would not receive a penalty until they felt guilt, understood what they had done, and owned up to the error.

This remarkable rule must be understood in the context of people living in close community, where everybody was known as an individual. Even if an offender could in theory commit a crime and get away with it, this would rarely happen. The option of fleeing was not viable. The Nhunggabarra could not survive on their own, without the support of their society, and the prospect of dying alone with no one conducting the proper ceremonies was too horrible to even contemplate: it would condemn a person to an eternal afterlife as a ghost. The kinship system ensured that the bad news would travel wherever one went, so moving to another community was not an option either. Thus, offenders had nowhere to hide, and sooner or later the pressure on them would become too strong. All adults knew the law very well, so they would know that they had committed a crime. Eventually, even the toughest person would cave in and would then take their punishment voluntarily. If the person died as a consequence, they were guaranteed the proper ceremonies and a place in the Warrambul.

Offenders were always punished by their own community, even if the crime had been committed against, or in, a neighbouring community. This crucial rule prevented vendetta behaviour. The Nhunggabarra law did not permit revenge and blood feuds against other communities: these would have rapidly thrashed to pieces the carefully balanced intra-community relationships.

RESPECT AND EXERCISING THE POWER OF KNOWLEDGE

A recurring theme in the Nhunggabarra law stories it is the importance of respect. The Crane and the Crow story told the Nhunggabarra to respect the integrity of other individuals and the Seven Sisters story taught men to respect women. The stories taught respect for diversity and respect for foreign people and other countries (the Black Swans and Big Buurra of Bayaami stories). The Willy-wagtail and the Rainbow story taught the Nhunggabarra to respect the needs of the vulnerable; the Southern Cross story taught them to respect the law; the Creation of Narran Lake story taught respect for life itself.

When Aborigines use the word 'respect', it does not carry the conventional meanings of today — that is, to convey a feeling of admiration of someone or obedience towards a higher authority. 'Respect' in the Aboriginal sense is an *action*, a verb; it means that you allow people to see you in 'your true form', as you are. You show your true self only to people you respect, people you think worth the effort, and who you consider as having the capacity to understand what you mean and who you are. Showing yourself as you truly are to another person is, as such, a sign of respect. I sometimes hear Tex thank a group of people *for the respect*. He is not thanking them, as most of them probably believe, for listening to him, but he is thanking them for allowing *him* to see *them* as they truly are.

Respect permeated one's understanding of what it was to be a Nhunggabarra person. At the core was a general respect for knowledge itself. Although knowledge was to be shared, it was so valuable and so powerful that if applied carelessly it could be very dangerous. Hence knowledge was apportioned according to one's level of maturity. Access to ceremonial knowledge was given gradually; both men and women had to prove themselves through initiation and they were not allowed access to certain types of knowledge until they had reached a certain maturity. Fourth level knowledge was taught only to people of special talent.

The respect for knowledge gave all knowledgeable individuals an automatic leader role. Their leader role, however, was balanced by respect the opposite way: leaders respected the integrity of others and had to lead without imposing themselves on others and without giving outright orders — a challenging concept to say the least! The followers would, in turn, respect the leader and not try to usurp the leader role.

STORY | THE BLACK SWANS

1. When Wurunna returned to his people he brought with him some hunting tools never seen by men. These, he said, were made in a country where there were only women and they had given them to him in exchange for his possum skin rug. They had told him that they would trade more hunting tools for more possum rugs. The people agreed to trade and to go to the women's country.

2. Wurunna warned his people that there were unknown dangers on the plain because he was sure the women were spirits – they had told him there was neither death in their country nor any night. However, Wurunna said there was an evil smell on the plain which seemed to have death in it.

3. Wurunna planned to smoke all the men so that no evil would be carried back to their people. Wurunna also arranged a plan for warning the men to leave if they stayed too long on the plain. He would take his two brothers with him and would turn them into two large swans. As there were no birds or animals on the plain they would be noticed quickly.

4. As soon as everyone was ready Wurunna would send these swans to swim on the lake opposite the women's camp. Seeing them, the women would be frightened and forget the men, who could then go onto the plain and get what they wanted. He told every man to take an animal with him and if the women tried to interfere, they should let the animals go and, again, the women would be distracted and the men could make their escape with the tools.

5. They set out – Wurunna and his brothers went to the far side of the plain and Wurunna lit a fire to smoke his people. From inside himself he brought out a large crystal and with its power he turned his brothers into two swans. 'Bibil, bibil,' they said. When the women saw the smoke they ran towards it crying, 'Wi-balu, Wi-balu,' but then they saw the two large white birds swimming on their lake and ran towards them.

6. The men seized the opportunity and took all the tools they wanted from the women's deserted camp but the women saw them and came angrily towards them. Then each man let go of the animal he had brought – far and wide on the plain went possums, bandicoots and others. While the women

chased the animals, the men dropped the possum rugs and, taking the tools, rushed towards Wurunna's fire.

7. The women, seeing the men leaving with all their tools, ran after them but the men passed into the darkness and smoke and the women were afraid to follow – there was no dark or fire in their country. The women were so angry they began to fight among themselves and their blood flowed fast so that it stained the whole of the western sky where their country is. Now, whenever the people see a red sunset they say the Wi-balus must be fighting again.

8. Wurunna now travelled on his journey to the sacred place where Baayami lived. He forgot about his two brothers even though they flew above him crying, 'Bibil, bibil', so that he would change them back into men. By the time Wurunna reached the sacred place, the swans were very tired and rested on a small lagoon.

9. The eaglehawks, messengers of the spirits, who were flying to deliver a message, saw the two swans on their own lagoon. In their rage they swooped down, drove their claws and beaks into the poor white swans, and then carried them far away from the sacred place. As they flew, they plucked out the feathers of the swans, which fluttered down the sides of hills and lodged in between the rocks with blood dripping beside them – these formed flowers which are now known as paper daisies.

10. The eaglehawks flew on until they came to a large lagoon near the big salt water. At one end of the lagoon were rocks on which they dropped the swans. The eaglehawks then remembered the message they had to deliver and left the swans almost featherless, bleeding and cold. The swans thought they were going to die far away from their country and their people.

11. Suddenly, they felt a soft shower of feathers falling on them, warming their bodies. High on the trees above they saw hundreds of crows similar to those they had sometimes seen on the plain but had believed to be a warning of evil. The black feathers covered the swans except on their wings, where a few white ones had been left. Also the down under the black feathers was white. The red blood on their beaks stayed there forever.

12. The swans flew back to their country and their people. Wurunna heard their cry, 'Bibil, bibil', and knew it was his brothers, although when he looked he saw not white birds, but black birds with red bills. Sad as he was to hear their cry, Wurunna could not change them back into men. His power as a wiringin had been taken from him for daring to go, before his time, to the sacred place.

The Black Swans story is one in the series with the *wiringin*, Wurunna, in the lead role. It describes the dire consequences of a seemingly innocent action – the trading of possum skins for tools. As is so often the case in Aboriginal stories, the story teaches by showing us the consequences of abuse – in this case, the abuse of the power of knowledge. It is a complex story with many messages and many lessons.

Most valuable for our purpose is what the second and third levels tell about leadership and the responsibility that comes from the possession of superior knowledge. We will therefore focus our interpretation on the leadership aspects.

1. Leader's motive: increase personal power

Wurunna, who started the chain of events, did so for all the wrong reasons. First of all, he should not have been in the women's country at all – personal curiosity and ego had driven him there, not the needs of his people. He desired the tools because the technology represented something different and it would have value as a new form of power. However, he did not understand the technology he was taking, or the women, or the customs of their land. He did not know the concept of trade – his only concept was to steal what he wanted.

The women were also wrong, for wanting the possum skins in the first place and for doubting that what they had was enough. They had the perfect world without appreciating it: no death, no cold and no darkness. But they wanted more – something new, a change. The women thought they were giving away something of no value to themselves – they did not need tools for hunting, because they did not hunt. They thought they needed the possum skins – but these brought the unexpected consequence of death to their country for the first time. For both Wurunna and the women the first exchange was useless – the women did not need possum rugs as it was never cold, and Wurunna's people already had all the tools they needed.

2. Play the xenophobia card

Wurunna was completely ignorant of the people he had just met. He did not even realise that the death he could smell on the plain was the smell of the possum skin rug, which he carried himself. His ignorance, however, did not prevent him from using the little he knew to instil fear in his own people – the fear of that which is different – so they would go along with him and his plans.

3. Use the position against your own people

Wurunna then abused his status position as a person of superior knowledge to persuade people to change without telling them why. He ruthlessly induced his own people to invade another country to get what he wanted. He even used his own brothers to protect himself and to achieve his own ends. He showed disrespect to his people by exploiting the power he had been given for his own benefit.

4. Manipulate the ignorant

Wurunna used innocent animals to achieve his ends. The animals were taken into a foreign country and had no choice but to follow him. The people followed blindly even though it was going against all they had been taught.

5. Conceal the true purpose

Wurunna again abused his knowledge and his power to generate 'smoke and mirrors'. He showed disrespect to the women when he confused and concealed the true purpose of his actions.

6. Ignore the risks

In their ignorance the people brought change that would last forever, without understanding the consequences of their actions. They brought anger to the women's country, and because they were blinded by their anger, the women became blind to the innocence of the animals – all they wanted to do was hurt them. By stealing the tools, the people brought dishonesty and disrespect into their lives.

7. When things go awry: blame the others

The women turned on each other as soon as something went wrong. By their actions, they brought chaos, dishonesty, distrust of each other, disloyalty and disrespect into their world. They realised the consequences of what they had done and tried to blame each other – but their realisation came too late for change. They made decisions without considering the consequences.

8. Turn a blind eye . . .

Wurunna finally walked away from the disaster of his creation. He even forgot his brothers. He was obsessed with the power that comes from unique knowledge, so he went to the place that might give this to him. He did not want to see what was happening around him or take any responsibility for his actions.

9. . . . and leave the followers to save themselves

The brothers now got into real trouble, but Wurunna ignored his team and everything that happened to them. He was focused solely on himself and what he wanted to achieve, so he did not see – or did not want to see – what he had done. Chaos and death followed him and he still did not see it.

The Black Swans

The painting is in four sections representing that the law comes in four parts. The top section shows Wurunna and the possum skins he took into the women's country. Their country is represented by the semicircles of dots surrounded by female figures.

The second section shows Wurunna talking to the men in his community, the gathering of the animals and his two brothers, who he turned into swans.

The third section shows the animals they let loose in the women's country and the two eaglehawks attacking the swans. It also shows the women in chaos and arguing among themselves, and the men taking their tools.

The fourth section shows Wurunna going to the mountain, represented by the triangular shape, and the crows giving their feathers to the swans, which then turned black forever. The red and yellow circles of dots throughout the first three sections of the painting represent the women's country (see colour plate).

10. The dire consequences

The pain of the brothers, Wurunna's team mates, was severe. They were suffering and it seemed they would die; but even worse was that if they died outside their country they would not be buried properly, an eternal curse.

The eaglehawks (the wedge-tailed eagle) were also wrong; they took power into their own hands and made two decisions they were not allowed to make: to punish and to decide what the punishment would be. They forgot the importance of their own role and showed disrespect to the Creator who had given them that role. They saw themselves and their own desires as more central than their role.

11. Help will be given to the remorseful . . .

Help comes from unexpected places. Because they now understood their mistakes and what had happened, the crows, who the brothers had thought were evil, actually offered them help. One of the morals of the story is that out of all the 'bad' comes a great deal of learning if we take notice of what is happening and if we take responsibility for what we do wrong. By facing our mistakes we learn. The story even offers comfort to those who have to live with bad leaders – they can expect help from high places!

12. . . . but not if we repent too late

Even Wurunna at last understood the consequences of what he did, but it was too late to change his actions. He would have to live with remorse, shame, distrust, guilt, disrespect and the loss of his powers – he had sacrificed all that we need to live a happy and fulfilled life.

So what would the ideal Nhunggabarra leader have looked like in pre-European times? Probably something like the opposite of

Wurunna. In telling us the worst, the story allows us to infer the opposite as the ideal to strive for.

The ideal Nhunggabarra leaders were governed, not by their ego-driven quest for personal power, but by a genuine motivation to serve their people. They respected all people; in particular they cared for the less knowledgeable and the less fortunate. They considered the consequences of actions and asked for advice before they acted; they did not try to conceal the true purpose of their actions and they reviewed the results. If things went wrong, they owned up to their mistakes, took personal responsibility for any negative effects and tried to compensate any followers who suffered. They acted with wisdom and broadmindedness in their relations with the communities outside Nhunggal country. They honoured and respected their differences and encouraged the people to learn from different ways of being and the different perspectives of other countries.

A LEADER ROLE FOR EVERYONE

As we noted at the beginning of the book, the Nhunggabarra people had an overall mission to keep all alive. This immense task was delegated to every single Nhunggabarra person by means of the law. Everybody had at least one major role to fulfil on behalf of the community. The wiringin, the medicine man or the 'clever man', had several unique roles, and in that sense was the most 'powerful' person of the community. But there was no excess capacity in the Nhunggabarra that the wiringin could draw upon for his services; he had to cater for his own sustenance and build his own camp, just like everybody else. His dwelling was no more elaborate than anybody else's and his clothes were just as scant as those of his community fellows.

The Nhunggabarra had no royalty, so there was no need for roles as aristocrats. And because they had no kings, not even chieftains, there were no organised wars that required armies. Hence, they did not need people who filled roles exclusively as warriors or soldiers.

Everyone had direct access to the spiritual world, so there were no roles for intermediaries like ministers, pastors, priests and or other clerics. Because they had no government, there were no roles as government bureaucrats. Since they possessed very little in terms of worldly goods, there were virtually no burglars and hence there was no role for a police force. And they had no role for a taxman, because they did not have any taxes.

The roles the Nhunggabarra did have included: teachers, child minders, story custodians, storytellers, dancers, painters, tuckandees (a 'brother' or 'sister' who acted as a back-up person), hunters, gatherers, net makers, basket makers, spear makers, fishermen and women, trackers, grain grinders, totem minders, medicine men and cooks.

All adults would know all the stories, and they would tell them freely. However, in educational situations only the custodians would tell the stories and the others would be silent. The most experienced hunter would be respected as the leader, but he would not order the other hunters to follow him; he merely made his decision known about the direction and target of that day's hunt. The other men would follow him, if that was their role. If they chose not to go, they would know they were breaking the law, but they were free to decide and the leader would not exert authoritarian power to make them follow him. The respect for both the expert's decision and for the individual's right to join or to refuse was absolute. The same would apply for most other roles. The roles were inherited and everybody would respect their role. No one would try to compete or take over the role of another person.

Was there then no chance for an individual to develop skills outside their inherited role? Yes: the primary 'career' was to devote more and more time in service to the community as a whole. This came naturally with age and the Nhunggabarra role models were the old people. They had with age grown into several vital roles – they functioned as teachers and mentors, conflict mediators, 'knowledge repositories', and as models of good behaviour. They were respected for their wisdom and superior knowledge accumulated over a long life.

An old person was respected, but not automatically influential. Nhunggabarra people were individuals just as Westerners and they would develop varying degrees of wisdom and knowledge. A very able spear maker and a woman well-versed in medicine would be greater assets to their community than the unskilled and would, as a consequence, be respected also in other matters.

Mary Gilmore describes a team of Aborigines who were felling and positioning a tree as a barrier in Wagga Wagga: 'Every man was alert; no man got in another's way; and each was captain in his own place.' Could more complex leadership tasks involving hundreds of people, such as large-scale hunting or fishing, work with this model?

Fishing at the fish traps in the Barwon River at Brewarrina is a good example. The fishing season was signalled by the floods receding, so people would gather around the traps without having to be called. Two people with the roles of 'watchers' would each stand on top of a rocky outcrop. When they yelled that they saw a good number of fish a whole group of men and women with the role of 'beaters' jumped into the river and formed a chain of bodies that covered the whole width of the river. Beating the water and shouting, they began to drive the fish in front of them upstream towards the trap area. The watchers directed the chain and when it entered the trap area, the 'beaters' turned 'catchers' and began spearing the smaller and medium-sized fishes, allowing the largest to escape. The fish were thrown up on the riverbanks, where another party took care of gutting them and preparing them for cooking.

Everyone knew their role – they had been doing this every year for as long as they could remember, and their fathers and mothers had been doing it before them. Their children were now with them, learning the ropes. There was no supervisor or project leader; all knew their roles and the roles were inherited. The same ideal applied to all organised activities involving several people: the work had to be done with as few directives as possible.

A multitude of roles created a multitude of role leaders and the law added support and authority to the role owners by also requiring respect for the person fulfilling their role. A person would have one major role and one was not allowed to usurp the role of this person. This meant that a leader was safe in the role — but only as long as they showed respect to the followers!

The Nhunggabarra person with a certain role had undisputed leadership and power in that field of knowledge, but at the same time they had to accept the leadership of others and be the follower in other knowledge fields. So every adult had both leader roles and follower roles at the same time — who had the leader role and who was the follower depended on situation and context. We could therefore call the Nhunggabarra's leadership style *context-specific*. It is not until very recently that this challenging form of organising has met the interest of business and academia.

The Nhunggabarra stories encouraged critical self-reflection among the leaders. The Black Swans story would have been performed in front of everybody in the community on a regular basis, and all people with access to the second and third levels of meaning would be reminded of the responsibility that comes with the leadership role and superior knowledge. The story thus functioned as a warning against abuse of personal power. As long as the story was kept alive, the meanings were traded from generation to generation and abusers would have a hard time getting away with their actions.

STORY | MIRRAI MIRRAI: THE SEVEN SISTERS

Angry because his people would not give him food when he wanted it, Wurunna had left his community in search of another group with which to live. He had encountered many strange and frightening things on his journey. His last encounter had so terrified him that he ran away as fast as he could. He was running so fast that he stumbled into a camp without first seeing it.

Frightened he looked around, but soon realised he had nothing to fear as there were only seven girls in the camp. They looked more startled than he was. The girls were friendly – they gave him food when they found out he was hungry and allowed him to camp with them for the night. Wurunna asked where the rest of their people were and what their name was. They replied that their name was Mirrai Mirrai and that their people were in a far country. They had only come to this country to see what it was like and after staying a while they would return home.

Wurunna was tired of travelling alone and decided that if he could he would steal a wife from among them. He left the camp as if leaving for good but hid nearby to watch for his chance. He saw the seven sisters start out with their digging sticks in hand. He followed at a distance, taking care not to be seen.

He saw them stop by the nests of some flying ants and, using their yam sticks, dig around the ant holes. When they had successfully unearthed the ants, they sat down to enjoy their feast, for these ants were a great delicacy to them. While they were eating, Wurunna crept up to their digging sticks and stole two of them.

When the Mirrai Mirrai had finished eating, they picked up their sticks and prepared to return to their camp. But only five could find their sticks, so these five started off, leaving the other two behind to look for their sticks and to catch up later. While the two girls' backs were turned, Wurunna placed the sticks firmly in the ground. When the girls turned around they saw the sticks and tried to pull them out. While they were struggling, Wurunna stole up behind them and seized them by their waists. The girls screamed and struggled but their sisters could not hear them and they could not escape Wurunna's grip.

Eventually, the girls quietened and Wurunna told them not to worry – that he was tired of travelling alone and wanted two wives, whom he would look after. But they must do as he told them. If they were quiet and went with him, he would be good to them, but if not, he would use his nulla-nulla to punish them.

The girls saw they could not resist so they travelled quietly with him, hoping that one day their sisters would come and steal them back again.

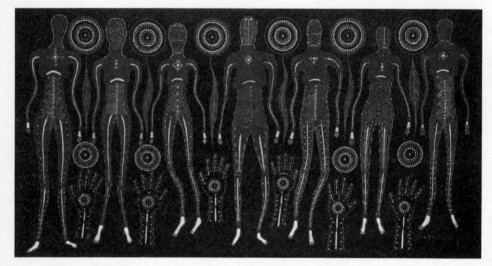

The Seven Sisters

The painting shows the seven sisters together in the sky with the designs on their chests being the learning and respect we get from them. The hands represent Wurunna and the two sisters he took, and the circles of dots, the community they came from. The designs on the women represent their way of doing ceremonies – each woman's design must be different. It also represents the fact that Nhunggabarra women only ever painted on their body. The various U-shape designs on their chests represent the different ways of communicating practised by different communities. By painting the designs on their own bodies they showed respect to all the different peoples they knew. The leaves represent the pine tree and the hands represent the community and families from which the girls came.

As the weeks passed, the girls appeared to be content with their new life, but privately they wondered if their sisters were still searching for them and they hoped they would be found eventually. One day, Wurunna was having difficulty starting a fire and he instructed the girls to get some bark from two pine trees nearby. The girls told him they must not cut pine bark. 'If we do, you will never see us again,' they said. Wurunna again ordered them to do as they were told. 'If we do, we will never return,' they replied. 'You will never see us in this country again, we know it.'

'Do as I say,' Wurunna said. 'If you run away, I will catch you and beat you hard – so go, do as I say.' The Mirrai Mirrai went to a tree and struck it hard, driving their gambu (stone axe) into the bark. The gambus immediately began to rise higher and higher in the pine tree; the tree began to grow, carrying the girls with it. Higher and higher grew the tree. Wurunna came to check on the girls and saw the tree growing, with his two wives clinging to the trunk high in the air.

Wurunna called to them to come down but they did not reply. He watched as the tree grew so tall that its top touched the sky. He saw the girls' five sisters reach down from the sky to help them up, telling them not to be afraid, but to join them and live in the sky forever. And there they have been ever since – the girls that Nhunggabarra people call Mirrai Mirrai, but who are also known as the stars, the Seven Sisters.

The first level of the story describes how the star sign, the Seven Sisters, was created. On the second and third levels, the Seven Sisters story explains the marriage law and the reason for it: marriage planning prevented men from stealing women by force from other communities. Such behaviour would have had disastrous effects both within a community, as well between the communities.

GENDER ROLES

European women, since the birth of the agricultural economy, worked alongside their husbands on farms. The industrial revolution added a female working class in the cities, and the women of bourgeoisie and nobility offloaded the onerous tasks of their households on to less fortunate sisters. However, women were denied the rights of higher education, universal suffrage and independent ownership of land and property, and access to many professions, among them medicine and the priesthood. Their contribution to the economy was not highly regarded.

In contrast, Nhunggabarra women were the principal contributors to their community's economy, responsible for up to 80 per cent of food production. They were expected to undergo full education, including extensive training in paediatrics, medicine and nursing, as well as ecology, biology and spirituality. Women would over time build up enormous practical knowledge about the medicinal plants and herbs of their country and their usage.

Nhunggabarra women were the teachers of all children up to the age of puberty. They conducted their own sacred ceremonies and they had a crucial role in greeting newcomers to the community. They were responsible for the short-term welfare of community members, from birth to death, in terms of sustenance. And because they were in charge of marriage planning they also controlled the 'long-term strategy': which combination of people was going to create the offspring best-suited to fill future roles in the community. Finally, when the Nhunggabarra had fulfilled their duty on earth, their land was inherited via the women. Women had the crucial role in mourning ceremonies in order to make sure the spirits of both men and women found their way to their home in the Warrambul.

The Europeans saw none of this. 'They consider their women as secondary objects, oblige them to procure their own food...and, on the march, make them beasts of burden,' Charles Sturt noted on his first exploration into New South Wales. He and the other white men and women, with their bourgeois and noble European backgrounds, completely missed the several key points about gender roles in Aboriginal society. They tended to regard male activities, such as hunting (which was the sport of aristocracy in their own countries), as having a higher status than female foraging and missed the fact that the women's efforts generated the bulk of the community's food.

And because men's ceremonies were visually more elaborate than women's, the Europeans drew the erroneous conclusion that Aboriginal men had the same religious monopoly as the European men enjoyed and male anthropologists dismissed women's ceremonies as 'love magic'. They did not realise that they − as men − were generally excluded from the women's more sacred ceremonies.

White men did not see in action the strong and powerful female network that worked the complex kinship and totemic system to ensure that marriages filled all the necessary roles of the Nhunggabarra and the communities that formed the cultural bloc. They did not learn about the tuckandee safety net. When the first settlers arrived, the Nhunggabarra's carefully crafted society infrastructure had already begun to disintegrate in the wake of depopulation. But the knowledge of how things were properly done remained: Tex's grandmother went through full initiation and the Nhunggabarra marriage planning system remained in place well into the 1900s. However, many ceremonies could not be performed to the full extent and gradually disappeared.

The Europeans also did not understand the main reason behind the men's elaborate initiation ceremonies and why they travelled and educated themselves much longer than the women. They saw it as another example of the men's high status. The law stories, however, reveal another view: the Nhunggabarra male ancestors are portrayed as reckless and aggressive and responsible for most mistakes. Hence, men need extra schooling and experience to mature and become responsible citizens in Aboriginal society. The men had to compensate for their lack of maturity and knowledge by learning from others and by conducting more ceremonies during their time on earth.

The European male scholars jumped to the conclusion that the Aboriginal women's role was onerous and of low status – they were 'profane', while the men were 'sacred'. Little did they realise that they only were seeing themselves in a mirror.

By and large most Western observers tended to miss the fact that women in Aboriginal society – before the arrival of the Europeans – lived and functioned on equal terms with men. There did exist *roles* to be filled by men and there existed roles that had to be filled by women, but interpreting these gender roles in Western 'status' terms is foreign to the Aboriginal mindset. Men showed respect for the female roles and women respected the male roles. Both were necessary for survival of the society and hence equal in value. Men and women were regarded as equal and different.

ROLE PLANNING AND RECORD KEEPING

As a Nhunggabarra person you were born into a role as a consequence of your kin and ancestry. Planning who were going to fill the roles in a community was the duty of all the women in the cultural bloc. They did this by maintaining a tight control of the complex kinship system and by planning the best combinations of kinship by means of marriage.

'Love marriages' may have existed before the Europeans arrived, but then only as exceptions. The family was the main production unit of the Nhunggabarra society and marriages had to be carefully planned. If the women got the planning wrong, the consequences for the community were dire; the family team might not function properly and a role might not be fulfilled or might die out.

How could they keep track of such an intricate web of relationships without written records? Or did they have a system?

The answer might be found in the 'mystery stones' that have been found in the Nhunggal region. While still in his teens and working at a station near Goodooga, Tex's attention was caught by an object protruding from the dirt in one of the paddocks, a stone cylinder with a conical end. It had inscriptions on its surface. He took it home and showed it to his grandmother. She said immediately, quite concerned: 'Return it to the place where you found it and bury it there.' Then she explained that the stone cylinder was used by the Nhunggabarra women to record all births, deaths and marriages in order to keep track of the totem and kinship relations of the communities, and that it must not leave Nhunggal country.

The first European to discover one of these stone cylinders was A.G. Brook, the owner of the Goondabluie station situated on Nhunggal country, between the Narran and Barwon rivers. He publicly exhibited his discovery in 1884. Since this time at least 500 stone cylinders have been catalogued. Many more are believed to be lying in storage on private properties. The farmer Lindsay Black, who published a first catalogue of the stone cylinders in 1932, was convinced that they had a ceremonial purpose and questioned all Aborigines he could find about them. He had to give up, when all he got were vague answers ('don't know') or fibs ('they were used to increase the supply of snakes').

The stones' cylindrical and conical form, similar to witches' hats, earned them a scientific name: *cylcons*. Their length ranges between 10 and 85 centimetres. More than a third of the catalogued stones still have visible inscriptions in the form of straight lines, circles, crosses and lines resembling various bird tracks. Most of the cylcons are made of sandstone or other soft and porous materials so many inscriptions may have disappeared. It seems they were buried shallowly, close to old campsites, generally not at old ceremonial or sacred sites, and they have been discovered as the soil erodes away. The finds have generally not been possible to date, but a cylcon has been found at the Cuddie Springs excavation, which suggests they have been used for at least 20,000 years.

If the cylcons were used by the Nhunggabarra for record keeping of kin they would have lost their function immediately when the infrastructure of the cultural bloc collapsed. This would explain why no one has seen the stones being used in any of the other Aboriginal communities in the area. Neither anthropologists nor archaeologists have been able to come up with a validated theory of their purpose.

Hence theories abound. The anthropologist R. Etheridge Jr, who studied the carved trees in the region, suggested they might be buurra message stones. Other theories that have been proposed are that they are death stones, burial records and phallic symbols(!). No theory suggesting their use for keeping record of kin has been proposed before now.

The world's first writing systems were accounting systems: they appear to have been responses to central planning challenges. The majority of the thousands of Sumerian clay tokens unearthed to date by archaeologists record numbers of sheep and amounts of grain. The

Mesoamerican writing systems that have been deciphered show detailed astrological data. This suggests that writing originated as a tool for kings and priests to keep control, for centralised powers to plan ahead for securing food resources and for predicting dates for critical religious events.

The vast Roman, Persian and Chinese empires would have been impossible to govern without writing so, not surprisingly, the central powers confined writing ability to a class of professional scribes. As the anthropologist Claude Levi-Strauss put it, ancient writing was developed 'to facilitate the enslavement of other human beings' – far indeed from the values of the Aboriginal societies.

Scholars have therefore normally found it easy to answer the question why the Australian Aborigines were non-literate and without writing systems: they were not controlled by secular or religious chiefs with planning requirements. This was, however, not true for the cultural bloc of the Nhunggabarra and their neighbours. They had one very complicated central planning task: marriage planning.

Planning marriages and finding the best combinations of kin among 26 communities, spread over an area probably exceeding 30,000 square kilometres, must have been an immensely complicated central planning task. It required specific and detailed information about how people in all the communities were related, a daunting record-keeping challenge which must have exceeded the capacity of the human memory.

Could the inscriptions in the 'mystery stones', the cylcons, be for this purpose? The inscriptions are not random: they are lines in patterns that resemble record keeping. Could the Nhunggabarra women and their female network have begun the first steps to developing a writing system for the same reason as the Sumerians and Mesoamericans – that is, as central planners needing to keep record? And was this record-keeping system lost when their society collapsed? This is what Tex's grandmother asserted. If the cylcons were 'women's business' it would have been impossible for white men to learn anything about it no matter how inquisitive they were.

MANAGING RISK

STORY | WILLY-WAGTAIL AND THE RAINBOW

Dhirridhirri lived by herself in a camp with her three little girls – she was a widow. One day Bibi made a camp quite close to Dhirridhirri. Dhirridhirri was so frightened of him that she could not sleep. She would watch Bibi's camp all night and if she heard a sound she would cry aloud, 'Dhirridhirri, wyah, wyah, Dhirridhirri.' Sometimes, she would be crying out all night.

One morning Bibi went to her camp to ask her what was wrong. Dhirridhirri told him that she was frightened because she was alone with her children and thought she could hear someone walking about. Bibi told her not to be afraid. But night after night the crying continued to happen.

Eventually, Bibi said to Dhirridhirri that if she was so frightened she should live with her daughters in his camp and he would protect her. But Dhirridhirri said she did not want to, and so her crying, 'Dhirridhirri, wyah, wyah, Dhirridhirri', continued night after night. Time after time Bibi asked her to share his camp but she always refused.

After a time Bibi thought of a plan to show Dhirridhirri how strong he was and how able he was to protect her and her daughters. He began work on a beautiful, coloured arch which he placed right across the sky, stretching from one side of the earth to the other. He called it yuluwirri (rainbow).

When the rainbow was firmly placed in the sky and showing its brilliance, Bibi returned to his camp to wait. When Dhirridhirri saw the rainbow she became even more frightened and fled with her children to Bibi's camp for protection. Bibi told her proudly that he had made the rainbow to show her how strong he was and how safe she and her children would be with him.

Even though Dhirridhirri was a little afraid of Bibi, she was also full of admiration for him, so she agreed to stay in his camp with her children. When, much later, they died, Dhirridhirri became the willy-wagtail who can still be heard crying out, 'Dhirridhirri, wyah, wyah, Dhirridhirri.' And Bibi became the brown treecreeper, who is always running up trees as if he wanted to build another yuluwirri.

Willy-wagtail and the Rainbow

The two large figures represent Bibi, the brown treecreeper, on the left, and
Dhirridhirri, the willy-wagtail, on the right, with the three children below them,
painted pink to represent sacred (see colour plate). The circles show how each
community is linked to another through the tuckandee. The arch across the top
of the painting represents yuluwirri, the rainbow, and the hands represent the
learning Bibi went through for his tuckandee. The diamond shapes are a traditional
Nhunggal country design.

This story tells how the Nhunggabarra managed risk: in this case the rule that everyone had the responsibility of looking after and teaching the children of the community. The story also describes the role of the tuckandee. Because Dhirridhirri and Bibi were turned into birds it means they were from the same group of totems. As the tuckandee, Bibi therefore was responsible for looking after Dhirridhirri and helping teach her children. By building the rainbow, Bibi showed that he was strong enough to protect them and that he could teach the children the proper way. The rainbow symbolises the tuckandee, which is there as an invisible support in times of need.

Both Dhirridhirri and Bibi were rewarded for not breaking the law – for showing respect to each other and for looking after the children – by being turned into the willy-wagtail and the brown treecreeper.

Low risk of starvation

In the 1700s the risk of starving to death was high, in general, worldwide. This is still the case in the twenty-first century in the developing world. A series of analyses during the 1990s confirmed that between 50 and 60 per cent of all childhood deaths in the developing world are caused either directly or indirectly by hunger and malnutrition.

Hunger is also the first risk that comes to a Western mind on encountering the harsh realities of the Australian outback for the first time: Europeans have had a hard time surviving in Australia. However, except during extreme drought, Nhunggal country was able to feed the Nhunggabarra quite well before their production model was disrupted by the Europeans' arrival.

Low risk of war

Aboriginal society seems violent when judged by today's standard: for example, capital punishment was meted out for offences that we would call minor today. However, provided a Nhunggabarra person did not break the law, they had a very low risk of dying at the hands of other people, since war, as the rest of the world knows it, was unknown to them. The Western mind finds this hard to believe until the Nhunggabarra society model and belief system are taken into account.

Their spiritual connection with the land made the idea of taking over another country completely meaningless. If a war campaign were to be successful it would only mean more work and more responsibility! War was against all that the Nhunggabarra law stood for and it violated the mission to keep all alive, which was shared by all the communities in the cultural bloc. The testosterone-fuelled young men would have got enough of an adrenaline surge from their long educational walkabout. And if we also add the close kinship relationships due to marriage planning, we have a model that virtually guaranteed peace among the communities that made up the cultural bloc. It seems quite unlikely that the Nhunggabarra were involved in wars with their neighbours.

Did the Nhunggabarra fight wars outside their cultural bloc? We do not know, although this too seems unlikely, because they would have had to cross the land of other people and combine forces with other communities outside their cultural bloc, a behaviour that was alien to them. We believe that the Nhunggabarra probably always lived in peace.

Australia-wide, before 1788, there exist no reports of European- and Asian-style aggressive warfare with the intention of taking over another country or of conquering an enemy — these wars belong to chiefdoms and kingdoms where individual motives of supreme leaders dramatically increase the probability of conflict. Also, Aboriginal fortifications were never discovered in Australia. Settlers reported intra-Aboriginal wars in the early 1800s in the New South Wales coastal areas, at least one involving several hundred warriors on each side. These wars, however, occurred after European arrival, when the society infrastructures had disintegrated due to diseases and when the communities were under severe stress because they had lost their land. It was as if the wars had come straight out of the rule book of the Black Swans story: the Aborigines fought each other instead of joining forces against their common enemy. The Nhunggabarra apparently knew quite well what could happen in a severe crisis, when the rule of law was no longer upheld, and had addressed it as best they could through their laws.

There exists no evidence of rebellions or serious challenges against the established order anywhere in Aboriginal Australia. Protests, such as they were, probably took place within the framework of the law, and if these differed from expected behaviours, adult protesters could expect sanctions.

The disintegration of Aboriginal societies due to diseases that spread ahead of the settlers meant that the Europeans never got to experience true Australian Aboriginal society. Although we have no final proof, most available evidence points towards a conclusion that pre-European Australia was a generally peaceful continent.

Low risk of disease

In early 1789 an eyewitness arriving at Port Jackson reported that 'an extraordinary calamity was now observed among the natives. Repeated accounts brought by our boats of finding bodies of the Indians in all the coves and inlets of the harbour…pustules, similar to those of smallpox, were thickly spread on their bodies.'

This was the first reported outbreak of smallpox and it was most likely introduced by the Europeans, because it occurred only one year after first settlement. Only three out of 30 to 50 people of the Cadigal band, which inhabited the territory immediately around the first British settlement, survived this epidemic.

Before the Europeans arrived the Nhunggabarra had no concept of many diseases common today. They did not know the common cold, for instance. The only serious diseases known to Aboriginal Australia were dysenteries and some arthropod-borne diseases. All other diseases were introduced on the Australian continent by the Europeans, except perhaps smallpox, which may have first been brought in by Malaccan fishermen, who traded with Aboriginal communities in northern Australia. The Europeans did not catch any indigenous diseases unknown to them upon arrival in Australia.

A large number of diseases with Eurasian and African origin were unknown in Australia. They include smallpox, rubella, mumps, diphtheria, measles, influenza, whooping cough, and tuberculosis. Also the two epidemic diseases with African origin – yellow fever and cholera – were unknown. Syphilis and malaria did not exist either.

The main reason epidemic diseases did not exist in Australian Aboriginal society pre-European contact is that many originate from domesticated animals. Many Eurasian epidemic diseases probably came about from the advent of agriculture and sedentary life some 10,000 years ago. For instance, pigs probably contributed whooping cough and influenza, smallpox came from camels and/or goats, and measles from cattle. Since the Aborigines did not domesticate any large animals, there was no environment in which epidemic diseases could develop.

The Nhunggabarra also had a high standard of food and a healthy lifestyle in general, which may be other reasons why they experienced fewer illnesses than the average Westerner living in Australia, Europe and the USA today.

A final clue suggests that serious diseases leading to death were not common. Sorcery, 'sung' on a person by a wiringin as punishment for a crime, was seen as the only cause of all deadly diseases, except death from old age. This suggests that disease in pre-European Australia was an extraordinary event requiring an extraordinary explanation. The introduction of European diseases among the Aborigines reduced their state of health dramatically: also, the Europeans were taken aback by the effects. This would explain why both settlers and anthropologists report that Australian Aborigines perceived a high risk of being hurt by sorcery.

The safety net: tuckandee

Traditionally, every Nhunggabarra person was born to a 'brother' or 'sister' in one of the surrounding communities. This person, your tuckandee, was not known to you, but they were taught all your law, religion and belief. The appointed tuckandees were given the relevant knowledge during their initiation process, but they would not know that they had learned anything that distinguished them from the other men and women of the same age group and they would never know unless their services were called upon. If a person died prematurely, the tuckandee would be called to that person's community to teach the children all the knowledge they needed to fulfil their role in the community.

Maintenance of the tuckandee institution was the responsibility of the women. It must have required them to keep record of existing kinship relations of all the 26 communities and to communicate on a frequent and regular basis with each other – an enormous challenge. Could they have accomplished this without written records? It seems unlikely. We believe the explanation lies with the stone cylinders described earlier in this chapter. However, how such records were kept and how the communication worked has not been confirmed by research.

BUILD COMMUNITY

Evolution theory has become a paradigm: it implicitly forms the mental model of laypeople, managers and scholars, irrespective of scientific field. For example, American anthropologist Elman Service explained that societies develop in stages from simple structures to more and more 'complex' ones as they grow in size. His classification in 1962 of societies into increasing levels of complexity as 'bands', 'tribes', 'chiefdoms' and 'states' has influenced social science scholars to our day. Though in his 1997 book *Guns, Germs and Steel*, Jared Diamond finds fault with the theory.

> The main problem with evolution theory is that it is a theory of biology. When applied to the human realm, such as societies populated by people with morals and free will, evolution theory can at best be regarded as a metaphor and its 'explanations' must be regarded with suspicion. Evolution theory lends itself too easily to the dangerous conclusion that the current state of humanity is the 'best' and that Western industrial societies are the most 'advanced', and it has been used to justify atrocities committed by colonising powers all over the world.
>
> Evolution theory is useful for painting with a broad brush, but it has to this very day prevented us from seeing the true achievements of the society of the Australian Aborigines.

The Nhunggabarra community

While we know fairly well the band organisation and nomadic life of the desert-living Aborigines, very little is known, besides traditional tales, about how the Aboriginal societies in the southeast lived before the Europeans disrupted their societies. It seems that people along the rivers were probably living a more sedentary life. There exist no trustworthy eyewitness reports about village living – only what the first explorers observed when passing by.

The Nhunggabarra were probably semi-sedentary; the whole community lived and moved together and they did not move camp very often during a year. People built wind-breaks of branches in summer and for the winter they may have built dome-shaped grass-thatched huts over light timber frames, and their camps may have resembled villages. Thomas Mitchell reported at least two such 'villages', one close to Brewarrina, possibly on Nhunggal land:

Their roads appeared in all directions . . . the buzz of population gave to the banks at this place the cheerful character of a village in a populous country.

A bit further along the Barwon River, Mitchell saw 'covered huts . . . large enough certainly to contain a family of 15 persons . . . There were also permanent huts on the banks, well thatched with straw . . . able to afford a ready and dry shelter in bad weather'. Mitchell once rode through a 'village', deserted by its inhabitants and describes in his diary:

They [the huts] were tastefully distributed amongst drooping acacias and casuarinae; some resembled bowers under yellow fragrant mimosa; some were isolated under the deeper shades of casuarinae; while others were placed more socially, three or four together, fronting to one and the same hearth. Each hut was semicircular, or circular, the roof conical, and from one side a flat roof stood forward like a portico, supported by two sticks . . . The interior of each looked clean and . . . gave some idea not only of shelter, but even of comfort and happiness.

These 'villages' would have been built in areas where the Nhunggabarra stayed for longer periods, such as the Narran Lake, where huge middens filled with crustacean shells and fish bones reveal the existence of habitation over a very long period. When the Nhunggabarra moved, they carried their essentials, but they left the wooden frames of the huts, sacred items belonging to a site and heavier utensils, such as grinding millstones, for until they returned next season.

How did the Nhunggabarra organise their society? What type of society was it? Elman Service uses the term *band* to describe a society of lowest complexity. The band has no permanent single base of residence. It jointly owns its land; it has no regular economic specialisation except by age and sex. There are no formal institutions, such as laws, police and treaties. The organisation is egalitarian, with no formal leadership and no upper or lower classes. Leadership is entirely based on personality, fighting skills, strength and intelligence. Although there is some similarity – for instance, the nomadic and egalitarian features – this model does not fit the Nhunggabarra organisation. As we have seen, the Nhunggabarra society was ruled by law, and leadership was sophisticated.

Service's next stage on the evolutionary ladder is the *tribe*, a linguistic unit of a few hundred people occupying a specific territory. The tribe is residential: even if foraging still brings in a proportion of the food, horticulture and domestication of animals provide a substantial contribution and allow and require more sedentary living. The tribe consists of several bands and more than one kinship land-owning group (*clan*), the members of which inter-marry. A tribe is not simply a collection of bands; the ties that bind a tribe are more complex. It is an association of a much larger number of kinship segments, which, in their turn, are each composed of families. This creates residential arrangements, such as villages consisting of family units occupying one house each. Tribal organisation allows higher population density, but the number of people in a tribe is still so low that all know each other by name.

In some ways the description fits: the Nhunggabarra and their neighbours spoke their own languages, so they did form linguistic units, and they had quite complex family and kinship relationships. However, they were not residential and they did not domesticate any animals except the dingo. Hence, they had not reached the tribe level of complexity according to Service. Still, there are features of Nhunggabarra society that are more advanced than the theory prescribes for the tribe, such as leadership and conflict resolution.

The issue of conflict resolution is generally regarded as the primary force driving hunter–gatherer societies to attain higher levels of complexity. Service (and Diamond) reason that in bands and tribes, almost everyone is kin, by blood, marriage or both. If two people get into an argument, they will both have relatives, who apply pressure on them to keep them from violence. However, if the size of the population grows beyond a few hundred to also include strangers, conflict resolution becomes increasingly difficult. In turn, people will grow fearful of bloodshed and they will demand security. This allows one or more strong individuals to emerge who, with promises of 'law and order', secure a monopoly on violence, take over law keeping and become *chieftains*, the first and least complex level of centralised government.

The Nhunggabarra people and their neighbours had no chieftains. Still, they seem to have been able to maintain well-functioning societies for tens of thousands of years, comprising maybe as many as 15,000 to 20,000 people, without resorting to the kind of feudal tribal violence that has characterised New Guinea or the African continent. There is no evidence of systematic blood feuds before the Europeans arrived and disrupted Aboriginal societies. This suggests that the Nhunggabarra and their neighbours had developed institutions for society building, as well as conflict resolution and decision-making processes, that worked also in more densely populated areas. The Nhunggabarra law stories prescribe many processes and institutions for resolving community conflicts, for preventing centralised power, for keeping intercommunity peace, for community welfare and for environmental care.

Consensus

The law stories outline several processes to minimise conflicts in the community. The combination of context-specific leadership and respect for everyone's role reduced power struggles. Telling the stories repeatedly kept everyone well aware of the law. The rule of law ensured that people who started conflicts were dealt with. But for very difficult and complex matters the Nhunggabarra probably used *consensus*.

Consensus is a gradual process of building both understanding and commitment. People do not have to necessarily agree with the outcome; rather, the aim is to generate everybody's agreement to *support* the outcome, to make them satisfied with the process by which it was achieved and to confirm that their ideas were considered and discussed.

Consensus is an unsurpassed conflict resolution mechanism and the ultimate power-sharing process; it ensures that everybody has a direct say in matters that concern them, which makes it 'more democratic' than representative democracy.

However, consensus becomes cumbersome on a large scale when more than a hundred people are involved. Hence, when a population grows above a certain limit a more complex organisation is required, where decisions are made by fewer people. In Western and Asian societies, chieftains emerged who acquired, or were given, absolute powers in secular matters.

The Nhunggabarra solution to the size problem was to split the community in groups according to roles. Within each group decisions were made according to the consensus principle. The men had the role to decide, by consensus, about hunting law, the women decided about marriage law etc. Spiritual law was the only area where one person, the wiringin, had the final say.

An example Tex tells from his childhood in the 1950s illustrates the principle.

Tex: *A young bloke married a woman of the same totem. This was unheard of and a serious break of the law and carried the death penalty. A call went out to all women looking after marriage law and they arrived from as far as Queensland. They sat down and talked for a couple of weeks to reach a decision. In the end the women decided not to punish the couple, because they agreed that they had to consider also the white people's law. No men were involved in the matter.*

Preventing centralised power

The shift from tribes to chiefdoms is regarded as the crucial step in governance. From then on societies developed more and more complex structures, characterised first by men of absolute power, later by centralised governments, and then gradually developing into the democratic state. The process has been accompanied by tyranny, rebellions, civil wars and conquests. The formation of the European states is a case in point: it was to take 7000 years from the advent of agriculture in southeastern Europe before the first version of representative democracy, Solon's constitution in Athens in 594 BC, returned at least parts of power to the common people.

This is the downside of centralised power that history teaches us: power given to the few will – sooner or later – be abused to serve the few. And once given away, power has almost never returned to the people. Still today, more than 2500 years after the advent of democracy, more than one third of humankind do not have the power to elect their governments.

The Nhunggabarra must have been acutely aware of the downside of centralised power, because the law stories contain a wide range of principles and rules that prevented individuals from rising to absolute power and we have already mentioned *context-specific leadership*, *respect* and *role-splitting*. Female foraging and gathering were not split into roles and this suggests that the Nhunggabarra were more concerned about potential power abuse by men.

Custodianship rather than individual ownership reduced the opportunities for individuals to grab surpluses and to build up individual fortunes. The allocation of roles was pre-planned through the marriage laws, which made 'career choice' a non-issue. One would know from childhood what role one was expected to fulfil on behalf of the community.

A community of communities

The Nhunggabarra and their neighbours were different communities, in different countries with a variety of languages and many diverse ways of communicating beyond language alone. They were different people, who did not have a common religion; all had their own stories about their origin and how earth was created. They were – as individuals – also quite dissimilar in physical appearance. They would have had similar tangible resources at their disposal, but they would be unevenly distributed; some, like the Nhunggabarra, would have had more land; some, like the Ngemba, would have had rich fish resources. Similarly, some of the people would have had very powerful and sacred sites on their land, with higher significance for another people than for their own people. These are all potential causes of envy and tensions between people.

Yet, there were also many commonalities: they were all hunter–gatherer societies, so they had similar challenges and they would understand the principles and functioning of another country. They all lived in an area with similar climate and soils, crisscrossed by rivers that flooded and dried out in a regular pattern. Their languages, although different, had a common origin. They probably shared a general view of the world and of the spiritual world, similar to some degree to Christianity in Europe. Many of their sacred symbols were the same; all would have had the Rainbow Serpent or Baayami in their creation stories, but his actions and roles would have been different. They shared the totem system with all other Australian Aboriginal communities and the same model for custodianship of their most valuable tangible resource, land. They may also have shared the mission of keeping all alive, although we cannot know.

In many ways the Nhunggabarra and their neighbours were no different to many other Australian Aboriginal societies that were neighbours and that shared similar living conditions. Yet, something that was perhaps less common was that the Nhunggabarra and the surrounding countries had developed a highly advanced level of cooperation, a community of communities. Despite their diversity, the communities were in many ways a 'cultural bloc'. We do not know how common these types of cultural blocs were in pre-European Australia. Maybe they existed only in the relatively densely populated areas or only in the southeast. There is evidence of at least one other 'cultural bloc' further south, along the Murray River.

To make collaboration happen in practice they had developed several processes and legal institutions, which tied them together, and we have already touched upon these earlier. The combination of the *marriage laws* and the eighteen- to twenty-year *journey of knowledge* for men ensured that all adult women in any one community originated from other communities, and at any given time some 20 to 40 per cent of all adult men (depending on assumed life expectancy) would have been 'journey men' from another community. All adult men would have walked practically all learning tracks around the cultural bloc and would have got to know quite well at least their kin in all the communities. This would have allowed an extraordinary blending of blood lines, friends, kin, knowledge and experiences.

The law against punishing people from other communities – the *anti-vendetta principle* – must have been a crucial peacekeeping mechanism, given the terrible and long-lasting effects of vendetta in other parts of the world. The tuckandee law was another trust-building mechanism. Who would unwittingly risk killing the knowledge safe-keeper of their children in a war? The Big Buurra, where everybody came together to jointly conduct a live learning experience, further reinforced both diversity and commonality. Even the *trade process* was organised to minimise sources of conflict.

The main benefit of all these processes was long-term peace. Other benefits were a richer knowledge base, livelier trade, a better safety net and a wider selection of marriage partners.

·

The conclusion is that the Nhunggabarra had developed conflict resolution/minimisation mechanisms that could work in a society of several thousand people – without resorting to centralised power. The large number of provisions put in place to avoid individuals rising to power suggests that the Nhunggabarra either had experienced central-ised power and reacted against it, or that the original law-maker was an extraordinarily wise ancestor (Baayami), who could foresee the unpleasant effects. Whatever the explanation, the provisions allowed the Nhunggabarra to avoid the 'chieftain option'.

Since the Nhunggabarra were integrated in a community of communities, their neighbours ought to have been organised according to similar principles, although it is outside the scope of this book to ascertain this. The law stories show how the Nhunggabarra and their neighbours coped better at higher levels of organisational complexity than a hunter–gatherer society *should* have according to theory. We believe the main reason for their accomplishment was the organisational architecture of their society. Beliefs and values, leadership and rules of law supported, reinforced and balanced each other *as a whole* – this has not been generally understood and definitely not been properly studied.

INNOVATION: LIVING AT A STONE-AGE LEVEL

The anthropologist A. Lang probably put into words the feeling of the early Europeans when in 1905 he wrote:

> As far as what we commonly call material civilisation is concerned, the natives of the Australian continent are probably the most backward of mankind, having no agriculture, no domestic animals, and no knowledge of metal-working. Their weapons and implements are of wood, stone, and bone, and they have not even the rudest kind of pottery.

The question that had puzzled Europeans ever since they arrived in Australia is: how is it possible that Aboriginal people, who seem perfectly intelligent as individuals, were living practically at a stone-age level?

Could the explanation be that Aboriginal society was completely unreceptive to, or that Aboriginal people had customs preventing them from adopting, new technology? Most laypeople and many historians share an explicit or secret (more common and politically correct these days) opinion that this was so. It is widely believed that Australian

The Creation (Rainbow Serpent)

Map Over Nhunggal Country

The Learning Track

How The People Got Their Totems (Big Buurra)

The Crane and the Crow

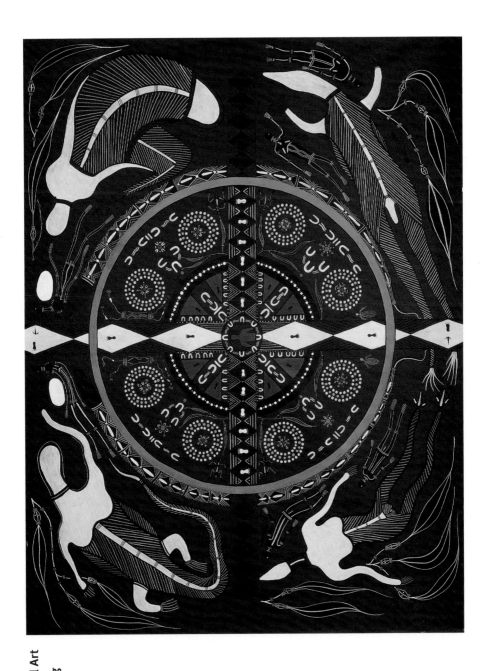

**The Four-level Art
of Storytelling**

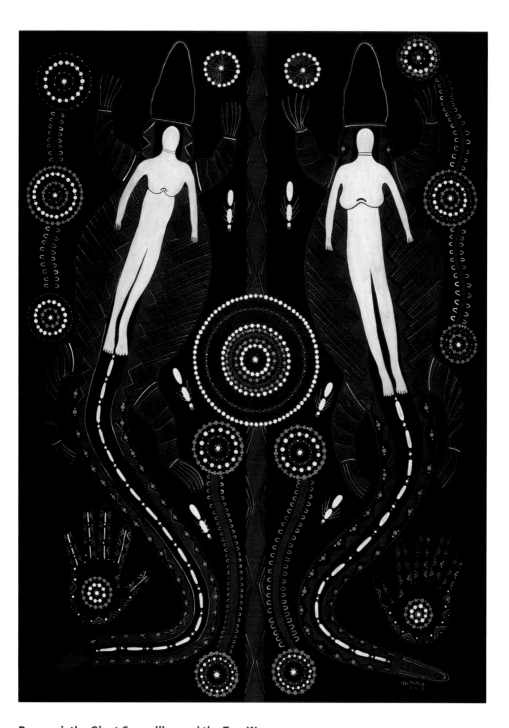

Baayami, the Giant Crocodiles and the Two Women

Journey of Knowledge

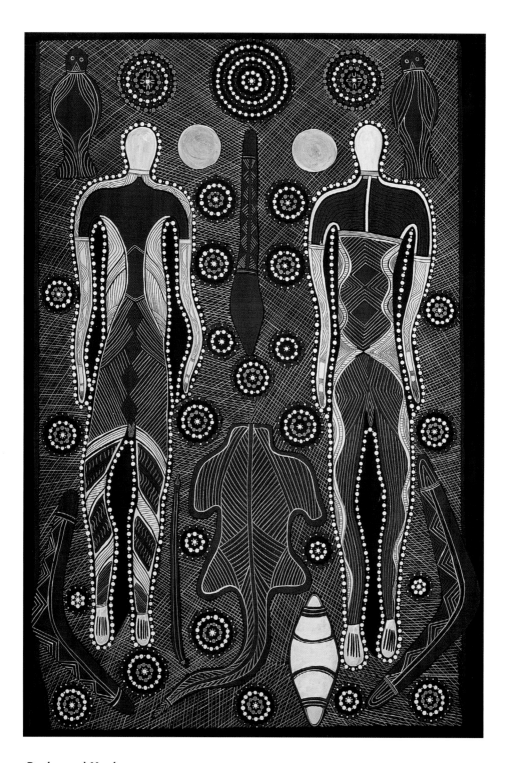

Baaluu and Muuboop

The Flower of Law

The Black Swans

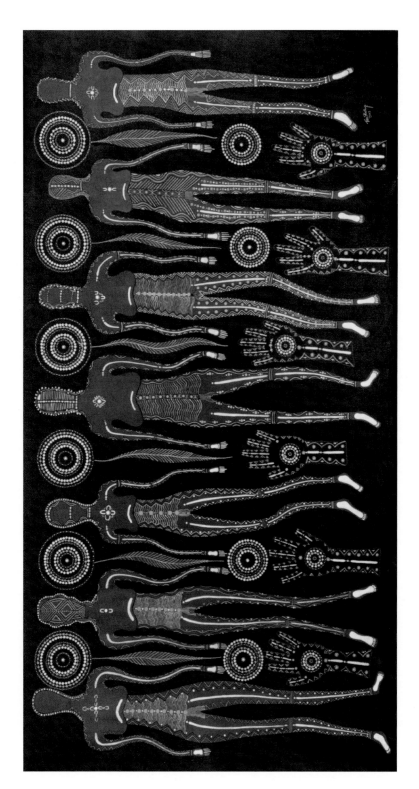

The Seven Sisters

Willy-wagtail and the Rainbow

How the Nhunggabarra Got Flowers

Vision for a Sustainable Planet: Our Actions on Lands and Rivers

The Southern Cross story (page 97)

The circle in the middle represents all the different communities. The two hands with white designs are the spirit that lifted the trees. The other hands are of the two men and the woman. The kangaroo designs show the law about how to cut the meat.

Aborigines shared ideological features that made them technological laggards; they were conservative; they were living in a great illusion – an imagined Dreamtime – not in reality, and not focused on practical ways to improve their day-to-day life.

The trouble with this theory is that it comes from a Western perspective, which sees 'development' in terms of tangible material wealth.

Let us first distinguish between *breakthrough inventions*, which are made for the first time, such as the first society or person that invented the padlock (for locking chests), and *incremental invention*, like a new improved variety of padlock or the adoption of the padlock for a new application (for locking doors).

That eternal Australian icon, the returning boomerang, is an example of an Australian Aboriginal breakthrough invention probably first made more than 10,000 years ago. A returning boomerang preserved for at least 9000 years was found in the peat bog of Wyrie Swamp in South Australia. Throwing sticks resembling the boomerang were invented independently in many places in prehistoric times, but the Australian boomerang remains the oldest one that has been proven to have a returning quality.

Australian Aboriginal societies' general reluctance to accept change could explain why they were still using stone tools even though metal tools had been invented elsewhere. But why did the Cape York Aborigines not adopt even bows and arrows, when they would have had many occasions to see the New Guineans using them?

The explorer Sir George Grey pondered over this very question, when in 1838 he watched the spear and the *wamara* (spearthrower) in the hands of an experienced Aboriginal hunter:

> The spear, when projected from the throwing stick, forms as effectual the weapon as the bow and arrow, whilst at the same time it is much less liable to be injured – and it possesses over the bow and arrow, the advantage of being useful to poke out Kangaroo rats and opossums from Hollow trees, to knock off gum from highly branches,

to pull down the cones from the banksia trees and for many other purposes.

Thomas Mitchell even observed an Aborigine on the Darling River using the spear as an oar: 'A native, when he wishes to proceed, stands erect, and propels the canoe with the short spear he uses in fishing; striking the water with each end alternately, on each side of the canoe, and he thus glides very rapidly along.' (Apparently inspired by Aboriginal technology, Mitchell went on to patent a 'boomerang propeller for steamers'.)

Both Grey and Mitchell noted the value of a multi-use tool compared to a specialised tool for someone who has to carry everything they own. Also, spears thrown with the spearthrower were no doubt much more effective than an arrow against the large marsupials of Australia.

Aboriginal people could be very fast in adopting a new technology with very complex follow-on effects. The British colonists brought with them British dogs when they arrived in Tasmania. Tasmanian Aborigines had never seen dogs, since the dingo had not made it to Tasmania. Within a few years, the Aborigines changed their hunting methods, increased the size of their huts to accommodate the dogs and even invented a new form of catamaran to transport them. This instantaneous acceptance of a new technology despite the profound social and psychological adjustments it required is evidence that the Australian Aborigines were not hostile to innovations.

Aboriginal people were also quick to adopt new materials from Europeans, even if the contact was indirect through trade. For example, the first use of glass predated European settlement. Aborigines at York Peninsula made knives from bottles they had discovered washed up on the beaches. They were also found to have used broken bits of glass to replace pieces of flint on their spears.

In reality, adoption rates of innovation show no pattern. Both native societies and Western societies differ greatly in ideology. Some of the New Guinean societies have quickly adopted new Western technology, while others have resisted. The reception of inventions also varies over time. Islamic societies in the Middle East today are relatively conservative, while in medieval times they were technology leaders and displayed literacy rates higher than contemporary Europe.

.

Innovation researchers usually identify at least five factors that determine how inventions are accepted by societies. The first and the most obvious factor is tangible economic advantage compared with existing technology. The Aborigines' rejection of the bow and arrow and their quick acceptance of the British dog seem to fall in this category.

The second factor is how easily the tangible advantages of an existing new technology can be observed. This is one reason why weapon technology everywhere tends to spread much faster than other technology. Bows and arrows got a boost when their efficiency as weapons in the hands of specialised troops was recognised in medieval warfare. Indeed, archaeologists have found evidence that hunting tool technology could spread very fast in Aboriginal Australia. The *wamara* (spearthrower) spread so fast that it seems to have been invented in many places at about the same time; the domestication of the dingo as a hunting dog also occurred so fast that, archaeologically, it looks like it happened simultaneously across the continent. On the other hand, the Aborigines, who had not experienced organised warfare before the arrival of the Europeans, were not attracted to bow and arrow technology.

Compatibility with existing tangible investments is the third factor. England was late in electrifying street lighting because of the huge investments already made in gas pipes, for example.

Compatibility with existing social values and beliefs is the fourth factor. For instance, American farmers value production efficiency very highly, so soil preservation innovations tend to take a backseat. Vested interests may also hamper innovation even if there are clear advantages. The notorious example of an intangible value factor is the QWERTY keyboard, which in 1873 was designed to slow down the typist because the mechanisms of the early typewriters could not cope with the speed of experienced users. Today, attempts to introduce better keyboards are still being rejected, mainly because of the intangible investments in typing skills already made by typists and typing teachers.

It is hard to say whether compatibility was an issue or not in Aboriginal society. Some evidence points to the opposite. Anthropologists are bewildered by the redundancy in Aboriginal technology, which cannot be explained in simple ecological terms. As is evidenced by excavations, Aboriginal people developed a huge variety of spears and spearthrowers – there was no lack of innovation there. But given that a single type of spear does an effective job, why have five or ten, all slightly differently barbed and named? Why all the variation in clubs and baskets? The available evidence suggests that rather than resisting change due to vested interests, Aboriginal toolmakers seem to have enjoyed experimenting with new materials and new applications.

Complexity is a factor that reduces adoption of innovations. A new technology that is difficult to understand or that requires considerable skill to learn spreads more slowly. This probably did not apply in Aboriginal Australia.

Finally, innovation researchers identify the fifth factor in how innovations are accepted by societies as *intangible value* such as a social or status value. A modern example is fashion and design. There is no economic advantage in buying fashion jeans, and designer frames do not help us to see better, but people are happy to pay double the price for them anyway.

Intangible innovations

In order to understand Aboriginal innovation we will need to add spiritual and intangible innovations. Modern-day examples of intangible breakthrough innovations are new music styles, such as jazz; new perspectives in art, such as cubism; new industrial innovations, such as computer software; and new society institutions, such as the limited-stock company.

Aboriginal societies made a wide range of intangible breakthrough innovations: multi-layered storytelling, ecofarming, rule of law, unique art styles, consensus, context-specific leadership, telepathy, hypnosis etc. These spread to cover the whole continent. The Aborigines were also eager to adopt European intangible innovations. They learned very quickly, for instance, how to trade according to market principles with the Europeans. New words such as 'horse' and 'white fella' spread very fast in areas untouched by white men, and tunes of popular English songs could be found woven into songs performed at corroborees.

Evidence from both archaeology and eyewitnesses thus back up a conclusion that the Australian Aboriginal people were not against innovation; on the contrary, when a new technology offered clear and observable advantages, they were very quick in adopting it and also in making the necessary indirect adaptations in their society – that is, they were good at incremental innovations. But this still does not explain why so comparatively few breakthrough innovations occurred in Australia compared to the rest of the world.

Breakthrough innovation is random

Historians do not agree on a pattern regarding breakthrough innovations and they have found myriad factors that influence innovation in societies – some of these factors have been found to increase the innovation rate and some have been found to decrease it, and opposing forces tend to occur simultaneously. This means that over a large enough area (such as a whole continent), some proportion of a society is likely to be innovative at any given time. This makes breakthrough innovation at society level unpredictable and random.

Once a useful breakthrough is made somewhere on a continent it starts spreading. Societies adapt the innovation and add to it incrementally. Simple incremental innovations occur independently in many places; there are many different independent inventors of

Aboriginal intangible breakthrough discoveries

Aboriginal intangible discovery	Western world innovation
Animals as teachers	Lost
Barter trade	Replaced by market economy in 1800s, but returning, driven by the internet
Community living	Rediscovered in the 1960s
Consensus decision making	Known, but largely replaced by autocratic leadership
Crystal healing	Rediscovered, but not generally accepted in society
Farming aligned with the ecosystem	No
Gender equality	Exists in theory but not in practice
Hypnosis	Rediscovered in the 19th century (Mesmer)
Individual spirituality	Known
Context-specific leadership	Rediscovered and on the increase
Knowledge-based organising	Rediscovered and on the increase
Learner-driven education	Developed in late 1900s
Life-long learning	End of 20th-century management concept
Medicinal effects of herbs	Discovered
Society mission to keep all alive	No
Model for a sustainable world	Possibly lost with the introduction of agriculture
Multi-layered storytelling	Possibly lost with the introduction of writing
Narrative maps	Map-making developed in both Asia and Europe
Rule of law	Discovered
Space–time concept	Discovered 1905 (Einstein's theory of special relativity)
Telepathy	Known, but not accepted by mainstream science
Welfare system and tuckandee	General welfare systems discovered
Zero per cent unemployment rate	Lost in the Industrial Revolution with the introduction of 'work'

padlocks and non-returning throwing-sticks. Complex breakthrough inventions, however, occur in only a few places. For instance, writing has only three or possibly four independent origins (Sumer around 3000 BC, Mexican Indians before 600 BC, China by 1300 BC and possibly Egypt around 3000 BC). All other writing systems have been shown to be adaptations of one of these. The phonetic alphabet, today the dominant writing system in the Western world, is a unique invention with only one origin – it arose among speakers of Semitic languages in the area of modern Syria.

Since innovation is random, mathematics rules. Size of population and accessibility of a land mass, without hindering oceans, are thus of great consequence. The huge Eurasian landmass supported rapid diffusion of technology and the continent's large population (six times that of the Americas and 230 times that of Australia) increased the probability that a creative individual was born and made a break-through. In contrast, the isolated Australian Aborigines received only drops of new technology from their neighbours and their small popu-lation reduced the number of potential breakthrough inventions.

Tasmania is a case in point. Around 10,000 years ago Tasmania was separated from mainland Australia by rising sea levels. Tasmania's 4000 to 6000 hunter–gatherers remained out of contact with any other people until the Dutchman Abel Tasman arrived in 1642. The Tasmanians then had the simplest material culture of any people in the world. Not only did they lack the technologies that the mainland Aborigines had invented since they were separated, they had also lost several of the technologies that they had possessed at the time of separation.

Jared Diamond draws the conclusion that it is Australia's geographical separation, not the intellect of its peoples, which is the main reason for their lagging behind other people in the world with regard to tangible innovations. His conclusion rings true. However, it misses one major point. The Australian Aborigines excelled in intangible innovations, or rather as they would have seen it, intangible *discoveries*.

In particular, one discovery stands out: a very advanced governance model for a sustainable world. Maybe the model was once discovered elsewhere as well; perhaps it was once even the original model for all peoples on earth. However, the model was everywhere obliterated by the combined forces of the human ego and 'guns, germs and steel'. Thanks to their geographical separation, the Australian Aborigines were allowed to finetune their model over thousands of years and they would gladly have handed over their showcase on a plate to the rest of the world had they not been so devastatingly interrupted before the Western world was ready for it.

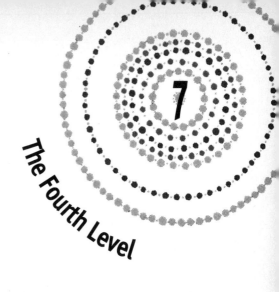

7

The Fourth Level

ANYONE WHO TRIES TO LEARN ABOUT the customs of Australian Aboriginal people cannot avoid the spiritual realm. Aboriginal people were (and are) deeply spiritual. They seem to have possessed psychic powers that are largely lost or considered taboo in mainstream modern Western civilisation. The ability to apply such psychic powers was the highest level of knowledge of the Nhunggabarra, the hidden fourth level of the stories that was revealed only to the wiringins, the men of high degree. The fourth level is the know-how about the spiritual realm — not only the knowledge about it, but the capacity to actually act outside the normal physical world.

The wiringin is generally referred to as 'medicine man' in English. Aboriginal people call him 'clever man' in English, a term that better describes his wide-ranging roles. Apart from his healing duties, he was also the custodian of the most sacred laws and stories, the 'chief justice', the highest spiritual authority, and a medium for contacting the spirits. Through personal ability and training he also had psychic abilities surpassing those of his fellow men and women.

Although the early white settlers recorded many accounts of his powers, anthropologists long dismissed the wiringins as 'humbugs', 'the greatest scamp of the tribe', or 'impostors', to mention but a few of the derogatory terms in the literature.

A.P. Elkin (1891–1979) was the first anthropologist to acknowledge that the wiringins did indeed have extraordinary knowledge and powers that science could not explain. He regarded the wiringins that he had personally met as outstanding personalities, and he wrote in 1945:

> Beneath the unkempt hair, above naked body or one clothed in the white man's cast-offs, and in an immobile face shine shrewd, pene-trating eyes – eyes that look you all the way through – the lenses of the mind that is photographing your very character and intentions. I have seen those eyes and felt the mind at work when I sought knowledge that only the man of high degree could impart . . . This clever man was definitely an outstanding person, a clear thinker, a man of decision, one who believed and acted on the belief that he possessed psychic power, the power to will others to have faith in themselves.

The wiringins were the only ones who learned the fourth level of the stories. They passed through very striking ceremonies and had experiences which gave them access to a special body of spiritual and esoteric knowledge. They had insight into the minds of their fellows, and by observation they built up a wealth of information about the members of their community, which they could draw upon when needed. They also learned from their teachers and from experience to distinguish curable illnesses from incurable ones. The wiringins were in Elkin's words, 'men of high degree'.

Their psychic abilities came from a combination of talent and a trained ability to consciously use the unconscious. The wiringins also had access to tools to enhance their ability and they had learned the practice: how to interpret dreams, how to ascertain what was happening at a distance or how to use hypnosis to make those present 'see' things they wanted. One such tool was crystals and the wiringin's first crystal was inserted in his body (usually under the skin in the abdomen area) during initiation. In the Black Swans story, Wurunna brought a large crystal from inside himself and with its power he turned his brothers into swans.

We know that the wiringins in general, regarded clear quartz as the most valuable crystal. It was the all-round tool, in that it was regarded to both improve connection with the higher self and amplify the healing energies of the wiringins. It could thus be used for healing on both the physical and psychic plane. Not much information has survived about the actual practices of the wiringin, primarily because they were held secret and never revealed to white men and hence rarely recorded.

The wiringins were credited with the power of flying through the air to distant places on earth, or to the Milky Way, where they visited the Ancestors and their spirits. They were said to be able to climb to the sky by means of a cord that emanated from their bodies. They were able to send their spirit helpers to distant lands and learn what happened there. They could send their own dream spirit to other places, travelling at extraordinary speed. An eyewitness account from the 1800s illustrates how their contemporaries experienced wiringin powers.

Soon after the white men came to Melbourne, a black fellow living near where Heidelberg now is, was nearly dead. His friends sent for Doro-Bauk [the wiringin], who lived to the west. When he arrived, he found the man just breathing ever so slightly, and his Murup [spirit] had gone away from him, and nothing remained in him but a little wind. Doro-Bauk went after his Murup, and after sometime returned carrying a possum rug. He said that he had been just in time to catch it around the middle, before it got near the Karalk (the bright colour of sunset, which is said to be caused by the spirits of the dead going in and out of the land of the dead). The dead man was breathing little wind when Doro-Bauk laid himself on him and put the Murup back into him. After a time the man came back to life.

It is not known how the Nhunggabarra wiringins learned their profession. Elkin describes three ways common to southeast Australia, all of them experiential. The wiringin could be selected in his early years because he displayed early signs of talent. Boys who showed a leaning towards the profession were given special training in spiritual matters and were tested, among other ways, by means of specially constructed sentences in conversation.

Another common way to become a wiringin was to inherit the profession. Descent alone was not sufficient, but a son of a wiringin would certainly be under special scrutiny from his young years for signs of talent. A third method, sometimes described to anthropologists, was an inner experience of being 'called'. It could come from a vision of the spirits. Such an inner calling could also be deliberately sought by sleeping in an isolated place, near the grave of a wiringin or in a sacred spot.

At some stage in the wiringin's education he had to go through a range of special initiation ceremonies. At the end of these ceremonies one wiringin said, cited by Elkin:

> Whereas previously I was blind to the significance of the seasons, of natural species, of heavenly bodies, and the man himself, now I begin to see; and whereas before I did not understand the secret of life, now I begin to know.

The training that followed was focused on diagnosing and treating illnesses, producing the crystals from the body, the spirits, and exercising psychic powers. To learn what was needed took many years and a long series of initiations. One also had to learn the knowledge in both word and action, so it could be passed it on. This was the only way to preserve the sacred heritage for the future of the community. The retention of these powers depended on self-discipline, such as avoiding certain foods and drinks.

The wiringins were few — only one or two per community. This means there might have been between 25 and 50 wiringins in the cultural bloc in the time before the Europeans arrived. They would have formed an esoteric 'community of practice', peers of special knowledge and colleagues with common concerns and responsibilities. They met occasionally at certain ceremonies and larger gatherings and they may also have collaborated on occasions of dire need. We know from the How the Nhunggabarra got Flowers story that they sometimes joined forces when they needed to contact Baayami and that they also climbed the Wubi-Wubi Mountain together to ask for help when the whole community was threatened, such as during severe droughts.

The wiringin's role was to be of service to the people of his community – he was not to generate a power position as he was not chief or king. As Elkin says: his unique knowledge and individual powers were to give his people faith in themselves.

There seems to have been people in most Aboriginal communities with relatively high degrees of psychic powers, even if they were not regarded as wiringins; one might call them 'specialists'. In some areas of Australia (not among the Nhunggabarra) the function of the wiringin was separated from those of the *spirit medium* or the seer. This person could foretell the future of events; they were able to bring the spirits to the camp of their people at night and they sometimes also composed songs for entertainment. Their role resembled today's psychic mediums and their performances could turn into fully-fledged séances. An eyewitness describes such an event:

The people were in the camps and strict silence was maintained by the direction of the medium. The fires were let go down and then the medium uttered a loud 'coo-ee' at intervals. At length a shrill whistle was heard, then the shrill whistling of the spirits, first on one side and then on the other. Shortly after, a sound as of persons jumping down to the ground in succession. This was the spirits and a voice was then heard in the gloom asking in a strange muffled tone: 'What is wanted?' Questions were asked by the medium and replies given. At this séance the questions related to the movements of absent friends and of enemies. At termination of the séance a voice said: 'We are going.' Finally, after all was over, the medium was found in the top of an almost inaccessible tree, apparently asleep, where he said the spirits left him when they went away.

According to the old Nhunggabarra people, there had existed very powerful female wiringins, but the profession tended to be exclusively male. Women were much more common among psychic specialists. Howitt describes a type of psychic surgery performed by a woman:

A native girl, Booroong, living in Sydney, paid . . . occasional visits to the lower parts of the harbour. From one of these she returned extremely ill. She was seated on the ground and one of the lines worn by the men, was passed around her head once, taking care to fix the knot in the centre of the forehead; the remainder of the line was taken by another girl, who sat a small distance from her, and with the end of it fretted her lips until they bled very copiously. Booroong imagining all the time that the blood came from her old head, and passed along the lines and ran into the other girl's mouth. This operation they called the be-anny and it is the peculiar province of the women.

Even if the wiringins and the specialists were the most skilled, all Aboriginal people knew medicinal herbs and they were able to treat everyday pains with a wide range of remedies. People were also quite sensitive to dreams about a person's totem, which could give precognitions of the whereabouts of distant friends.

Stories about telepathy are common. Elkin recounts this story told to him by an Aboriginal man:

When a man is down on the plain and I am on the hill, I look towards him while I am talking. He sees me and turns toward me. I say, 'do you hear?' I will my head from side to side glaring at him, then turning I say, 'come on quickly'. As I stare at him fixedly, I see him turn as he feels my stare. He then turns, and looks about while I continue staring at him. So I say, 'Walk this way, right along here, where I am sitting.' Then he walks right up to me where I am sitting behind a bush.

I draw him with my power. You do not see any hand signs or hear any shouting. At last he comes up and nearly falls over me. I call out so that he will see me. He says: 'you talked to me and I felt it. How did you talk so?' I explain, he adds: 'I felt towards you while you were talking to me, then I feel that you were there.' I answer, 'True, it was in that way that I talked to you,' and he felt those words and also that power.

Older people had often developed precognition and there are many stories about remarkable acts. Jimmie Barker, a Muruwari man, tells about several such experiences from his childhood in the early 1900s, when he was living at a mission near Brewarrina. On one occasion his family was camping several days' walk away from the mission when one of the old people at night uttered a loud grunt and then fell silent. The next morning Jimmy was told that they had to return immediately, because something was wrong at home. When they returned they learned that one of the old people had died.

The Nhunggabarra, as had many other Aboriginal people, had a custom of mapping out the whole body to classify relations, such as father, mother, sister's child etc. This system was used for various purposes. Elkin describes one:

If an involuntary twitching occurs in the body part associated with the class of father, the person immediately abstracts himself from all surrounding interests and letting his head droop forward, as I have seen, enters a condition either of receptivity or of free association. After a time he becomes satisfied that such and such a person in the prescribed relationship will arrive before long. The information has 'come' to him.

Australian Aboriginal people seem to have been able to control their body temperature. The explorer Thomas Mitchell marvelled:

On that freezing night, the natives, according to their usual custom, stripped off all their clothes, previous to lying down to sleep in the

open, their bodies being doubled up around a few burning reeds.
We could not understand how they could lay thus naked, when the
earth was white with hoar frost; and they were equally at a loss to
know how we could sleep in our tents without a bit of fire to keep
our bodies warm.

To the Aborigines of today there is nothing exceptional about
gaining information via telepathy or inner search. Tex describes, for
instance, how his father taught him to find his way home if he got lost.
Tex learned to meditate over his father's totem (emu). He learned how
to still his mind and visualise the emu moving in the country. The
right direction then came to him. As his father said: 'When you get
lost a spirit makes you see things backward.' He used this method
several times in his days as a drover and it still works well for him in
the bush.

STORY | HOW THE NHUNGGABARRA GOT FLOWERS

After Baayami had left the earth, all the flowers that grew on the plains, on
the stony ridges and on the trees, died. The earth looked bare and desolate
without flowers and only the people could remember a time when flowers
bloomed. And without flowers, there were no bees and so, no honey, and
the children of the Nhunggabarra people cried for something sweet.

There were only three trees where the bees still lived and made honey,
but no one was allowed to touch anything on the trees because they were
the sacred trees onto which Baayami had carved all the laws and religion
of the Nhunggabarra people.

Baayami saw that, although the children cried for honey, the people had
not touched the sacred trees and he was pleased. He said he would send
them something sweet which, in times of drought, would come on the box
tree and gulabaa tree. And that is how the white sugary specks came to be
on the leaves and how the sweet sap came to run down the bark of these
two trees, so that the Nhunggabarra children would always have something
sweet to eat.

How the Nhunggabarra Got Flowers

The three wiringins who climbed the mountain, with the designs illustrating the ceremonies they had to do at each stage of their ascent. Their footprints are shown in the diamond shapes representing the steps they found in the cliff. The spirit with feathers at the top left of the painting represents the two eaglehawks, Baayami's messengers, while the figure on the right is the spirit that took the wiringins to Baayami in the Warrambul. The bullroarer between them represents the voice the wiringins heard, while the three sacred trees from which it was made are represented by the three vertical diamond designs, with the two hands representing Baayami making the bullroarer.

Around the three wiringins at the bottom of the painting there are only sparse circles of white dots, representing the blossoms dying. The white dots on the leaves are the sweet nectar eaten by the children, when there was no honey being made by the bees. The red and yellow circles of dots at the top of the painting represent the wiringins scattering flowers all over the country when they returned from the mountain (see colour plate).

However, the wiringins still longed for the sight of flowers and decided to find Baayami and ask that the world be made beautiful again. They travelled across the Nineteen-Mile Plain to Wubi-Wubi Mountain and climbed to the summit using the footholds which had been made in the rock. On reaching the summit they saw a stone excavation containing a freshwater spring and, after drinking the water, felt immediately refreshed from their gruelling climb.

They then saw several circles of stone and, stepping into one of them, heard the voice of Baayami's helper, Wallaguroonbuan, asking what the wiringins wanted there. Having told their story the wiringins were lifted through an opening in the sky to the Bullima, a beautiful place where flowers never ceased to bloom. They were told to gather as many flowers as they could carry and take them back to their people.

Baayami told the wiringins that never again would the earth be bare of flowers, that through all the seasons a few flowers would be sent by different winds. Yarragaa Mayrraa, the east wind, would bring the flowers in plenty – so when the east wind did not blow the flowers would not be plenty, but there would always be a few. And when the flowers were few and the bees made little honey, then the sweet clear wahlar would flow from the trees, and the sweet white specks would form on the leaves, to take the place of honey, until the flowers were plentiful again.

And the wiringins took the flowers back to their people and scattered them over the land, and wherever those flowers fell, that kind of flower has grown ever since. This place, where the Nhunggabarra people learned of the flowers and where the wiringins scattered them, is still called Ghirrawiin, the place of flowers.

THE SPIRIT OF WUBI-WUBI: A TOUCH OF THE FOURTH LEVEL

Being the only mountain on the vast flat dry plain, Wubi-Wubi is visible from afar. It is the only mountain between here and the Queensland border some 150 kilometres north, so it is an impressive sight. It must have been an awe-inspiring view for the Aboriginal people, since their land and the land surrounding the mountain consists entirely of flat plains. Charles Sturt was also impressed when he passed through here. He climbed the mountain, as the first white man in 1828, and named it Oxley Tablelands because of its flat top.

Wubi-Wubi Mountain is situated on Ngemba land southwest of the Nhunggabarra. The Nhunggabarra man would have seen the mountain at least once in his lifetime, when he stayed with the Ngemba during his walkabout, but in general the Nhunggabarra would have travelled here rarely. And no one would have even dreamed of climbing the mountain, because it is one of the most sacred places on earth. Wubi-Wubi was the last place on this earth that Baayami stayed, before he travelled to the Bullima in the Warrambul (the Milky Way), where he still resides today. But before he left, he said that if the Aboriginal people ever wanted to contact him, they could do so from the mountain. The How the Nhunggabarra got Flowers story describes one such contact.

This is the first time Tex has been this close to Wubi-Wubi. When he grew up in the 1950s and 60s the mountain was still considered a place the Nhunggabarra went to only in dire need. In the time before European arrival, only the wiringins were allowed to climb the mountain and then only if they had a mission of great magnitude and needed to contact Baayami. When we approach, Anne, concerned, asks Tex how he feels. 'I'm all right,' he assures us, and he is visibly full of excitement and expectation, as indeed we all are.

We slowly approach the mountain on the narrow dirt road, when we suddenly see a rare sight in front of us: two wedge-tailed eagles, the mythical eaglehawks of the Black Swans story, the messengers of Baayami. They spread their huge wings and take off slowly and majestically up towards the mountain. 'Where might they be heading and with what message?' is a thought that probably passes through the minds of all three of us.

We can follow the birds, because in front of us the road now starts the steep ascent towards the top. The mountain has two adjacent tops, with the highest being 309 metres above sea level, which is less than 200 metres above the plain. But rocky outcrops rise quite steeply on all sides, so it is not a straightforward climb. The new road has been cut deep into the rock and a tarmac stretch leads us east up to the highest top of the mountain, where a telecommunications company has built a communication antenna.

The mountain top around the antenna is quite flat, full of small sharp-edged stones; the view is magnificent over the vegetation-clad flat land. No signs of human activity are visible. To the northeast I spot something that looks like a dry, open desert-like plain without vegetation, and I ask Tex what it is. 'The lake!' Tex exclaims. 'Just as in the Black Swans story!' He and Anne take off full of energy, trying to find the rockpools.

Tex and Anne return, disappointed. They have seen some small rockpools, but nothing spectacular. We decide to descend and start driving down the road. We suddenly detect a small dirt track leading off the tarmac towards the other, slightly lower, western part of the mountain and we turn into it. There, in front of us, we see the eagle-hawks again! They fly on the same level as we are walking, soaring on the up-winds around the mountain, only metres away from the solid ground, where the mountain veers off steeply.

The farmer who today owns the mountain and lent us the key to access the mountain road has built a picnic and camping area on a slab of concrete, complete with a gas grill, a place for a campfire, a kitchenette and even a flushing toilet (!). It is brand new. A bit further away we notice mounds of rocks that seem to have been piled up over a 1000-square-metre area. The middle of the mounds forms shallow basins, the biggest some 10 metres in diameter and no more than a couple of metres deep. The bottoms of the basins show signs of having held water. We are in no doubt: we have found the rockpools in the story!

Charles Sturt, on his second climb of the mountain in January 1829, called them 'hollows...that deserve particular notice' in his diary. Each rock is flat, about the size that can be lifted by a man, so the rock pools could be the work of a group of determined men. Or, could it be that Baayami has thrust a spear into the hard rock surface, turned the spear, and then lifted it, as it says in one of the stories?

Tex carefully studies the ground for stone chips from worked tools, the certain sign of an old Aboriginal campsite, but he finds none.

Wubi-Wubi is not a place where Aboriginal people came to live for long periods. This was for wiringins only.

The stone circles should be nearby. I test a few spots with my pendulum, the instrument I have been using to detect possible geomagnetic fields. The rockpools test positive, possibly indicating the presence of watercourses beneath the bottoms, but the other areas of the rocks test negative, like the rest of the mountain. The area around the picnic spot is a sandy flat with a few scattered rocks. It is the best place for camping, with a view, and it would have been the perfect location for a stone circle. Some stones are lying around – these have clearly been moved to make space for the concrete slabs and the machines during the time of construction.

Tex spots a few large boulders further away, which appear to have not been moved. With a bit of imagination they could form a circle. I test the imagined centre with the pendulum. It turns vigorously positive. I walk to the periphery of the imagined circle and test outside it. The pendulum swing turns negative. I move the pendulum from outside the circle to the inside. The pendulum immediately shifts from negative to positive. By walking around the periphery with the pendulum I am able to determine the exact extension of the whole circle. Have we found the spot from which the wiringins contacted and then travelled to the spirit world?

I decide to take a picture of 'the circle'. It is late in the afternoon and the sun is setting in the west and when I aim the camera I notice that my shadow is cast straight into the circle. Something tells me that this is an important moment and on impulse I ask Tex and Anne to join me, so the shadows of all three of us fall into the circle. We try to fit the shadows of our heads in the centre.

According to Nhunggabarra belief, the shadow is one of the four spirits of a person and we are very careful to ensure our shadows do not cross each other. By letting our shadows fall into the circle we are in effect allowing our spirits to enter a possible danger zone. We are very silent. I take the picture. It is hard to express what we feel and why we feel it, but Tex's comment covers it well: 'I would not like to

On top of the sacred mountain.

spend the night here.' The sun is setting rapidly in the northwest and the eaglehawks have disappeared. Time to get moving.

In the evening of the next day, back in our Goodooga base camp, I go through my photographs to catalogue them. I note a strange spot on the picture of us at the stone circle. It looks like a dark object with fuzzy edges in the sky.

What is it? I can immediately rule out a flaw in the camera, because none of the other pictures contains a smudge. I can also rule out it being a reflection of the sun in the camera lens, since I was pointing the lens away from the sun. None of us had seen anything in the sky when we took the picture. We had obviously been focused on getting our shadows right in the circle, but something of that size suddenly appearing in the sky would definitely have caught our attention.

I run the picture through software with a number of different filters in my computer. The results reveal that the spot consists of an oval core surrounded by several layers, which make it resemble a vibrating or rapidly turning 'hole' surrounded by vibrations of another density.

The 'ring' has a connection behind it with something further away. The whole thing looks like a tube with the opening directed towards us and the rest of the tube connected behind the opening into the distance.

I show the picture to Tex and Anne. Tex makes some estimates and says: 'Can you see the direction of the connection? Southeast. That's where the Southern Cross and the Milky Way would be visible in the night sky.'

We get goose bumps . . .

8

The Spirit of Death Arrives...

SOME TIME, POSSIBLY IN THE LATTER part of 1828, a group of young Nhung-gabarra men saw a small group of people approaching their country. They were white! And they were accompanied by monsters! The young men fled heads over heels back to their camp to report their sighting.

The white men were probably from explorer Charles Sturt's party, who reached the southern-most part of Nhunggal country on their first journey, carrying their supplies on carts pulled by bullocks – huge animals never before seen in Australia. Other Aborigines seeing white men, bullocks and carts for the first time were often paralysed with terror. As Mitchell describes from one of his journeys: 'I remarked that he trembled so violently that it was impossible to expect that I could obtain any information from him.' Mitchell got used to Aborigines being terrified when he met them and he put it down to superstition and general cowardice.

One wonders how Mitchell would have behaved had he seen a group of spirits announcing death and accompanied by terrifying monsters on his doorstep! Because this was probably what the young Nhung-gabarra men perceived: the white spirit *Wanda* arriving. Many

Aboriginal stories describe Wanda, the spirit of death, a white-skinned terrifying ghost who in a prophecy comes to earth to live on Aboriginal land and brings death and devastation to all people.

Before the Europeans arrived, the indigenous people of Australia did not regard themselves collectively as 'Aborigines', but as members of smaller local cultural groups. From their point of view, earth as they knew it extended outside their own cultural bloc of communities but they had no concept of people from different worlds.

Many other Aboriginal people connected white colour with death and mourning, even if not all had the story about Wanda. For them, the only logical explanation was that the white-skinned Europeans must be their deceased relatives, who were returning from the Warrambul to their previous homelands, loaded with new goods. After their first terror, many Aboriginal communities therefore treated the first Europeans as their kin, not as strangers. It was, however, hard to explain why the white people behaved strangely and unpredictably and did not appear to recognise their kin or the places where they once lived. An Aboriginal man asked the explorer Eyre: 'Why are the dead so ignorant, or so forgetful so as not to know their friends?' The only explanation was memory loss, since the spirits had fragmented souls. In this way the white men could at least be placed in some kind of established framework and incorporated in the Aboriginal moral order.

The Nhunggabarra old people of course knew about Wanda and the extreme danger of becoming involved with white men, but when they heard the young men's breathless account about the white people, they scolded the men. They had lost a valuable opportunity – they should have stayed, observed, made contact and learned. All went to the place of the sighting and carefully studied the wheel tracks and hoof marks and covered them with leaves and branches to preserve them for future learning.

The story about the Nhunggabarra young men's first contact with white men survived through the generations and was told to Tex by his grandmother.

This marked the end of Nhunggabarra society – within a year the epidemics were to hit them. When Thomas Mitchell's party travelled through the area three years later, the Nhunggabarra and many of their neighbours were already severely decimated by disease. Soon the first settlers arrived and with them a long period of suffering, massacres, pain and humiliation. That story, however, is not ours to tell.

The prophecy about Wanda came uncannily true. But as the stories also tell: there is no end, there is no past and no future, there is only the time of creation – *Burruguu* – and after creation there is only experience.

NHUNGGAL COUNTRY TODAY

I am walking with Tex across the Bhoda property in Nhunggal country, a sunny day in April. The dry red soil is covered by the ubiquitous galvanised burr, the typical plant on degraded soil in this part of Australia – it is some ten to twenty centimetres in height with sharp thorns that trash our shoes, socks and trousers. There are a few scattered trees and no edible grass: the millet grass gave up in the mid 1900s, and in 1974 the last white sheep farmer sold out of the area. After 100 years of European-style farming, what used to be a huge paddock for sheep was by then completely degraded and the whole property of 130,000 hectares could only sustain a maximum of 3000 sheep.

The property we are walking on occupies roughly one-tenth of original Nhunggal country. Today this land sustains four families of 21 people in total; together with people in industries and services the land sustains some 30 to 40 people. The same land would have fed a minimum of 50 people with Aboriginal methods prior to 1788, and maybe as many as 200.

The story is repeated all over Australia. Not long after the Aborigines had stopped tending to the landscape the Australian soil degraded rapidly. The reason is soil erosion. New topsoil forms very slowly and the annual soil erosion from industrial farming vastly exceeds annual soil formation; the world average is more than 30 times more soil lost than formed. In Australia the topsoil layer is thinner than in most parts of the world and less resilient to erosion. In many parts of Australia it did not take the graziers and grain growers long to flush what little there was straight into the sea. One generation of cattlemen sufficed to convert the Birdsville Track region in South Australia into desert, although it had sustained Aboriginal economy for thousands of years. After the Aborigines were gone it took only a few years for the scrubs to reappear and the grass to turn sour on the high grasslands in the rainforest in Tasmania that the explorer Henry Hellyer in 1827 deemed perfect pastures for sheep farming. Sheep farming stopped there by around 1845. On the open plains in the highlands of north Tasmania the settlers were increasingly frustrated by the growth of scrub, which by 1890 had obliterated most of the open land.

The sheep farmers are not to take the sole blame for the ecological disaster, however. Today it sounds incredible, but successive Australian governments imposed land clearance obligations on the farmers and minimum stocking rates, forcing them to keep a minimum number of sheep per acre as a condition of holding a lease. In the late 19th century stocking rates were three times higher than considered sustainable today; earlier (not necessarily reliable) figures suggest rates up to ten times higher.

For a short period, while the sheep were depleting the grass and eroding the land, cattle and sheep farmers made Goodooga the boomtown of the early 1900s and the biggest town in the area. Today the farmers are all but gone as providers of jobs and wealth and Goodooga is a sad shadow of its past glory.

The property we are walking on is currently owned by the Nhunggabarra community and managed by Tex's brother. Tex's father and the local Aboriginal community started a rejuvenation program here in 1997. The first thing they did was to get rid of the irrigation pumps. The idea is to let the land recover some of the lost topsoil, then to rebuild the original vegetation with Aboriginal methods and slowly start farming based on sustainable and ecological practices. After seven years of efforts there are positive signs. The Nhunggabarra staple food, pigweed, has returned. Patches of the first foxtail grass are also visible; even strands of millet grass are beginning to show up again.

One would have thought that Western innovators would have invented a farming technology more suited to Australian country than grazing by now. Instead, cotton was brought into the region.

COTTON: HI-TECH, NO-TOUCH

A traveller in northwest New South Wales can only marvel at the laser-levelled cotton fields irrigated by huge dams and channels; the towering bales of cotton waiting to be taken to the gins; the enormous harvesters on the fields and the narrow roads. This is high-tech, high-investment industrial farming, Western style.

There is unease, however, among the local people which is expressed in private conversations and in the town pubs. Their apprehension is justified. Protected by high walls and moats, with access to the fields only via a bridge, the newest cotton fields resemble medieval European defence systems. Fifteen years of relentless expansion has backlashed and the cotton industry is under siege. The moats and the walls are huge extra investments built in desperation to reduce water evaporation and to protect the environment against runoffs from fertilisers, pesticides and herbicides. The effect has been considerable: Australian cotton farmers produce more cotton per litre of irrigated water than any comparable country. But cotton is the thirstiest crop on earth: in water consumption it beats even rice.

The cotton farmers pump their water from the second largest river system in Australia, the Barwon–Darling. The Darling River is an Australian national icon, an 'extraordinary river...with the finest water...and without which those regions would be deserts, inaccessible to and uninhabitable by, either man or beast,' as Thomas Mitchell noted lyrically in his journal. Grass covered the riverbanks and huge river gums shaded and cooled Thomas Mitchell's party that thirtieth day of May 1835. Today the age-old river gums are doomed, clinging precariously with their exposed roots to slumped naked banks. Mitchell saw 'water being beautifully transparent, the bottom was visible at great depths, showing large fishes in shoals, floating like birds in mid-air'. I see only a turbid stream filled with opaque silt, which allows no fish to breed and no light to penetrate to the plant life. Invisible poisonous run-offs from fertilisers, pesticides and herbicides fill the river.

After 170 years of Western-style farming the Darling River flood plains are dying and the wildlife sanctuaries in the wetlands that Mary Gilmore describes in poetic terms are no more. The photosynthetic activity of the plants is the main source of food in the food chain, but it is now so severely disrupted that ecological experts regard the river as doomed, its ecosystems deprived of the sustenance that comes from floodouts and wetlands.

As the graziers were first to discover, Australian soils lose their organic and microbiological components very easily. The farms in the area had been flushing their soil into the Darling for a hundred years when synthesised nitrogen arrived on the scene in the 1960s; the result was to increase the rate of erosion even further. The land, degraded and meagre to start with, rapidly lost its biodiversity when synthetically fertilised; the soil became acid, unproductive and a large proportion of the fertilisers and chemicals ended up in the river system. The farmers then added pesticides and herbicides. The cotton industry is now completing the tragedy with new generations of fertilisers and pesticides.

An aeroplane at low level above a cotton field catches my attention and I stop to admire the pilot's acrobatic manoeuvres. He is spraying something, perhaps Endosulfan, the pesticide for the heliothis caterpillar, which eats the fruit of the cotton plants. The caterpillar promptly arrived in Australia together with the introduction of cotton. Despite the pilot's undeniable skills and precision work, some of the spray and the run-offs will find its way onto properties further away. In

1996, 25 farms in New South Wales and southern Queensland were put in quarantine when high levels of Endosulfan residues were found in their beef.

Endosulfan has been identified as a carcinogen and the herbicide Atrazine as a neurotoxin and public pressure will eventually force the farmers to stop their application, but the harm to the ecosystem is already done. The cotton industry is now setting its hopes on the next innovation – Ingard, a cotton variety genetically modified to withstand the heliothis caterpillar. The trouble with GM cotton is that plants containing natural insecticides may harm beneficial insects as well as the insect pests they are designed to target. Such secondary effects have of course not been properly studied.

The use of massive volumes of water to irrigate the world's thirstiest crop on the driest continent on the planet can only be described as folly, and the reckless application of fertilisers and pesticides tell a story of a hi-tech industry not in touch with reality or humanity.

The Nhunggabarra 'Recipe' for Sustainability

THE NHUNGGABARRA – AND MOST LIKELY other Australian Aboriginal societies – had developed something the industrialised world is still struggling with: a truly sustainable society on earth. Isolated on the Australian island continent, they had developed and finetuned their model. It had withstood and proven its sustainability over tens of thousands of years of dramatic events until their economy was destroyed by a force coming from outside their system.

We may disagree about the reason their society model survived for so long. Was it because of ancestral design (the Nhunggabarra view) or due to lack of progress (as many Westerners suspect)? Was the cause evolution (argued by social and natural sciences) or even a series of random events? Whichever explanation one prefers, let us focus on the resulting model and set aside the issue about the process of achieving it. We can distinguish economic, ecological, social and spiritual elements in the model.

A striking feature of the Nhunggabarra society is their knowledge-based economy. Because food and a few personalised tools were the only tangible production that scientists and economists recognised and were able to measure, these scientists and economists long

The Nhunggabarra 'Recipe' in Summary

Mission
Keep all alive

Core Belief: All are Connected
- 'All are connected' (Ancestors, people, animals, plants, sky and earth)
- Timelessness (time arrow is an illusion)
- Eternal life and reward in the Warrambul (when one's mission is accomplished on earth)
- Individual spiritual relationship with Ancestors – no formal religion, no gods, no devil or hell
- Spiritual world is mirrored in landscape on earth – no tangible religious monuments

Core Value: Respect
- For knowledge itself (learn about the responsibility required before access given)
- For knowledgeable individuals (defer to more knowledgeable people)
- For all individuals (do not impose your own view on other people)
- For knowledge diversity (learn from foreign people)
- For the rights of foreign people and countries (do not conduct conquests)
- For the leadership role of other individuals (do not usurp the role of another person)

Economy: Intangible
- Production and consumption are primarily intangible
- Tools and equipment made of natural materials – recyclable
- Tightly coupled teams (families) are core production units
- Intangible processes to keep all alive (stories, ceremonies and dances)

Ecosystem: Care

- Ecological farming methods – 'ecofarming'
- Natural medicine
- Regulation of population
- Nomadic life (to reduce human pressure on the ecosystem)

Primary Resource: Knowledge

- Life-long learner-driven education
- Eighteen-year knowledge journey
- Status from knowledge – no status in material wealth
- Knowledge safe-keeping (tuckandee, role-splitting)

Leadership: All Have a Role

- Context-specific leadership – all have a leadership role to play
- Impersonal role allocation (via planned marriages)
- Processes to prevent individual power monopolies (role-splitting, respect)
- Knowledge-based organising (focus is on creating, sharing and maintaining knowledge)
- Consensus decision-making
- Gender equality through roles
- Rule of law and enforcement of sanctions

Society: Build Community

- Fuzzy country borders – 'country ends where the story ends'
- Networking processes for keeping peace (buurras, knowledge journeys, marriage rules)
- Individual career (to take on more responsibility for functionality of the community)
- Generosity and sharing (reinforced by kinship rules)
- Custodianship of land and knowledge – no individual ownership
- Collaborative methods for increasing productivity
- Widows, orphans and elderly cared for by the community

dismissed Aboriginal economy as producing very low value. What they missed was more than half the economy – that is, Aboriginal society's very high production of intangible value: education, knowledge, art, law, entertainment, medicine, spiritual ceremonies, peacekeeping and social welfare.

Nomadic life and an emphasis on intangible production and consumption ensured that the ecological pressure of the economy was kept low. The Aboriginal people's ecofarming methods were built on intimate knowledge of the ecology of the land, so they were indistinguishable from nature itself. Consequently, they were dismissed as 'primitive' both by arriving settlers and by scientists into our day. It is only due to the very latest advances in ecological science that their methods are now being recognised. A particularly interesting feature is that their mission to keep all alive ensured that they maintained the breeding stocks, that the methods for trapping mimicked nature, and that methods that did have a considerable impact, particularly fire, were carefully managed to maintain the ecosystems.

The result was a society in balance with its natural and social environment.

By examining the Nhunggabarra society an impressive architecture is revealed – a well-designed, comprehensive societal structure, where every element supports the whole. With a spiritual belief that 'all are connected', the core value 'respect' follows naturally and ecosystem care is hence not only a matter of immediate survival, but also the reason for existence – the mission to 'keep all alive'. Production of intangibles is how the mission is fulfilled. Nomadic life is less harmful to the fragile Australian ecosystem than agriculture. Making individual know-how the decisive power factor, and keeping a tight rein on men's ego-drive spreads leadership roles; building community also outside one's own country keeps the peace and increases survival rates.

Is it not 'too good to be true', an ideal picture, an after-construction? I am admittedly applying organisation and management theory concepts on the Nhunggabarra society – in that sense it is an after-construction. I am not implying that the Nhunggabarra openly discussed spirituality, legal principles, values and leadership style in these particular terms. Unlike the Western world of today, their society seems to have been so finely tuned economically, ecologically, socially and spiritually that the laws of their society had to change only slowly, and in response to changes in climate and environment. In the short term at least, the laws were unquestionable. The Nhunggabarra credited Baayami for their achievement; Western scientists cite evolution.

I have used the law stories as the main source, and so in that sense the focus in the book is on the 'ideal': how the Nhunggabarra were meant to behave. Of course, the Nhunggabarra society was not an egalitarian utopia populated only by idealistic people with altruistic motives. On the contrary, the law stories reveal that the Nhunggabarra knew the consequences of criminality, power abuse, over-exploitation and war only too well and had done the best they could to prevent them. Hunter–gatherer societies are often called 'egalitarian', which is true in terms of material wealth. But when we consider the significance of individual knowledge and intangible wealth, a society emerges with equality in tangible terms and inequality in intangible terms. It is a society for ordinary human beings – a carefully balanced model with checks and balances and reinforcing loops.

One such loop is the *power loop*, with many mutually reinforcing and counter-balancing drivers. The Nhunggabarra community was no democracy, but they still had developed power-balancing processes: consensus, context-specific leadership and know-how organising are principles that can surpass representative democracy if properly implemented. At the very least they should have prevented power abuse and given reasonable guarantees that individual concerns could be raised. Knowledge was for the benefit of the community and it was too powerful to be handled carelessly. A person had to be initiated to get access. This gave power to older people. But they, in turn, were kept in check by the requirements of consensus and that those with more knowledge must show respect for other people. The respect for knowledge also made it hard for charismatic men to grab positional power and it further reinforced community-oriented values. Their educational walkabout kept testosterone-fuelled younger men busy during the years they might be a threat to the existing power structure, and when they returned to their home community they were too mature and had accumulated too many relationships in the neighbouring communities to start wars against them. Role-splitting functioned as a glue to keep the community together, and alongside context-specific leadership, it reduced the risk of monopolies of expertise and reinforced community orientation. The general lack of tangible goods reduced leaders' temptations to seek material wealth for status and people's temptation to engage in conspicuous consumption of material goods. Men's short-term power positions were checked by the women's long-term control over their marriage-partners-to-be and the roles that their children would have. And the wiringin was always the last resort in any power dispute.

The *value-creation loop* is driven by the Nhunggabarra's emphasis on intangible production and consumption. Their spiritual preferences over and above material wealth increased the demand for intangibles such as art, education and entertainment, and reduced greatly the demand for status in the form of worldly goods, monuments, churches and palaces. This minimised ecological pressure and improved food production.

The value-creation loop is closely linked with the *knowledge-building loop*, which starts with the knowledge of Nhunggabarra's Ancestors contained in the landscape and the animals and plants that populated it. Through observations, the Nhunggabarra learned how to best sustain the landscape and animals and plants. This knowledge accumulated in the stories, songs and ceremonies. The stories in their turn became material for intellectual query and individual self-reflection, which reinforced the connections between nature and individuals. The tuckandee system and role-splitting guarded against the risk of losing knowledge and protected it across generations.

Spiritual principles that emphasised the interconnectedness of all and everything were crystallised in the mission of keeping all alive and the value of *respect*. Mutual respect — sideways, upwards and downwards — was the glue that kept society together and functioned as a check and balance against power abuse. At the core was the absolute respect for the integrity of the individual — which was balanced by the requirement of the individual to respect the community. Both the mission and the value of respect furthered peaceful relations with neighbouring countries. Because people and animals were one and the same, the requirement for respect was extended to all living beings and also extended to respecting other people's opinion — that is, a respect for diversity.

How the Nhunggabarra arrived at their model is less important for us than their accomplishment. Their organisational architecture proved virtually impossible to break from within. The only way to crush it was intervention from the outside.

The Nhunggabarra model may be the 'original blueprint' for organising, the 'natural' design for human society. Is this how governance of sustainable societies in general might have looked if the societies had been allowed to evolve undisturbed by outside aggression and influences of competitive and self-serving power seekers?

KNOWLEDGE-BASED THEORY

It is very difficult to measure intangible value. Economists generally avoid this problem by only considering value that can be measured in money terms. Traditional economists therefore consider the value of an animal to be the economic value it provides. Production is measured in financial terms and the value of a trade transaction is measured by the financial value inherent in the good. According to traditional economics, the Nhunggabarra did not produce much of economic value except food and some tools.

Another problem is that intangibles sometimes behave in an opposite way to tangibles. For instance, cars and machines tend to depreciate in value when they are used, but intangible resources often grow when they are used and depreciate when not used. For instance, if one stops speaking a language or leaves one's profession, the competencies gradually dissipate or become obsolete. A third issue is that proficiency in a language or professional competency requires huge intangible investments in training and education. These assets are embedded in individuals and measurable in financial terms only with high uncertainty, so traditional economics circumvents the problem by not recognising them as assets with a value.

Knowledge-based theory does not back off from considering value only because it is hard to measure. It recognises that value tends to generally have a substantial intangible component. The value of the ability to speak another language can be in increasing the enjoyment and experience of holidays, or it can be used to generate salary as a language teacher, interpreter etc. Whether one converts the intangible value to financial value depends on the context and is a matter of choice.

Intangible value is generated when new knowledge is *created* (innovation) and *shared* between people (collaboration). Intangible value is also created when knowledge is *converted* from one form to another.

In present-day societies we convert more and more of the knowledge held in people's heads to information and store it as digital records; examples are 'lessons learned' repositories and databases storing customer information. This makes sharing fast and efficient. The Nhunggabarra converted their knowledge about the world to stories, songs and dances that they shared with each other and from one generation to another. Our companies convert market data to information – by analysing customers' buying patterns they are able to serve market segments better. The Nhunggabarra observed their 'customers' – by analysing the behaviour of animals, for example, they learned not only about the animals and how to sustain them, they also converted their observations to knowledge about themselves.

For the Nhunggabarra, value was in the action-generating features of knowledge, so the definition of knowledge we use is *a capacity to act* — know-how and competence can be regarded as synonyms. Intangible value grows each time a transfer or conversion takes place, because the capacity to act does not leave the creator. The knowledge I learn from you adds to my knowledge, but it does not leave you. Thus, from an organisational or society viewpoint the capacity to act effectively doubles each time knowledge is shared. A bit simplistically one might say that knowledge shared is knowledge doubled and that the more *flows* we can generate between the intangible resources, the more value is generated.

There are many barriers against value-generating knowledge flows, as members in 21st century organisations and societies will know first hand — the crucial barrier is lack of trust. Will the knowledge I share be used against me? Will my relative competitive position be jeopardised? Another issue is closeness in context: it is obviously a lot easier to share knowledge in a society where you know the background of everybody and speak the language. Therefore, the full potential of value creation can probably never be achieved in real life.

THE NHUNGGABARRA'S KNOWLEDGE-BASED APPROACH

The Nhunggabarra mission to keep all alive gave them three 'customer segments' to serve: the totems (animals), the plants and the land. They also knew what they had to do: keep them all alive or the individuals and the community would collapse.

The Nhunggabarra, as individuals, had to learn everything worth knowing about their 'customers', otherwise they could not fulfil their needs. They had three collections of resources at their disposal: the people with their capacity to act, the tools and ceremonies, and their 'customers' who could be observed. They had to build their know-how in performing the ceremonies and they had to learn the proper execution of ceremonies or else risk the ceremony losing its power. A society that kept its harmony both inside and in its dealings with other communities was crucial: they had to tend to an architecture that was sustainable long-term. Last but not least, they had to keep themselves alive, otherwise their struggle was pointless and the whole world would go under anyway.

The Nhunggabarra had many methods for ensuring the flow of the capacity to act between individuals: buurras, storytelling, learning tracks, initiation, songs, dances, artwork, ceremonies, walkabouts, learner-driven education, to mention but a few. Education was imperative for an individual to function as an adult in this society; in particular, the demands on every man to learn were very high – men were not regarded as fully functioning adults until the age of 32. We can compare this with the present-day Western world, where the highest degree awarded in the education system (doctor) can in Australia be accomplished as early as the age of 24, and very few achieve it.

The Nhunggabarra used their skills and other individual capacities to improve animals' capacity to grow and multiply. They cultivated the countryside to increase land suitable for animal habitats; they created breeding sanctuaries and performed reciprocity ceremonies (for instance, the 'sorry dances' in preparation for a hunt).

Knowledge flowed the other way, too. The Nhunggabarra people learned from the animals, the earth and the plants. The totem system ensured a group of dedicated and knowledgeable individuals, who would always act in the best interest of their totem animals. Education also gave the Nhunggabarra insights into the relationship between various animals and the best vegetation types for sustaining them. Features of the landscape served as navigation aids.

The Nhunggabarra also converted the knowledge they learned from their 'customers' into better tools and processes, such as new natural medicines, new songs and new paintings. They invested time and creative effort in developing new tools and traps. Over time they also adapted the stories to changing circumstances.

The tools and processes helped the Nhunggabarra to be better hunters and gatherers. Tangible tools, like the spear and the wamara, enabled them to hunt more effectively; ceremonies prepared them for the hunt; stories supported their navigation in the landscape; the law ensured that the community functioned socially.

Animals, plants and the earth contributed considerable knowledge to the stories (they populated the stories, they functioned as mnemonics), the law (the totem system was inspired by the animals) and the tools (in the form of tangible materials). The animals even inspired the Nhunggabarra's language; many words in the Yuwaalaaray/Yuwaalaayay language are derived from or inspired by animal sounds.

Many methods were implemented with a dual purpose: to both sustain the 'customer' and to sustain the 'mob'. The fire tool was crucial in sustaining the animals' habitats and improving the topsoil for edible plants for both animals and humans; the fish traps ensured survival of the breeding stock and provided food simultaneously; the ceremonies reached and communicated with the animals' spirits; the law made sure that the Nhunggabarra moved around so they did not deplete the animal stock, the vegetation or the soil.

The stories, the songs, the ceremonies were all aligned under one spiritual paradigm and they supported each other. A story would be supported by a song and a painting and a dance; tools would have multiple uses and also feature in stories and ceremonies.

The Nhunggabarra spent a large proportion of their most productive resources on building community and common context. In addition, the mission emphasised a holistic view, which maximised value creation. A crystal clear mission that is embraced by all people would be the envy of most present-day organisations, not to mention societies. And the mission was kept alive too; by telling and retelling the stories, by acting and living it in everyday life, in a society of high transparency, where equality reigned.

Knowledge-based theory allows us to see what the Nhunggabarra did with all their 'free' time: that their value generation, production as well as consumption, was primarily intangible.

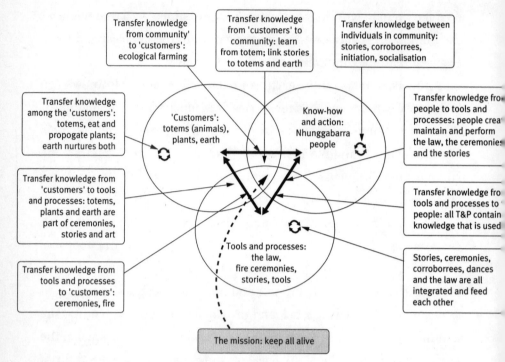

The Nhunggabarra's knowledge-based strategies.

HOW GENERAL IS THE MODEL?

What happened to the Easter Island population? We now know that it may once have numbered 15,000 people. Why did the Viking society of Greenland die out? The powerful Anasazi of New Mexico? The enigmatic Maya? At the peak of their society the Maya may have numbered 15 million people on the Yucatan peninsula. However, when the Spaniards arrived in 1524 there were only some 30,000 people left. How did such a large population and sophisticated society just disappear? Jared Diamond investigates in his 2005 book *Collapse* if there were any common causes. He concludes that collapses of these societies had many roots, but the common cause was environmental degradation initiated by deforestation. Agriculture allowed higher food production than hunter–gathering; however, tilled land came at the expense of the forest and the wildlife, which were crucial for keeping the ecological systems in balance. Increasing populations also required more and more wood for cooking, houses, palaces, temples and tools.

The disappearance of the forests changed the microclimates and the ecology, causing droughts and rapid soil erosion. Ever growing populations continued to extend tilled lands further and further into more and more marginal areas until even a minute change in climate was enough to prompt a catastrophe. The trigger factor leading to the final downfall was often a change in climate, such as a prolonged drought.

New findings unearthed by archaeologists also shed some light on the role played by the leaders. What did the leaders do when their societies faced dwindling food supplies? Two responses to the escalating disaster have been uncovered: one was to live the 'Great Illusion' as long as possible, until the society eventually collapsed 'overnight' in an archaeological sense. The secular leaders increased their consumption of luxuries and priests built more temples. The other approach could have been picked from the 'Wurunna rule book': the leaders blamed innocent bystanders and sent their people to wars against neighbouring peoples or started civil wars against each other.

So far there are few surprises in the analysis. The societies that collapsed seem to have followed the path 'explained' by evolution theory – that is, when resources grow scarce, wars and internal fighting and destruction follow.

However, there exist a few old societies that managed to survive for quite long. They include the highland societies of New Guinea and the tiny South Pacific island Tikopia. The New Guinea highlanders operated sustainably for tens of thousands of years as hunter–gatherers and then for another 7000 years as farmers in small communities separated by huge mountains. Tikopia has sustained a population of 1200 people for almost 3000 years without succumbing to the seemingly inevitable disaster scenario that is waiting around the corner of every society based on agriculture. Both are people who at the time of European colonisation were dismissed as 'primitive'. The New

Guineans lived in thatched huts, wore little or no clothing and lacked writing; their tools were all made of stone, wood and bone. Hence evolution theorists still score them lowest on the scale. Both societies, however, have managed to avoid the vicious spiral of population growth and environmental degradation which threaten us living in 'advanced' industrial societies.

One important ingredient to their success is that the survivors started with favourable environmental conditions, such as wet climates and good soils, which can cope with degradation caused by agriculture. In Tikopia's case the soils are refilled by the volcanic dust from other islands. The New Guinea highlands are blessed with copious amounts of rain, and Tikopia enjoys more rain than other Polynesian islands.

The defining difference between the sustainable and the collapsed societies, however, turns out to be their organisation, leadership and ecological knowledge. The key organising principle has been to keep the population in balance with environmental impact. New Guineans practised at least five methods for regulating the population: using forest plants for contraception and abortion, sexual abstinence, natural lactational amenorrhea and infanticide. Constant small-scale wars also kept the population growth in check. Tikopian methods in earlier times included coitus interruptus, abortion induced by abdominal pressure, infanticide and celibacy. They even practised suicide. The belief that the population must be carefully managed is still very strong on the island and at least one annual ceremony is carried out by the chiefs to preach an ideal of zero population growth.

The leadership principle in both societies has been and is still a very flat power hierarchy. New Guinea highland villages had no kings or chiefs. Their leaders were 'big men', who by force of personality were more influential than other men, but they lived under the same conditions as everybody else. The big men could not make decisions on behalf of any individual. Decisions were (and still are) made by means of consensus.

The third principle is a very high level of ecological know-how. New Guinea highland farming methods are so sophisticated that

European agronomists still do not understand why the highlanders' methods work there and why European farming technology fails. The methods are highly specialised and so customised to each patch of land that people must grow up on the farms and learn the techniques first-hand to be able to farm successfully.

The similarities with the Nhunggabarra are striking. Ecological know-how and flat power hierarchies are obvious parallels. However, the starting condition, favourable environment conditions for sustainable agriculture, did not exist in Australia. The Australian Aboriginal people's wisdom in not trying to develop agriculture is therefore apparent – they would most likely have suffered the fate of the collapsed societies. Instead, the Nhunggabarra, one of the communities with more favourable environmental conditions, developed their hunter–gatherer society into a very 'complex' version beyond what has been generally understood and appreciated. This is an impressive achievement, which suggests considerable organisational and leadership skills.

10

Sustain our World!

CAN MODERN INDUSTRIALISED SOCIETIES LEARN ANYTHING from the Aboriginal model for sustainability? An argument against this is based on the 'survival of the fittest' theory of evolution: *The tragic fate of the Australian Aborigines shows that their model for society was not 'fit to survive'*. This argument, however, misses the point. Evolution theory is not a social theory; it explains only the *biological consequences*. Biologically, the Australian continent was a world almost cut off from the rest of the planet, and therefore very vulnerable to an invasion of alien microbes. This is also what happened in reality – the Australian Aborigines succumbed rapidly to the range of epidemic diseases that hit them almost simultaneously. Those who survived became immune and then bestowed immunity on their children. How would our bodies and societies today cope if a dozen alien microbes from outer space suddenly fell on our planet? Of course we do not consider an alien invasion from outer space very likely, yet this is exactly what happened to the Australian Aborigines when the 'alien' Europeans landed on their shores.

However, the *social consequences* of European arrival on the Australian continent cannot be explained by evolution theory. To do so is to classify humans as animals or microbes without free will and morals. There was nothing 'evolutionary' about the European expeditions that colonised the Americas, Africa and Australia — they were initiated and funded by people, who exercised their free will and chose conquest and plunder rather than cohabitation and trade.

Another argument is that *our societies are so 'advanced' by comparison that we have nothing to learn from 'less advanced' societies*. But what is 'less advanced': to sustain the world, or exploit it; to care for nature, or pollute it; to build community, or empire; to produce intangibles (art, knowledge and relationships), or tangibles (cars, computers and guns); to develop natural remedies, or synthetic medicine; to 'work' two to five hours a day to afford one's lifestyle, or eight to ten hours a day?

A third argument against modern industrialised societies learning from the Aboriginal model is not as easily dismissed: *we cannot learn from the society of the Australian Aborigines because it was too different from the modern industrialised world*. This is a very complex argument, which must be divided into three sub-arguments.

The first sub-argument is that *Western societies are 'open societies'. We cannot implement solutions from 'closed' societies*, such as the Nhunggabarra and their neighbours. The concept of open and closed societies was popularised by Karl Popper, who applied his 'critical rationalism' from the philosophy of science on societies. The 'open society' is a rational ideal: societies populated by free individuals who, protected by a framework of law, propose and make responsible, rational decisions based on science and so achieve better societies for everyone. Popper contrasted it with 'closed societies', which tend to be marked by their taboos and obligations, which exempt individuals from moral problems; there is never any doubt about how to act. The Nhunggabarra society was probably more closed than open, but this could be because they had found a model that worked, were happy with it and very careful not to change, while Western societies still have not found a model that works. One must also question how open Western societies really are. Why, for example, have the free individuals not seen fit to make the decisions required to stop polluting the environment? How 'rational' is that?

The second sub-argument is linked to the first and has to do with the role of free will in an open society: *the Nhunggabarra model will not work in Western societies, where individuals are free to pursue any role in competition with others.* Individual freedom and competition have given us a world of privately held corporations, which compete against each other on a global scale. What's more, in Western societies people today have a wide selection of spiritual convictions to choose from, and this freedom to choose is one of the treasured features of modern society. The Nhunggabarra did not have this choice.

The third sub-argument is that *Western corporations provide us with material affluence and unprecedented variety and choice of goods. We cannot return to an Aboriginal society.* It is true that a return to a hunter–gatherer society is no solution, but as we will outline in more detail below, material affluence does not seem to make people in Western societies happy. Another facet we will look into below is that we — just like the Nhunggabarra — enjoy intangibles more than material goods. Most of the production in Western economies is already intangible — most services, for instance — and becoming more so by the day.

These two last arguments are not easily dismissed. They tell us that the Nhunggabarra recipe cannot be implemented as a whole. Still, the Australian Aborigines have shown the way: a sustainable world requires a model where the elements fit holistically and strengthen each other. Can we develop one that will work in our complex and open modern societies? We will discuss some of the possible elements of such a model that uses the Nhunggabarra 'recipe' as the starting point.

Modern quantum physics teaches that *all are connected*, and after the communication revolution in the last decade no one can deny that people on the planet influence each other — be it for better (cultural exchange and knowledge) or for worse (pollution and terrorism). We are better informed today about the state of the world than ever before and able to collaborate across all borders. This is one of the reasons why protesters against the corporate laissez-faire version of globalisation can mount considerable support in practically no time and start a process of adjustments. The interconnected world is still in the making, and backlashes against it are mounting, but the trend towards more interconnected people and countries is a long-term inevitability.

There are other trends that show surprising and encouraging similarities between modern Western societies and the Nhunggabarra. As our consumption of services grow, our economies rapidly become more *intangible* and *knowledge* becomes the *primary resource*. In the wake of this trend there are also signs that the command-control *leadership* model, which has dominated since the birth of the modern corporation in the 1800s, is coming full circle – back to versions where individuals are more in control of their own worklife.

No changes in an open society can be implemented against the values of individual freedom and competition. We do not have sufficient space to dwell in depth on such vast topics. We will only explore two positive balancing elements of the Nhunggabarra model: the value of *respect* and the process of *community building*.

But we have to start with *ecosystems*. The contrast between Australian Aborigines' *sustaining* attitude and the modern industrialised world's ruthless *exploitation* of the planet's ecosystems cannot be starker – and this is bad news for us, because the current extensive and rapid depletion of the planet's ecosystems is the defining point of our future. Humanity is living what could be the last days of a 'Great Illusion'.

EXPLOIT OR SUSTAIN?

The profusion of life in an ecosystem is staggering. One square metre of good grassland soil contains around 1000 each of ants, spiders, wood lice, beetles and larvae; 2000 each of earthworms and millipedes; 8000 slugs and snails; 20,000 pot worms, 40,000 springtails and 12 million nematodes. The life forms underground weigh more than those above ground; the equivalent of a dozen horses per acre. They all work to sustain life as we know it and there is little in terms of substitutes for their activities.

Try to imagine the technologies and investments required to produce oxygen, regulate the chemical composition of the atmosphere, and the oceans, and convert solar energy into raw materials, just to mention a few. It cost US$200 million just to keep eight people alive for two years in Biosphere 2 with a minimum of services (Biosphere 2 was designed as an airtight replica of earth's environment).

The sum total of the ecological systems that support life can be called 'Natural Capital', a concept suggested by Paul Hawken and Amory and L. Hunter Lovins. Natural capital is different from human-made capital in that it cannot be produced by human activity and we, in the Western world, tend to overlook it. We can live perfectly well without giving a thought to the photosynthetic cycle that reproduces the oxygen that we breathe. We can admire the river from our car window without caring about the fact that the asphalt under our wheels covers an area that was once a wetland with an ecosystem that sustained a rich bird life and a huge variety of fish and crustaceans.

Depletion of natural capital today is rampant and goes on all around us, but we don't notice it because the changes are subtle. Drawings made by artists in the early days of European settlement in south-eastern Australia display a pristine, lush and open landscape that is so alien to most modern-day Australians that, for many years, it was thought that the English artists had not quite been able to draw the Australian environment properly.

Today's bushland tourists in Nhunggal country don't miss the freshwater lobsters that no longer breed in the Darling River, the fish that no longer swim or the birds that no longer fly, because they don't know they were there in the first place.

We do not miss the 500 kilogram turtles outside Cuba, because we, living today, never saw them. The seas were so thick with giant turtles that Columbus's ships even ran aground on them. Reefs swarmed with 400-kilogram groupers outside Florida's coastline 500 years ago;

there were so many oysters that their combined capacity filtrated all the water in Chesapeake Bay every five days. The final blow has been the last hundred years of industrialised fishing; humans have flattened the coral reefs and scraped the seagrass beds bare. A dead zone larger than New Jersey now grows at the mouth of the Mississippi and all the cod fisheries there have collapsed.

We do not know and we do not care as long as someone else picks up the bill. The UK politicians do not feel responsible for their coal-fired electricity industry's sulphur-dioxide emissions, which are driven by the winds to the west coast of Sweden and fall as acid rain, killing the forests and dissolving heavy metals that pollute the ground-water. And if the UK's people allow politicians to turn a blind eye, why would the power plant managers care?

But it is harder to understand why power plant managers do not care about the fact that they are filling the lungs of their children and spouses with mercury, a dangerous neurotoxin, which is known to slow mental development. A US nationwide study conducted in 2004 by the University of North Carolina has revealed that one-fifth of the American population is surrounded by mercury levels above the EPA recommended limit. The biggest source of airborne mercury is coal-fired power plants.

We in the Western world live in a 'Great Illusion', not in reality. We behave as if the ecosystem comes free of charge and we also run our economies and allow our politicians and company leaders to live the illusion. A part of the problem is that our systems to measure wealth mislead us. We have elaborate systems for measuring the financial wealth created, but we have no idea about the simultaneous wealth destruction in natural capital.

Since we do not measure and charge for the cost of natural capital, a large proportion of the financial capital in the world and most of the physical infrastructure that we are so proud of have been generated by depleting the earth's natural capital. Cotton is Australia's second largest agricultural export earner after wheat, but the numbers only 'work' because the cotton farmers do not pay the cost of replenishing the water and the other natural capital they are exploiting.

Our 'progress' is on a daily basis, adding to a huge unmeasured and unaccounted for liability that we are handing over to our children.

Consistent environmental decline is reported by the Living Planet Index, a tool developed by WWF International to measure the health of forests, oceans, freshwater systems and other natural systems. The index shows a 35 per cent decline in the planet's ecological health between 1970 and 2000.

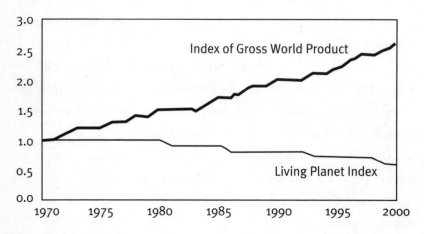

Economic activity and ecosystem health. (Worldwatch Institute Yearbook, *State of the World*, 2004, p. 18)

We have a tendency to think of the Western world of material wealth as 'advanced'. But our progress is to a high degree — unknown how high — an illusion, because companies do not take the real costs into account. Our 'progress' must be devalued by the depletion of the natural capital and by the steeply rising health costs of caring for the victims of 'progress', such as asthmatics, coronary disease sufferers, diabetics, the obese and stroke victims. And we have not even begun to address the climate issue, because the leaders of the USA, Australia and China prefer to live under illusion rather than in reality.

How many of the innovations today are only rectifying problems caused by the innovations of yesterday? What is our *real* progress – the net progress, after taking all these costs into consideration?

INNOVATION: RESPONSIBLE OR RECKLESS?

Innovation is the mantra of today and 'innovation economy' is the latest buzz phrase. Western company managers and governments push employees and citizens to innovate or die in the competition race and consultants happily offer advice and write books on how to innovate or die. Remember Wurunna of the Black Swans story? The story has a twist: Wurunna's actions, although performed for the wrong reasons and with dire consequences for all involved, still achieved a major benefit – breakthrough innovation of tools. This is a common theme in the Nhunggabarra stories: when someone breaks the law it some-times generates an innovation as an unintended side-effect. It shows that the Nhunggabarra knew very well both the risks and the advantages associated with innovation; they knew that breakthrough discoveries are made when someone breaks the existing rules and that the conse-quences therefore are unpredictable.

This is the darker, other side of innovation – the environmental and societal consequences of the introduction of new products. These consequences are not given much weight by corporations, and govern-ments have tended to turn a blind eye, too.

Little has changed in this respect since the 1950s when farmers in the US midwest resisted the government-funded introduction of the newly invented pesticide, DDT, on a large scale. One of the farmers claimed that DDT killed the worms, too, and he did not want to lose them, because they fed the singing birds. He was scorned of course. Among those ridiculing the farmers was a young Everett Rogers, who at the time took the first steps in an academic career that would make him one of the world's most renowned experts on innovation. He, who once labelled the midwest farmers 'traditionalists' (i.e. lowest on the innovation scale), now believes the bird-loving farmer was right all along.

Rogers is concerned that research into innovation is fundamentally biased pro-innovation; the premise is that the consequences of innovation are always beneficial and the indirect effects are never studied. However, the few studies into the full impacts of innovation that have been made show that indirect consequences are much more common than we like to believe and that they are generally both unanticipated and undesirable.

The indirect effects of the large-scale application in the 1950s of DDT are now widely recognised as disastrous. Surely, nothing similar could happen today? Societies must by now have rules in place that prevent such disasters? But consider this: safety data are only available for fourteen per cent of the most common chemicals in Europe. About 3000 chemicals now used daily across the European Union may never have been tested – the producers do not have to provide test data for chemicals introduced before 1981. New proposed EU regulation is not surprisingly under heavy attack by the European Chemical Industry's Council, CEFIC. It represents 40,000 companies and claims that the planned reforms threaten 1.7 million jobs. 'The philosophy behind the new chemicals policy still appears to be too one-sided in concentrating on environmental and health protection,' says CEFIC.

The illusion of the 'innovation economy' drives company managers to resist restrictions and ignore lessons of the past. And consultants, who do not have to take responsibility for their advice, thrive in a climate of recklessness. The bestselling *The Innovator's Dilemma*, by the latest innovation guru Clayton Christensen, teaches readers to pursue 'disruptive technologies' – that is, new and radically different products – while not offering one word on responsibility or indirect effects.

But can our world afford more reckless innovation? What is the next disaster-waiting-to-happen around the corner? Is it going to be electromagnetic pollution from mobile phones and wireless internet, computer and telecommunication (ICT)? Do telecommunications companies feel responsible for their introduction of extremely high and unprecedented levels of high-frequency electromagnetic radiation to unsuspecting societies? The tobacco companies are still denying their responsibility for millions of lung cancer victims; the oil companies and the oil-burning power-generating companies do not feel responsible for the alarmingly high mercury levels in people and fast-food executives feel no responsibility for their customers' obesity. What responsibility will the ICT industry and the local governments take for the indirect health consequences of wireless communication?

Nhunggabarra law required people to be responsible for how their actions affected people in both their own community and other communities. The Nhunggabarra 'recipe' for sustainable progress was to be selective and to consider consequences before introducing a new technology into society. As the Nhunggabarra taught: with unique knowledge comes unique responsibility.

WESTERN ECONOMIES ARE BECOMING INTANGIBLE

During 2005 the number of mobile phone users passed two billion, one-third of the planet's population. The other run-away technology in the last decade is the internet, with its ability to combine communication and information content. Both technologies support intangible consumption; they allow people to communicate, to share knowledge and to collaborate. Despite the fact that mobile networks and internet connections rely on high-tech hardware to function, the only reason to buy the hardware is the intangible service it offers.

Between 60 and 80 per cent of the value added in the OECD countries' gross domestic product of 2003 came from 'services' – that is, intangibles such as education, health, retail, transport, hotels, restaurants, art and entertainment. Manufacturing corresponds to less than twenty per cent of value added in OECD economies today and agriculture less than five per cent.

The shift away from tangibles as generators of wealth began in the early 1960s around the time when Galbraith criticised the materialistic American society in his book *Affluent Society*. America and the other Western countries are not consuming less material goods today – on the contrary. But not only are the growth markets intangible, even tangible goods are becoming less 'hard'. Intangible software has for many years been replacing tangible hardware in consumer goods from toys to cars to buildings. It is more than ten years since the value of ICT components surpassed the value of steel in a BMW. Fashion and design determine prices of mobile phone headsets. And so on. Competencies and knowledge of people, relationships with customers and other stakeholders, image in the marketplace, and intangible institutions, such as the internet, rule of law and democracy, are the wealth generators of our times.

However, intangibles still remain unaccounted for in countries' public accounts. Investments in intangibles have been treated as input (i.e. as a cost) rather than as investment that produces an asset. Some improvement has taken place. Since 1999, the US Bureau of Economic Analysis has included software in its measures of business investment. Gross business investment in software in 2002 was over $180 billion, which makes US gross domestic product nearly 2 per cent higher than it would be if intangibles were not counted at all. Although there is some progress, measuring of intangibles is still in its infancy and can only be approached by indirect means.

The economist Leonard Nakamura of the Federal Reserve Bank in Philadelphia is one of the few who have made a serious effort in this respect. He estimates US private investments in intangibles (design, software, ideas, artistic expression and marketing of new products) to have been a minimum of US$0.5 trillion, more likely US$1.0 trillion in 2002. By comparison, investments in tangibles – that is, equipment and fixed assets that same year – were US$0.93 trillion.

The trend is visible also in stock market valuations. Intangible assets have replaced tangible assets as wealth generators in industrial companies that make up the Dow Jones Index. Despite the downturn in

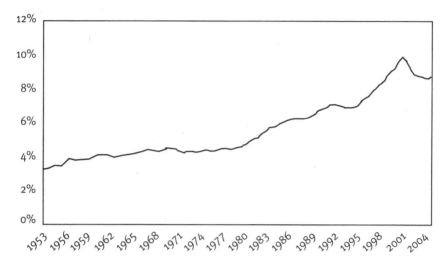

Estimated total intangible investment in the USA, 1953–2004. (Nakamura 2004)

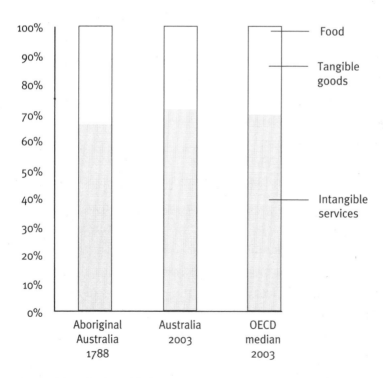

Composition of value added in Australian GDP, 1788 and 2003. (Estimates based on the time usage and OECD)

stock markets since the 'dot-com bubble burst' at the beginning of the 21st century, share prices remain on historically high levels compared to their underlying asset value as reported in annual reports.

The conclusion is that our economies are becoming more and more driven by intangible factors. As our economies 'advance', intangibles drive a larger and larger share of value creation. Is there not a delightful – and promising – paradox in this? Industrial economies are approaching the conditions of the Nhunggabarra society, the 'first' economy. The composition of the Australian gross domestic product in 2003 and 1788 look remarkably similar. Intangibles were the main products in Australia in 1788, just as they are today. The main difference is a higher proportion of value added in 2003 coming from tangible goods.

FREEDOM TO CHOOSE: FOR EXCESS OR HAPPINESS?

Logic suggests that having options allows people to select precisely what makes them happiest. The USA is the country of unparalleled individual freedom, of more opportunities and choice than any other country on earth, so Americans should be the happiest people on earth. This is however not the case.

It is obvious that some choice is better than none. To be able to choose between two cereals is better than having only one choice. But what about having 273 different cereals to choose from as Americans had in 2004? Studies by social scientists reveal that increased choice and increased material affluence have been accompanied by decreased happiness in the US, as in most other affluent societies. As the GDP more than doubled in the last 30 years, the proportion of Americans describing themselves as 'very happy' declined by about five per cent, or by some 14 million people.

The Nobel laureate psychologist Daniel Kahneman and his colleague Amos Tversky were in 1984 able to show that bad feelings from losses are felt stronger by people than good feelings generated by gains. Barry

Schwartz and colleagues followed up this research by designing experiments that show people may also suffer regret from the option they finally settle on. They conclude that the worry over future regret is a major reason why people feel less happy in affluent societies. And the more options one has the more likely it is that one will experience regret.

Twenty years of studies have confirmed beyond doubt that more economic growth does not improve levels of happiness in a country. The three main conclusions from all this research, summarised by Australian Clive Hamilton in his book *Growth Fetish*, are that, above a certain level of national income, people in richer countries are no happier than people in poorer countries; that in any given country rich people are not happier than those with moderate incomes and that when people grow richer they do not become happier.

An excess of alternatives causes stress also in other ways. In 1999, US teenagers were asked by the *New York Times* and CBS News to compare their experiences with those that their parents had at the same age. Fifty per cent of children from the more affluent households said their lives were harder, due to high expectations and 'too muchness': too many activities, too many consumer choices, too much to learn.

RESPECT: BALANCE AND STRENGTH

As we have seen, many of the Nhunggabarra laws are summarised by a single word: 'respect'. Respect is, however, an oft-forgotten concept in Western societies today. Not much has changed since the postwar generation threw the concept overboard in the 1960s. Respect is still commonly perceived as deference to inherited status and traditional hierarchy; as driven by duty and honour and avoidance of shame; a means to avoid punishment. Respect is seen to encourage static and impersonal behaviour. Rarely do we regard respect in the Nhunggabarra terms: the glue of society; as a powerful means to create symmetry, balance, empathy and positive relationships between individuals; and as a means of avoiding competitive behaviour.

Respect is an unknown concept in organisations, which, instead, are characterised by competitive behaviour among individuals. It is believed that competition enhances individual performance and this is true to a degree. However, competition within an organisation has many negative consequences, which reduce performance for groups of people and organisations and therefore for societies as a whole. One is that people will avoid sharing their knowledge with others, but keep it to themselves as a means of building individual competitive advantage.

Internal competition also adds to workplace stress and health problems. In Australia, the total cost of workers' compensation claims for stress-related conditions is estimated at over A$200 million every year. Research by the UK Health and Safety Executive, the government body regulating worklife risks, conducted from 2004 to 2005, has indicated that about half a million people in the UK experience work-related stress at a level they believe is making them ill: up to 5 million people in the UK feel 'very' or 'extremely' stressed by their work, and work-related stress costs society about £3.7 billion every year.

The value of respect could be a positive balance on individual freedom; it does not require legal intervention, because it works on an individual level. In the organisation of respect, employees are expected to respect the integrity of other employees' points of view and to not impose their own view on their colleagues. They are expected to respect the leadership role of other individuals and not try to compete for the position of another person. They are expected to accept the authority of knowledgeable people, but not to defer to people of mere positional power. Employees are asked to learn from customers and other stakeholders and to respect and appreciate the diversity of knowledge they provide. They are expected to respect other market players and not to behave dishonestly against them. They are actively discouraged from competing with each other.

In an organisation of respect, leaders behave with a high level of respect for the integrity of their employees. They encourage all staff to treat their customers with respect and not try to sell products and services of low value. The leaders respect the environment and make sure that their products and services do no harm.

In the society of respect, the speed limits in front of the school are obeyed. The person at the supermarket checkout is regarded with friendliness; the person blocking your way, with consideration; the old people are treated with humanity and care. And perhaps most difficult: in the society of respect we throw out our masks and allow our fellow humans to see us as we truly are.

LEADERSHIP: CAN ALL HAVE A ROLE?

Below is a modern leadership ideal from the interpretation of the Black Swans story with only a few words changed.

Today's leaders should be driven not by their personal ego-driven quest for personal power, but by a genuine motivation to serve their people. They must respect all their people, in particular the less knowledgeable and the less fortunate. They must be considerate and ask for advice before they act; they must not conceal their true purpose and they have to review the effects of their actions. If things still go wrong, they are expected to own up to their mistakes, take personal responsibility for the negative effects and make sure they compensate those who suffered. They are supposed to act with wisdom and broad-mindedness in their relations with people outside their own country or company. They should honour and respect their differences and encourage their people to learn from different ways of being and different perspectives of other countries or companies.

How many of today's leaders spring to mind? We probably have in our minds – fed by admiring business journalists – an image of 'The Leader', who makes strategic business decisions, acquires competitors, and supervises and controls a range of middle managers, who, in their turn, make operational decisions and supervise and control the employees. Large organisations have up to ten such layers. They represent what organisation theorists call the 'command–control model' (others have used less flattering labels, such as 'psychic prison' or 'machine').

The command–control model is the dominating hierarchical structure in the industrialised world and we recognise it from the large corporations as well in public sector bureaucracies. It is widely believed (among managers) that it is the only form that really works. Business language is littered with battlefield terminology ('strategy', 'battle for market share', 'chain-of-command', 'wars for talent', 'marketing warfare', 'exploit weakness' etc.), revealing the army as the origin of the command–control organisation. It is probably as old as the history of organised wars – that is, it may go back as far as the first chieftains and the first farming societies, approximately 9000 to 11,000 years ago. In the command–control model the role of the leader is similar to the chieftains' in the first agrarian societies.

In contrast to the command–control model, the Nhunggabarra model for organising was a combination of *context-specific leadership* and what I have called *knowledge-based organising*; depending on the situation and level of know-how, everyone in society had a leadership role in a specific area of knowledge. Most of a day's routine tasks probably followed this principle. As long as the events returned on a regular basis the Nhunggabarra even seem to have been able to organise big and complex events, such as the Big Buurra, with this leadership model. What can be more efficient and effective than organisations where everybody knows their roles and fulfils them without orders and supervision?

For creating commitment and coherent action in more complex non-routine issues the Nhunggabarra probably used the *consensus process*. The Nhunggabarra therefore spent considerable time and resources upfront to achieve consensus, but once consensus was achieved very little was required in terms of control.

Knowledge-based organising, a rapidly growing alternative to command-control leadership, has attracted considerable interest among organisation theorists for several years. These knowledge-based organisations resemble the Nhunggabarra organisational form. They are organisations with no tangible production; their highly educated and skilled employees produce only intangibles, and leadership tends to be more context-specific. They are found in business services, such as accounting and advertising, in information, telecommunication and computer technology, in research (both public and corporate), and in the entertainment and performing arts industries. In growth terms private knowledge-based companies have outperformed the manufacturing industry and other service industries since the 1970s.

In the first ever study made into the organisation and leadership of such organisations published in *Managing Knowhow* in 1987, Tom Lloyd and I distinguished ten success factors which are still valid to a large degree.

1. *Day-to-day leadership* by a person visible in the organisation and recognised as an expert in the core knowledge area of the business. The similarity with the Nhunggabarra is 100 per cent; the old people and the wiringin were visible and present.

2. *Quality and quality control.* True experts do not accept inferior quality. The Nhunggabarra did not have supervisory control. Their quality control was self-assessment, a very advanced form only possible in organisations with a flat hierarchy and high levels of trust. The Nhunggabarra even had independent quality control; tuckandee and role-splitting ensured that knowledge was not corrupted. I note 100 per cent similarity.

3. *Respect for know-how.* By this I meant that the power hierarchy is based on individuals' levels of know-how, not on positional power, which makes leadership roles context-specific, particularly in the professional/technical areas. What I have learned from the Nhunggabarra is that respect is a much broader concept. Still, the similarity

is 100 per cent; the Nhunggabarra's hierarchy was context-specific and based on know-how.

4. Combination of professional and managerial know-how. Leaders must possess organising know-how, but they are respected because of their professional expertise. The Nhunggabarra display a clear organisational ability in their architecture, so their leaders must have possessed both, but we do not know. I assume a cautious 50 per cent similarity.

5. A strong, well-defined culture. Characteristics of a well-defined culture are that all employees know what their organisation stands for and what their mission is. There is no doubt about 100 per cent similarity; the Nhunggabarra had a clear mission and their culture was reinforced on a daily basis.

6. Focus on core know-how. By this I meant that the 'professional conglomerate' is impossible. The Nhunggabarra had to be multi-skilled, but each person focused on fulfilling their role. (Every man knew how make spears, but he did not do it unless it was his role.) I believe the connection is clear here; 100 per cent similarity.

7. Know-how preservation. There have to be processes in place to keep the key people from leaving. We have seen that the Nhunggabarra had elaborate processes for securing know-how, and key people did not/could not leave; 100 per cent similarity.

8. Developing the people. The only way to stay successful long-term is to develop the organisation's people. I have come to broaden my understanding and would today include resources such as customers and intangible tools and processes. The Nhunggabarra comply with even a broader definition; there is 100 per cent similarity.

9. Processes for changing key people. This is a sticky problem for a knowledge-based organisation. It will not survive if the key people are not replaced. Again the similarity is 100 per cent. The marriage laws ensured that all roles were filled long-term and the Nhunggabarra grew into roles and leadership automatically as they grew older.

10. Stable organisational structures. An intangible production requires stable administration processes. There is 100 per cent similarity with the Nhunggabarra; their model survived thousands of years.

So, by my reckoning, the similarity between the new breed of knowledge-based organisation and Nhunggabarra society is a striking 95 per cent.

If the current trends hold, knowledge-based organisations will become the dominant type of organisation in the future. This is encouraging, because it suggests that the command–control organisations that have dominated since the advent of the agriculture society may be coming to an end. It may mean the downfall of corporate chieftains and a return to 'natural' organising principles. By 'natural' I mean the kind of organising that people would gravitate towards unless they were predisposed through experience to another form of organising.

We know that hunter–gatherer societies precede the first agrarian societies and the chieftains. Hence the organisational form of hunter–gatherers should be the oldest on earth, the first, and even the 'natural' way of organising common human activities.

COMMUNITY BUILDING THE EUROPEAN WAY

The European Union is a new kind of community never before seen in history. The 26 member states have handed over much of their sovereignty to a transcontinental state-like community that is becoming legally, commercially and culturally borderless. Most of the continent has done away with customs and immigration controls. Billions of euros are invested in making the borderless infrastructure work on the ground in a network of bridges, tunnels, ports and rail lines.

The similarities with the Nhunggabarra and their bloc of 26 communities are striking. Just like them the EU consists of countries with languages so different that many of the people do not understand each other. The EU is comprised of people who do not have a common religion. Europeans are, as individuals, quite different in colour, complexion and physical appearance. Europeans have similar tangible resources at their disposal, but they are unevenly distributed; some, like Sweden and Finland, have more access to fresh water, some like the UK and Germany, have more access to coal. Some of the countries, like Italy, have very powerful and sacred sites on their land with high significance for people in other countries. These differences have in the past caused envy and countless wars all over Europe.

There are also many commonalities between EU countries. They are all industrialised societies, so they have similar challenges and they understand the functioning principles of another country. Most of the European languages, although different, have a common Indo-European origin. Many of European sacred symbols are the same; all have 'God' or 'Allah' in their creation stories, but God's actions and roles are different. Europeans share an understanding of what 'family' is and they have similar models for ownership of land and other assets.

Like the Nhunggabarra, Europe's foundation is community building and collaboration, not military force. To European citizens in general warfare is an outmoded concept.

The EU is leading the efforts to reduce greenhouse gases on the planet and is driving its companies to implement more ecological practices in transport, use alternative energy sources and test chemical substances more rigorously. Despite its critics, the new European currency, the euro, must be regarded a success. It was smoothly introduced and the euro is now on par with the US dollar as a reserve currency for central banks.

A new 'generation E' of 20- to 30-year-olds has emerged for whom a borderless Europe is taken-for-granted, who travel extensively and work everywhere, particularly in the service industries. Just as the young men in Aboriginal communities did in their cultural bloc, the young 'E' men and women immerse themselves totally in the diversity of cultures. In *learning by living together* the generation E are showing the way to a new form of education, with a curriculum that could have been taken straight from the Nhunggabarra: 'practical geography' (how to navigate in a new country and where the essential sites are located); 'practical survival' (where and how to find work, food and a place to stay); and 'practical Medicine' (new ways of maintaining health).

Along the way, the E generation is finding marriage partners in other countries to a degree never before experienced in Europe and fulfilling another of the Nhunggabarra ingredients for keeping peace – without the need for marriage planning.

LESSONS THAT CAN BE LEARNED

The Nhunggabarra recipe for a sustainable society was a holistic model, where the elements both reinforce and balance each other. The Nhunggabarra kept a lid on individual egos and prevented competition by collaborative processes. It was a low-energy/low-impact model well-suited to the vulnerable ecosystem of Australia.

Industrialisation and the innovation of market economy let the genie out of the bottle and unleashed both individual freedom and competition. These expansive forces have powered the Western industrialised world to an unprecedented level of production and population, but only by exploiting the energy resources of the planet and at the cost of depleting the ecosystems. The Western world has still – after 10,000 years of agriculture – not been able to develop a farming technology that does not harm ecosystems. The Nhunggabarra were able to develop both sustainable food and tool production. We living in the world today are doomed unless farms and industries become truly sustainable. It is not that we do not have the resources – it is that, unlike the Nhunggabarra, we are still living in an illusion.

Democracy brought a balance of power to Western society and the crucial privilege of common people to change their political leaders. But the restraining forces on the new type of leaders, chairmen and managing directors of corporations are currently inadequate. It is as if some people shift morals when they enter the corporate world. The corporate greed that time after time brings shame to leaders would be an impossible behaviour in a society where people respect each other. This is one more lesson industrialised modern society can learn from the Nhunggabarra.

There is also a point beyond which innovation becomes reckless: when there is lack of concern about people's health, for society and the natural environment, and when the hidden costs surpass the benefits of new products. Something seems to be lacking in the corporate boardrooms – a sense of responsibility? It should certainly be food for thought that their products do not make their high-volume customers – those in the richest industrialised countries – any happier.

But perhaps boardrooms are becoming obsolete. One of the more inspiring accomplishments of the Nhunggabarra is that they were able to pull off complex organising tasks with non-hierarchical leadership. If they could, why can't we? Context-specific leadership and knowledge-based organising are on the increase in Western corporations, particularly those that produce intangibles. Consensus is actively applied by conflict negotiators and peace arbitrators in trouble spots on earth. This highly decentralised style of leadership is also being rediscovered in voluntary non-governmental organisations. A society with leadership roles for all does not have to be the privilege of the Nhunggabarra.

Another lesson worth considering is that the Nhunggabarra and their neighbours were able to build a community of communities with a very high level of interdependence. The rise of democracies since the fall of the Iron Curtain has encouraged a whole range of new collaborative initiatives around the world, spearheaded by the example of the European Union.

SUSTAIN OUR WORLD

What could a sustainable modern society look like? Some of the keywords of the Nhunggabarra were 'respect', 'intangibles', 'community

Vision for a Sustainable Planet: Our Actions on Lands and Rivers

The painting shows how our actions on the land and rivers are also felt in the oceans, where the river meets the sea. The painting features the sea turtle and the freshwater turtle. The oceanscape is contained within the freshwater turtle and the riverscape within the sea turtle, to show the connectedness and interdependence of everything.

building' and 'ecosystem care'. How could we make these concepts our own in order to sustain *our* world? What can we do as individuals?

When we apply these concepts for sustainability we change our buying patterns for material goods, demanding more natural materials, ecofarmed food and ecoproducts that don't pollute the environment, because we care about our own health and the health of our neighbours and community — even when the products cost more. We stop buying products containing untested synthesised materials and untested chemicals and make sure that we recycle our waste. We invest in houses heated and cooled by renewable energy and buy environmentally friendly, low-energy cars rather than those that infer luxury and status.

We put pressure on corporations and governments to make our current industrial methods more ecological and to increase the habitats suitable for animals and plants by moving over to ecological farming, ecologically farmed food and responsible forestry.

We select schools with learner-driven education for our children and schools that encourage teamwork, respect and collaborative behaviours. We encourage our children to learn by living in other countries. Ecology becomes the new major subject on their curriculum.

As employees we require respect for our integrity and have the courage to stand up against environmental abuse and require our corporate leaders to act and innovate with responsibility. We respect our colleagues and collaborate rather than compete.

As politicians we make the whole legal system work in favour of the global environment, because we care about our own country as well as neighbouring countries, and we create tax systems and laws with that mission in mind. We dismiss fear-mongering politicians, who spend our taxes on arms.

As organisational leaders we act with social consciousness and ecological responsibility towards the planet and focus innovation accordingly, both because we care personally and because we are given direction through changing buying patterns. We launch products that do not harm the ecosystem, because we respect our customers and care about their safety – not because we are afraid of lawsuits. We encourage collaborative behaviour in our organisations, because we have seen that it is profitable; we avoid reckless innovations, both because we feel responsibility and because we know that the laws ensure that such behaviour will cost us dearly.

As scientists we apply our minds to problems that concern the survival of the planet, because we know better than anyone what is required. As farmers we begin ecofarming, because we notice the increase in demand and also because we care about the run-offs from our farms.

In short – all of us living in the Western industrialised world change our habits and begin actively to sustain the world.

Utopia? It need not be. We have vastly more resources at our disposal than did the Nhunggabarra. We also have a very powerful and dynamic added resource: financial capital. We have more human capital than ever in the history of this planet and we also have more physical and social infrastructure. All we have to do is allocate our resources differently. The choice is ours.

Happiness surveys were not invented at the time of the Nhunggabarra, but allow us to finish our book with the following quote by James Cook taken from his journal after his first visit to Australia in 1770:

> From what I have said of the Natives of New Holland they may appear to some to be the most wretched people upon Earth; but in reality they are far happier than we Europeans . . . They live in a Tranquillity which is not disturbed by the Inequality of Condition. The earth and Sea of their own accord furnishes them with all things necessary for life; they covet not Magnificent Houses, Household-stuff etc, they live in a warm and fine Climate and enjoy a very wholesome Air, so that they have very little need of Clothing and this seem to be fully sensible of, for many to whom we gave Cloth etc to, left it carelessly upon the Sea beach and in the woods as a thing they had no manner of use for. In short they seem'd to set no Value upon any thing we gave them, nor would they part with any thing of their own for any one article we could offer them. This in my opinion, Argues that they think themselves provided with all the necessaries of Life and that they have no Superfluities.

We do not know whether the Nhunggabarra built the first sustainable society, but we are reasonably sure they built the longest lasting society. It is now up to us to not let ours be the last.

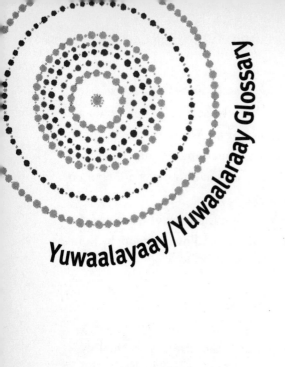

Yuwaalayaay/Yuwaalaraay Glossary

THE *GAMILARAAY / YUWAALARAAY / YUWAALAYAAY DICTIONARY* is a language-revival dictionary with most of the words coming from historical sources and we have drawn upon it to create our glossary. The aim has been to use a consistent, easily understood orthography (writing system) which reflected the careful pronunciation of the words — this could best be done where there was good pronunciation of the word on tape or by current speakers. In many cases this pronunciation was not available, in which case a 'best guess' was made as to the interpretation of the previously written word. For instance, in many cases 'u' in the first syllable becomes 'a' in current orthography. Some words that Tex learned as a child are used in the text instead of the YW orthography although they are not found in the Dictionary or are spelled differently: these words are marked in italics. Other known spellings and words are in brackets beside an entry.

Baaluu
Moon

Baayami [Baayame]
The first and most powerful wiringin

Baayamal [Baiamul]
Black swan; Nhunggabarra totem
animal

Balima [Bulima, Bullimah]
Also known as the 'Coalsack',
formation in the Milky Way

Barran
Boomerang; returning throwing stick

Bawurra
Red kangaroo

Bhoda [BAWURRA]
Red kangaroo; Nhunggabarra totem
animal

Bibi
Brown treecreeper bird

Bigibila [Piggibilla]
Echidna

Biiwii [Bidgee]
Sand goanna; Tex's totem animal

Birran-bili [Birrangulu, Birra-nulu]
One of Baayami's two helpers who later
became **Nullawa**

Bundi
Club

Burruguu
Time of Creation; used here instead of
the word 'Dreamtime'

Buubiyala [Bogiala]
Low tree with sweet berries

Buurra [Bora, Boorah]
1) Initiation ground; 2) Initiation
ceremony

Coolamon [Guliman]
Dish

**Coorigal [Guligal, Gawurragiil,
Gurraagal, Gurragiil] Springs**
1) Sacred site at Angledool; 2) Bee
droppings on the ground from their
nest in a tree

Cunnan-bili [Ganhanbili]
One of Baayami's two helpers

Dhaluraa
White-browed wood swallow also called
'tree manna-bringing birds'

Dhamarr [Dumer]
Pigeon; Nhunggabarra totem animal

Dhinawan [Dinewan]
Emu; Nhunggabarra totem animal

Dhirridhirri [Deereeree]
Willy-wagtail bird

Gambu
Stone axe; tomahawk

Gamilaraay [Kamilaroi]
Community and language of the
Gamilaraay people

Ganhanbili's hair
Pigweed; Nhunggabarra staple food

Garraagaa [Gahragah]
Crane

Garriya [Kurria, Gurria]
Giant crocodile

Gayamay [Gayami]
Women's word for the Buurra spirit

Gayandaay [Gavandy]
1) Bullroarer; 2) Men's word for the
Buurra spirit

Ghirrawiin [Ghirraween]
The place of flowers

Gugurruwan [Googoorewon]
The site of the Big Buurra

Gulabaa [Goolabah]
Coolabah tree

Gundhi [Goondi]
Hut made of branches and leaves

Maadhaay [Madhi]
Dingo

Mabu
Beefwood tree

Miyaymiyaay [Mirrai Mirrai]
1) Little girl; 2) Seven Sisters stars
(Pleiades)

Muboop [Buluurr]
Frogmouth owl

Murrula [Moorilloh]
Pointed club

Muruwari
Neighbouring people west of Nhunggal
country

Muyaay [Mooyi]
White cockatoo

Ngiyambaa [Ngemba]
Neighbouring people south of
Nhunggabarra

Nhungga
Kurrajong tree

Nhunggabarra
The people of the Nhunggal country;
also known as the 'Narran people'

Nhunggal
The country of the Nhunggabarra
people

Noondoo ranges
1) Sandy hill, northern part of
Nhunggal country; 2) Property name

Nullawa
One of Baayami's helpers, previously
Birran-bili

Tuckandee [Dhagaandi]
Your 'brother' or 'sister' in another
country; your children's support in
case of your death

Waan [Wahn]
Crow; one of the Nhunggabarra totem
animals

Wahlar
Sweet sap from trees

Wamara [Woomera]
Spearthrower

Wanda
1) Spirit of death, ghost; 2) White man

Warrambul
1) The Milky Way; 2) Sky world;
3) Watercourse

Wiringin
Medicine man; clever man

Wirri [Wirree]
A small bark dish or bowl cut out of a
tree

Wubi-Wubi [Oobi-Oobi]
The sacred mountain where Baayami
stayed before he departed for the
Milky Way. English: Mount Oxley

Yarragaa
Spring wind

Yarragaa Mayraa
Eastern wind

Yiilaman [Neilahman]
Shield

Yuluwirri [Yuluwirree, Yuluwarri, Euluwirri]
Rainbow

Yurrti [MAA]
Totem

Yuwaal
No (old form)

Yuwaalaraay
One of the languages/dialects spoken in Nhunggal country

Yuwaalayaay
One of the languages/dialects spoken in Nhunggal country

Australian/Aboriginal English

Billy
Teapot made of tin with handle for boiling tea over open fire

Boomerang
Returning throwing stick. YR/YY: *Barran*

Corroboree
Educational meeting with entertainment. YR/YY: *Yuurrma-y* (verb)

Eaglehawk
Wedge-tailed eagle

Kurrajong
Tree, widespread in eastern Australia

Yabby
Australian freshwater crayfish

Further Reading and Research Notes

THE WRITTEN SOURCES FALL BROADLY INTO three categories: journals written by the early explorers, archaeologists' accounts, and reports by anthropologists.

The reports of the early explorers are invaluable because the explorers were in the areas before other white men and sometimes before the epidemics hit. Many of their observations are quoted in the book because they reported what they saw, dryly and succinctly. However, their interest was in the land more than in the people, and they passed through only briefly, so most of their journals are of little use for our purpose.

Whenever possible we have used archaeologists' accounts. The archaeologists' methods and instruments today enable them to draw stunningly detailed conclusions about how a society would have functioned. However, their frame of reference is counted in thousands of years, so they can generally only give a broad picture.

Anthropology has for many years been the main source for understanding the society of Australian Aborigines. The anthropological primary research instrument is participant observation – to live with the people of the culture, participate in their lives, while at the same time acting as the observer. This is unrivalled as a source when the society exists. But anthropology struggles when the society under study has undergone dramatic changes, as was the case for Aboriginal Australia. Also by their mere presence, they, as outsiders, influenced the behaviours of people, who were likely to behave, if not differently, at least more self-consciously. An extra problem was the fact that the Aboriginal people have understandably not always been partial to being objects of scrutiny, so anthropologists were given access only to parts of their culture. More recent anthropologists have reinterpreted many of their early colleagues' studies of Aboriginal culture.

1. IN THE BEGINNING . . .

There were several sites involved in the Creation. The one we visited is situated at the Tago Springs in Queensland, just north of the border with New South Wales, on a property recently purchased by the National Parks and Wildlife Service. The site is currently under a recovery program since the spring's water flow has been severely affected by the previous owner's attempt to excavate the spring and create a permanent lake.

At least two different water-holding frogs are found in Australia (Clarke 2003: 140, 144).

Burruguu

The Aboriginal author Mudrooroo (1995) strongly criticises the term 'Dreamtime' as misleading. Sources for the Nhunggabarra Burruguu account were (apart from the oral sources): Berndt & Berndt (1999: 453–86), Myers (1991: 52–4) and Lawlor (1991: 47–9).

Space–time

Nancy Williams and Daymbalipu Mununggurr (1989: 70–83) describe the conceptualisation of time among the Yolngu people of northeast Arnhem Land. The people have several ways to express time: the movements of the sun and moon describe the time of the day and night; season refers to the time when wind direction, temperature, cloud formation etc. coincide.

The ancient ceremonies, songs and stories describe the proper behaviours in relation to land and people today. In performing them, the Yolngu claim the greatest authority is that of continuity: it has always been thus. They also place their trust in the recollections of their parents and other old people about the past.

The conceptualisation of space–time is from Einstein's work on relativity (*Scientific American*, Sept 2004).

Tonkinson (1978: 138) supports the similar notion when he states that by denying the human innovatory component in their cultural development and by adopting a cosmic rather than chronological notion of history, the Aborigines in effect claim primacy for religious conceptions of causation, being and purpose. He also confirms that the essentially spiritual basis for life, while depriving people of credit for independent creativity, does not deny them individuality.

Mission: Keep all alive

I have not been able to find a written reference from other Aboriginal communities with an identically phrased mission 'to keep the world alive'. Wandjuk Marika is close in the foreword to Isaacs (2005): 'Our people must preserve [the areas where the mythical beings left their life essence] or the animals, plants and people cannot survive.' Also Tonkinson (1978: 138–9) comes close when he says that a major feature in Aboriginal spirituality is 'submission to a sacred purpose', and about the Mardu people of the Western Desert: 'This power [of the spiritual beings] is available, more or less automatically, to all those who conform to the master plan for life originally formulated by these spiritual beings.'

The intangible and spiritual priorities of the Aborigines are well established. The main written source is Berndt & Berndt (1999). Also Clarke (2003: 15–30), R. Jones (quoted by Lawlor 1991: 61) and Flood (1999: 273–5) have contributed.

Sustaining the earth

The first white man's account of fires in Australia was by Dutch explorer Jan Carstensz, who, sailing along the Cape York in 1623, noted that smoke from Aboriginal burning obscured the sight of land. Both captain Matthew Flinders and the French explorer Nicolas Baudin, sailing in the Great Australian Bight, noticed in 1802 that the skies were constantly smoke-filled from Aborigines burning off the vegetation.

Quotes about smoke and fires come from Mitchell (1839, vol. 1: 53), James Cook in (Reed 1969: 151) and Mary Gilmore (1986: 183–90). Rhys Jones (1969) coined the term 'fire-stick farming' to describe the Aboriginal method of low-intensity burning as a means of farming.

Australia's vegetation has highly evolved mechanisms to regenerate itself after fire. Some species even require fire to crack their nuts before they can grow (Flood 1999: 251. 139; Mulvaney & Kamminga 1999: 59; Jones 1969; Blainey 1997: 71–82).

Quote about 'the first region on earth' is from Mitchell (1847: 174).

Sustaining the animals

A 'sorry dance', performed by more than 30 men, was observed and photographed by Gillen and Spencer (Lawlor 1991: 303).

Descriptions of the elaborate death and burial ceremonies among Australian Aborigines are found in Berndt & Berndt (1999: 453–86). The Nhunggabarra did not have the custom common to other Australian Aborigines of prohibiting the mention of dead peoples' names.

Stories in Arnhem Land prohibit burning regeneration habitats for fire-sensitive vegetation (Flood 1999: 251).

2. THE COUNTRY IS A STORY

Sources on climate have been Flood (1999), White (1999) and Blainey (1997: 85–90).

The link between story and geography is crucially important everywhere in Aboriginal Australia, confirmed by Myers (1986b: 54–72). Berndt & Berndt (1999: 33) mention that Aboriginal stories are useful in establishing traditional country borders and that they have seen and used such 'maps'.

Learning tracks in the landscape

The diamond shape in the Learning Tracks painting is an original form that has been found on carved trees in Nhunggal country, one tree (now lost) from Angledool was illustrated by Etheridge (1918: plate XXXIII).

The location of the sacred trees is confirmed by Langloh Parker (1905: Ch.VIII), who writes that: 'One day he [Baayami] was chopping a big Coolabah tree close to Weetalibah [Witilliba] water-hole, which tree, much to the horror of our blacks, was burnt down a few years ago by travellers.'

The combination of stories and the tracks between sacred Nhunggabarra sites described in this book is *not* what in Aboriginal English has become known as 'songlines'. Nor are they – with the possible exception mentioned below – 'ley lines' because they are not straight. The nearest description is 'tracks where learning took place' and therefore we have given them a new name: 'learning tracks'.

It is possible that Baayami's track between Angledool and Coocoran lakes could follow what is called a 'ley line' or what Paul Deveraux calls a 'spirit line', because the track follows a seemingly straight line.

Sources: Gerber (2001) discusses medical evidence for the effect of energy fields on the body. Deveraux (2001) discusses and describes ley lines and spirit lines.

The Nhunggabarra: the people that 'disappeared'

We do not know all the names of the communities that lived here prior to European contact or indeed their exact location. Tex learned the number of communities to be 26 and their approximate location from the Big Buurra story and from the old people, who were the sources of the stories, but there is no independent confirmation of the number of societies, their names, nor their location.

The close association in languages, stories and beliefs between the Yuwaalaraay, the Muruwari and the Ngemba is confirmed by Jimmie Barker (1977: 29).

Tex knows the traditional boundaries of Nhunggal country from the stories and the old people. However, the 'Nhunggabarra' name does not appear on any of the lists compiled by anthropologists. Tindale does not mention 'Nhunggabarra' in his work on Australian Aboriginal tribes (1974), nor does another main source on tribal names (Howitt 1904). The name of the people occupying the area that we identify as 'Nhunggal country' is instead referred to as the 'Ualarui tribe' by Tindale and he ascribes 12,000 square kilometres as the size of their country, which is the same size inferred from a map drawn by Tex. Also the geographic location of Tindale's 'Ualarui tribe' is identical: 147°25'E x 29°30'S.

The map of Aboriginal 'nations' compiled by Horton (2000) includes the area and the 'Ualarai tribe' under the Kamilaroi 'nation group' and does not mention any version of the Nhunggabarra name.

Tindale (1940, 1974) is the main source of tribal names in Australia. He claims to have personally visited some 400 tribes all over Australia in the 1930s and earlier. However, the original communities in this area of New South Wales had disappeared maybe a hundred years before he visited, and he would have had to rely on the memories of descendents of survivors and early settler sources. The people he met would not have spoken their own language to a foreigner; they would, out of respect, have tried to communicate with him in the language of the people from the countries in the direction from which he had come. Such habits did not make research easy.

Aboriginal people sometimes referred to themselves to white people as 'we are the people having xx for "no"'. For instance, one of the two words for 'no' among the neighbouring people east of Nhunggal country is *gamil*. Tindale found what he was looking for; something he could use as a standard. So he lumped together all the people he came across on his travels who used *gamil* for 'no' into one 'tribe', and called them the 'Gamilaroi' (Kamilaroi) tribe, speaking the 'Gamilaroi' language. His concept also fit into European ideas in the early 20th century about an ideal 'nation' with one people speaking one language. He then applied the same approach as a standard across all peoples in Aboriginal Australia.

The problems become evident when one notices that another Gamilaroi word for 'no' is *marayrr*, which looks like a dialectal variant of one of the two words for no, *maayrr*, in the Yuwaalaraay/Yuwaalayaay language. The *GY/YY/YR Dictionary* lists *yuwaal* as an old form for 'no', but Tindale (1974) records the Ualaroi language negative as *wongo* and criticises Radcliffe-Brown in 1930 for having erroneously recorded the Ualaroi word for 'no' as *yual*.

Hence, many of the Aboriginal tribal names used today are theoretical construc-tions, which were originally never used by the Aborigines themselves. The name 'Ualaroi' might even have been a mistake from the beginning: Howitt (1904: 56–8) mentions the 'Wollaroi' living along the Barwon–Darling River from Walgett to Bourke (i.e. the southernmost part of Nhunggal country). The name 'Wollaroi' has in many sources been confused with that of a neighbouring people, the Weraerai, (Walarai). The latter is included by Horton (2000) in the Kamilaroi (Gamilaroi) 'nation group' together with the Ualaroi.

According to Tindale (1974) the following tribes populated the area:

Name	Location	Area size (km²)
Baranbinja, Barranbinya	Bourke to Brewarrina on northern bank of Darling River	3,100
Koamu (Guamu, Kooma)	South of St George on the Balonne River to Angledool, Hebel and Brenda; west to Bollon and Nebine Creek. Mathews (1902, in Tindale 1974) included the people of this tribe with the Ualarai in his study of his 'Yualeai' language	15,600
Kamilaroi	Walgett NSW to Nindigully Qld; at Moree, Mungindi, Mogil Mogil, Narrabri, Barraba, Gwabegar and Come-by-Chance; on headwaters of Hunter River	75,400
Kula,Gunu, Kornu	Chiefly on the western bank of the Darling River from near Bourke to Dunlop, Warrego River to Enngonia	12,700
Muruwari, Murrawarri	Barringun NSW and Enngonia on Warrego River, Brenda and Weilmoringle on Culgoa River; at Milroy; south to near Collerina. Extensively in NSW extending north to Mulga Downs and Weelamurra in Qld	16,400
Ngemba	South bank of Barwon and Darling rivers from Brewarrina to Dunlop; on Yanda Creek; south to head of Mulga Creek; on Bogan River	17,200
Ualarai (Yuwaalaraay/ Yuwaalayaay)	On Narran River from Narran Lake to Angledool; southwest to near Walgett; on Birrie and Bokhara rivers, southwest to Brewarrina; their western country fell between the Culgoa and Birrie rivers. Koamu speaks a similar dialect	12,000
Weilwan (Wailwan)	Southern side of Barwon River from Brewarrina to Walgett; south along Marra Creek and the Castlereagh, Marthaguy and Macquarie rivers; south to Quambone and to near Coonamble	13,000
Weraerai, (Walarai)	North side of Gwydir River from Moree to Bingara, northward to Warialda and Gilgil Creek; west to Garah. At Yallaroi; on Macintyre River from Inverell to north of Wallangra. Often confused with the Ualaroi	10,700

The area identified by the Nhunggabarra old people as occupied by the Nhunggabarra and their neighbouring communities may once have been vastly larger than the approximately 30,000 square kilometres they suggest. Even if we exclude the Gamilaroi in the table above, the areas of the other eight tribes in the region mentioned by Tindale cover 100,000 square kilometres according to his estimates. However, there exist no independent sources to corroborate country borders and all estimates of country sizes are therefore tentative and contested. For instance, Muruwari country is 16,400 square kilometres according to Tindale (1974), while the map drawn by Muruwari man Jimmie Barker (1977), who lived from 1900 to 1972, is approximately 30,000 square kilometres in size and includes areas in the west and south, identified as Baranbinja, Gunu and Kunja tribes by Tindale. Tindale's estimates and definitions are used by Horton (2000), except for the Ualaroi (Yuwaalaaray/Yuwaalaayay), which is included in the Gamilaroi 'nation'.

One of the Nhunggabarra neighbouring communities is the Gamilaroi, which is allocated a huge area on Horton's (2000) map, much larger than in Tindale's table above. The communities in the cultural bloc would probably have included some of the westernmost communities, which Horton includes in the 'Gamilaroi nation', but no names have survived.

Berndt & Berndt (1999: 28–32) criticise Tindale's approach and point out that in many areas the people did not have a name which can be translated as an exact equivalent of a 'tribal name'. They propose the term 'linguistic unit' or 'dialectal unit' would be more appropriate, particularly where the languages, dialects and customs link into each other, as for instance in the Western Desert and in Arnhem Land. Their terminology therefore fits also for the Nhunggal country and their neighbours with both interlinked languages and interlinked customs.

The Nhunggabarra name has not disappeared entirely, however. It is referred to as the name of the main southern group of Yuwaalayaay speakers by two of the sources of the *GY/YY/YR Dictionary*, Ginny Rose and Greg Fields. Nhunggabarra is also known as the name of a group of people, who settled at the Bangate Station when their land had been occupied by the white settlers. It was from them that K. Langloh Parker, the wife of the station owner, collected the Nhunggabarra stories in the late 1800s. The name is also referred to by Ross et al. (1986: 52) as the Nhunggabarra tribe settlement at Angledool.

Irrespective of the name of the people, however, the conclusions in the book remain the same.

The ASEDA catalogue at *http://coombs.anu.edu.au/SpecialProj/ASEDA/* has also been useful as a source.

Population size

A lively debate exists among anthropologists and archaeologists about the size of the Aboriginal population at the time of European arrival in 1788.

The first population estimate was made by the anthropologist Radcliffe-Brown in the *1930 Australian Statistical Yearbook* (pp. 687–96). He was writing at a time when the Australian government was starting to ask itself how severe the decrease in Aboriginal population had really been during the 1800s. Radcliffe-Brown's purpose was to make a minimum estimate. For his calculation, he divided the Aboriginal population in three groups: tribes (people who speak a common language and practise same customs), subtribes (which have differences of dialect within a common language), and hordes (land-owning groups who owned and occupied a common a territory with known boundaries). He then estimated an average number of people per horde for the territories and arrived at the number of the tribe or subtribe. His definition of a 'horde' as a subtribe has been heavily criticised and it is not correct for our purpose because, at least for the communities constituting the cultural bloc, the land-owning group was not the same as the group occupying the territory.

The major problem with his work for our purpose is that there is so little data from the area we are interested in. Radcliffe-Brown spends only ten sentences on the Aboriginal population of New South Wales and refrains from examining the 'scanty data available'. He observes that an original population, estimated by the governor at the time to have been around 1500 between Botany Bay and Broken Bay, was practically extinct by 1845. He quotes a man who was one of only four survivors of a tribe that in 1810–21 counted about 400 individuals – a death toll of 99 per cent! Without further analysis, Radcliffe-Brown then concludes that the coastal part of New South Wales 'contained about 25,000 Aborigines, speaking more than twenty different languages, and that the rest of the State had about 20,000. To be on the safe side we may put the total for the whole State at 40,000'. This is the equivalent of only 0.05 people per square kilometre for a state that is 801,600 square kilometres in size.

Radcliffe-Brown gets support from the contemporary anthropologist A.P. Elkin (quoted by Berndt & Berndt 1999). He also arrived at a total population of around 300,000 for the whole of Australia at the time of European contact. He assessed the coastal population before European settlement to be around one person per 4–5 square mile (or 0.08–0.1 per km²); his figure for the tribe arid inland Ungarinjin is about one person to eight or nine square miles (0.04–0.05 per km²).

Radcliffe-Brown's conservative approach is likely to have yielded far too low numbers over all; the anthropologist Harry Lourandos (1997) showed from a detailed scrutiny of the journals by the explorer G.A. Robinson that the population of the Western District of Victoria in 1841 could have been 8000, double Radcliffe-Brown's earlier estimate for the region.

Low estimates by anthropologists have also been challenged by the economic historian Butlin, who in 1983 claimed that the effects of introduced epidemics such as influenza, whooping cough and common cold were much more devastating in the densely populated southeast than the first Europeans perceived. Those diseases were not recognised as being as lethal as they later proved and their effects were not as easily detected as those of the more spectacular disfiguring diseases of smallpox and syphilis. Based on survival rates of viral diseases, he estimated that only 50 to 60 per cent of the 1788 population of New South Wales were still alive in 1805 and he arrives at a population estimate four times higher than Radcliffe-Brown for the whole of New South Wales (approx. 160,000) and around 1 to 1.5 million for Australia as a whole (Butlin 1983: 82ff; 1993: 138–9).

The historian Richard Broome (2005) has tested Butlin's estimates for Victoria and accepts them, but they have been criticised as too superficial by anthropologists. However, at least for New South Wales, Butlin's estimates are much more detailed and more carefully argued than Radcliffe-Brown's. It is even possible to argue that the death rate in New South Wales might have been higher than Butlin suggests, because it was the first territory in Australia to be affected by disease. One indication is that the death toll from the first reported smallpox outbreak in Botany Bay in 1789 was around 90 per cent. Radcliffe-Brown recorded the 99 per cent death rate at Botany Bay mentioned above. Death tolls of 90 per cent have also been recorded among native Indians in America after the first Europeans arrived as noted by Clarke (2003:192–193) and Diamond (2004).

The explorers' journals have also been used for population estimates. The archaeologist Harry Allen compiled all explorer sightings of Aboriginal groups living around the Darling River and came up with an estimate of one person per 0.8 to 1.6 kilometres of river frontage in 1972. Keen (2004: 112) analyses Allen's material and comes up with an estimate of one person per 30 to 60 square kilometres, or 0.016–0.033 people per square kilometre, an estimate that is lower than even Radcliffe-Brown's. The explorer sightings in this area were made after the epidemics had passed through, however, so they tell about the effects of the diseases. But they cannot be used to estimate the size of the population before European contact.

Service cites Steward's 1955 estimate that population density is generally one person or less per square mile (0.4 people per km²) for bands and says that patrilocal bands vary in size from around 25 to 30 people to at least over 100.

The anthropologists R. Berndt and C. Berndt say that it is difficult to generalise beyond saying that in the northern areas there could have been fluctuation between 0.5 and 2 persons per square mile (0.2–0.8 per km²) and in riverine and coastal areas between 3 and up to 10 persons per square mile (1.2–3.9 persons per km²). Berndt and Berndt consider the larger figure may be far too high.

Archaeologists also argue higher population sizes based on archaeological evidence. The archaeologist Josephine Flood (1999: 79) discusses archaeological evidence and arrives at an estimate of around one million people for the whole continent or even higher. Mulvaney (1999: 69) discusses both anthropologists' and archaeologists' evidence and makes a consensus estimate: around 750,000.

The table shows that estimated population density seems to vary by approximately a factor of five between fertile and arid areas. Nhunggal country and most of the other communities of their cultural bloc were situated in the semi-arid but relatively fertile flood plain areas, which suggests that estimates from other river communities would apply.

A closer inspection of the various estimates suggests that Radcliffe-Brown's estimate for New South Wales as a whole stands out as far too low. Given that Butlin's estimate would be relevant as an average for New South Wales with both fertile and arid areas, we should apply a factor of two to three to reach an estimate for more fertile areas; suggesting a population of around 15,000 people for the whole cultural

A collection of estimates of Aboriginal population sizes, 1788

		Persons per km²	Nhunggal country	The cultural bloc
			12,000	30,000
A.P. Elkin				
Fertile coast	(high estimate)	0.097	1159	2897
	(low estimate)	0.077	927	2318
Arid inland	(high estimate)	0.048	579	1449
	(low estimate)	0.043	515	1288
Radcliffe-Brown				
Fertile Swan River		0.193	2318	5794
Fertile Goulburn/Murray		0.155	1854	4635
New South Wales total		0.019	232	579
Victoria		0.050	606	1515
H. Lourandos				
Western Victoria (2–3 times Radcliffe-Brown)		0.101	1111	3030
Berndt & Berndt				
Fertile Riverine and coastal areas along Darling River				
	(low estimate)	1.159	13,906	34,764
	(high estimate)	3.863	46,352	115,880
H. Allen / I. Keen				
Explorer sightings after diseases along Darling River				
	(low estimate)	0.017	200	500
	(high estimate)	0.033	400	1000
N.L. Butlin				
New South Wales total		0.200	2400	6000
R.H. Steward				
Hunter–gatherers in general		0.386	4635	11,588
E. Service				
Average 500 people per 'dialectical tribe'		0.433	5200	13,000

bloc of 26 communities. This would fit in well with estimates made based on both E. Service and R.H. Steward, by which we arrive at a similar number from a different angle. We cannot accept Berndt & Berndt's estimate as the maximum; it stands out as very high and might even be a misprint considering the text surrounding their estimate. A more reasonable maximum would be around 20,000.

Given that the Nhunggabarra populated the largest territory of the cultural bloc – around 12,000 square kilometres (a fairly large proportion of which was not fertile) – they must have numbered more than 1000, possibly up to 2000 people.

A total population of 15,000 to 20,000 for the cultural bloc would make gatherings of many thousands of people quite feasible; Dame Mary Gilmore (1986: 162) recounts the gatherings at the Brewarrina fish traps: 'Two of my uncles said they once witnessed what they reckoned were five thousand blacks assembled, and people who were older said that before the massacres began there were even larger gatherings.' (She was born in 1865, so the gathering may have occurred some time before.)

Large-scale violence against the Aborigines started with the first explorers. Members of Thomas Mitchell's party were the first white men known to kill Aborigines in this part of New South Wales. In the night of 11 July 1835 they shot and killed at least two Aboriginal people on the Darling River south of Bourke, one of them a mother carrying a child. After the event, anxiously waiting for a counter-attack that never materialised, Mitchell entered some 'melancholy reflections' in his journal: 'I regretted most bitterly the inconsiderate conduct of some of the men. I was, indeed, liable to pay dear for geographical discovery, when my honour and character were delivered over to convicts, on whom I could not always rely on for humanity.'

Thomas Mitchell was uncannily prescient. The first settlers – most likely with a convict background – probably arrived in the early 1840s. The exact date is not known, except that land commissioner Roderick Mitchell published in 1845 that the names Narran, Bokhara, Birie and Culgoa had been made known by stockmen, scouting for new country. Lawson Station near Brewarrina was established 'long before 1847'; Brenda Station, the largest in the area with at one time 120,000 hectares stretching into what is now the state of Queensland, was established in late 1849 to early 1850 (Ross et al. 1986: 70–1). The township of Brewarrina was proclaimed in 1863. The situation is described by Ross et al: 'No form of law and order was present to protect the Aborigine. Shooting of Aboriginal men was a common occurrence. Many of the Aboriginal women were captured and abused by the white men. Many of the station hands were ex-convicts...few if any had any wives. They were a breed of men accustomed to hardships and the cruelty of the convict era.'

Historian Henry Reynolds, who was the first to seriously investigate the effect of the violence in *The Other Side of the Frontier* (1981), estimates that more than 2000 whites were killed in a series of wars lasting up to the 1930s. By comparing historic records he estimated that, on average, ten Aboriginal people died violently at the hands of whites for every European death, and hence that 20,000 Aboriginal people were killed in total in Australia. Historian Richard Broome (2005: 81) makes an estimate for Victoria of twelve Aborigines killed for every white person.

One of the most infamous of the massacres of Aborigines in the whole of New South Wales occurred on Nhunggal land at Hospital Creek, 15 kilometres north of Brewarrina very soon after first white settlement. Peter Dargin writes that a posse of white stockmen 'rounded them up like cattle, old and young, on the Quantambone plain [now called '19-mile Plain'], and shot them, there was about 400, and that was how Hospital Creek got its name'. The reason for the massacre remains obscure, but it possibly involved alleged cattle theft.

We will never know how many Nhunggabarra died at the hands of white men in the first hundred years, but if 400 people were killed in one single massacre there must have been many more.

The large shell middens around the Narran Lake also suggest a country that once supported quite a large population for a very long time. The middens are protected as a cultural heritage site and have not been excavated, but they are huge – one that we studied measures some 100 metres across; the length is at least 400 metres and shells and bones from eighteen different animal species have been found, some of which are extinct.

Finally, the law stories show that the Nhunggabarra had developed processes, rules and institutions to cope with much larger populations than a few hundred people and at much higher levels of organisational complexity than a 'band'. We thus believe that our estimate of a pre-contact population in the areas populated by the 26 communities is the most likely option and justifiable, but it is considerably higher than 'conventional wisdom'. What speaks against it?

One possibility is that Tex's grandmother was wrong and that there were fewer than 26 communities in the cultural bloc. Such an error will reduce the total number of people, but it will not change the estimate of the Nhunggabarra population, nor any of the conclusions in the book.

Another possibility is that the 26 communities were not, as we have assumed, 'sub-tribes' comprised by a number of 'hordes' (Radcliffe-Brown) or 'dialectical tribes' comprised by a number of 'bands' (Service), but that the whole area was one 'tribe' or 'dialectical tribe' comprised by 26 'hordes' and/or 'bands'. This reduces the population estimate by a factor of 10 – that is, the whole cultural bloc would have consisted of 26 hordes/bands of 50 to 80 people, totalling some 1500 to 2000 people – and would imply that the Nhunggabarra 'horde' were a maximum of 150 people. This is lower even than a population estimate based on Radcliffe-Brown's average and it would be in conflict with other evidence. Such a small group of people would not have been able to maintain a different language, the law and the sophisticated societal infrastructure that the stories tell.

Yet a third possibility is that the communities in the cultural bloc were of a mixed nature, both 'tribes' and 'bands'/'hordes'. This is the most likely alternative to the main hypotheses, but it is not possible to investigate within the framework of this book. It would reduce our population estimate, but again would have little impact on our conclusions.

Sources of population estimates: Radcliffe-Brown (1930: 687–96), Elkin (cited in Flood 1999: 79), Butlin (1983: 114–39), Berndt & Berndt (1999: 23–33), Flood (1999: 79ff), Mulvaney & Kamminga (1999: 66–9), Service (1971: 58), Stewart (cited in Service 1971: 58), Lourandos (1997: 37), Tindale (1974).

Quotes from Sturt (1983: 68, 93), Mitchell (1839, vol. I: 26, 218, 241).

Quotes about the massacres are from Ross et al. 1986 and 'Aboriginal Fisheries of the Darling–Barwon River' by Peter Dargin, *www.breshire.com/about/1007/1029.html*, accessed 29/12/04.

Origins

Archaeologist: Jim Allen estimates the first occupants arrived in Australia 35,000 to 40,000 years ago, Sandra Bowdler claims 40,000 years ago, while Rhys Jones and Josephine Flood have arrived at the highest figure, 55,000 to 60,000 years ago, an estimate Flood considers conservative. They all agree that the first colonisation was along the coasts. Flood (1999) dismisses in her introductory chapter the sensational claims in 1996 that people have been in Australia for 116,000 years as based on incorrect interpretation of luminescence data.

Sources: Flood (1999: 28–29, 39–54, 93), White (1997), Clarke (2003: 9ff)

The Nhunggabarra language

Linguistic researchers comparing, grammar, vocabulary and sounds consider all except two or three of the Australian Aboriginal languages as members of one and the same 'proto-Australian' language family, called 'Pama-Nyungan'. The exception is a small group of languages around the Darwin area. The relationship between the Pama-Nyungan languages can be compared with the Indo-European language family, which comprises most of the European languages. The proto-Australian languages are as different as the Indo-European languages Greek, Russian and English. The use of sign language was also widespread – in 1897 the anthropologist Walter Roth described 198 different hand signs used by Aboriginal people in northwestern Queensland.

The estimated number of languages is based on the linguists' criterion that two forms of speech which are mutually intelligible should be considered dialects of one language. Linguists' criteria are not necessarily accepted by the public. The linguists, for instance, class Danish, Swedish and Norwegian as one language comprised of three dialects, a concept the populations of those countries would vigorously contest on nationalistic grounds. The Norwegian language even exists in two versions, Nynorsk and Bokmål, after a bitter language fight at the turn of the 20th century.

The languages have also been spelled Ualaroi (by Tindale), Yualeiai and Euahlayi (by Langloh Parker), but we apply the standard of the new YW Dictionary (2003).

Sources: YW Dictionary (2003), Blake (1981), Flood (1999: 233), Clarke (2003: 39–41), Berndt & Berndt (1999: 39)

Knowledge fair: the Big Buurra

The reports about the big gatherings at Brewarrina are from Gilmore (1986).

3. THE KNOWLEDGE IS IN THE STORY

K. Langloh Parker (1978) first published the Nhunggabarra stories she had collected as 'Kinder Märchen' (children's stories) in 1896 and 1898.

Flood (1999: 28, 141, 180, 189–92, 212–15) relates geological evidence that backs up events told in stories.

The key to the archives: the four levels

Judging from other cultural areas in Australia (Berndt & Berndt 1999: 389–92), the Nhunggabarra stories may once have counted several hundred. The total number of Nhunggabarra stories known by Tex and/or collected by K. Langloh Parker makes up less than one hundred, so a considerable proportion is probably lost.

Aboriginal stories cover all types of themes. Stories in the A.W. Reed collection (1982, 1994), assembled from many parts of Australia, explain physical features of the landscape, and how human beings and animals became as they are. Some are arranged as sagas, with Ancestors travelling in the landscape. Some tell about disasters, many about tricksters and malignant spirits. There are also tales of amorous adventure and illicit love and stories about relationships normally tabooed, such as incest and intimacy between a man and his mother-in-law. However, such themes are conspicuous by their absence in the Nhunggabarra stories published by Langloh Parker. She may have censored the selection, since they were to be published for children.

Berndt & Berndt (1999: 387–408) acknowledge that very little work has been done on 'Aboriginal oral literature', as they call it. The first anthropologists, such as W.E. Roth, dismissed them as the occupation of women and for men who were 'too lazy to do anything else'. Also, in the few cases where stories have been considered worthy sources, the interpretation has been from the white man's scientific perspective – for instance, the anthropologist J. Mathew in 1899 interpreted a story about the eaglehawk and the crow as 'expressing the moiety cleavage' (cited in Berndt & Berndt 1999).

Well-meaning efforts, but devastating from an interpretation point of view, have also been made – for instance, the collection of stories published by A.W. Reed (1908–79), who in the 1960s rewrote the original texts of many Aboriginal stories in 'admiration for the men of old'. He appreciated the poetic quality of the stories, but he never got beyond the first level of interpretation. See A.W. Reed (1982, 1994).

Also Langloh Parker is today accused by the Nhunggabarra older people of embellishing and anglicising the stories. Langloh Parker's version of the story 'How the Nhunggabarra got Flowers', recorded before 1895, is longer and contains more details than the version of the same story that Tex learned in the 1960s (see chapter seven).

Langloh Parker never penetrated beyond the first level, because she was not allowed access to the keys to the hidden meanings of the stories she collected. Not even esteemed anthropologists like Ronald and Catherine Berndt, who testify about the continuity and consistency of stories they had encountered over a period of twenty years, were unable to 'unlock' the multi-layered interpretations, and their accounts of stories remain first-level only. They do acknowledge (1999: 33) that the stories are useful in establishing traditional country borders and that they have seen and used such 'maps'.

In some ways the Nhunggabarra stories resemble Aesop's fables because they are populated by animals. A fable is a short story or folktale with a moral at the end. One might therefore say that Aesop's fables contain two levels of meaning, the moral being the second.

Owner versus custodian

That 'a boundary is to cross' was pointed out by Nancy Williams in an article in Williams & Hunn (1982: 131–54).

4. LEARNING THE STORY

The initiation site at Coorigal Springs

We know that initiation ceremonies varied considerably across Australia. The eyewitness accounts of initiation ceremonies used as sources for this book are found in Howitt (1904: 509–642, 643–77), Berndt & Berndt (1999: 165–87); K. Langloh Parker (1905: Ch. IX). They describe dramatic events over several days, where the boys were submitted to actions which exposed them to pain and fear. Symbolically, they were 'killed' and then 'resurrected' as young men.

Langloh Parker's (1905: Ch.VIII) description of the initiation ground does not say where it is situated, but there was only one in Nhunggal country, so it should have been the site at Coorigal Springs.

A note on dowsing. From geology it is well-established that the earth is crisscrossed by shifts in geomagnetic energy fields or energy currents. They are caused by watercourses and cracks in the soil under the surface, abrupt changes in the magnetic character of rocks etc. Many energy fields in the earth are man-made these days, such as power lines, water pipes etc. We know that the nervous system in the human body is sensitive to these energy flows, although people of the modern world are generally not consciously aware of such influences. Since ancient times two instruments, the pendulum and the dowsing rod, have been used to search for energy fields in order to find water, also known as 'to divine' for water. A dowser can follow the magnetic effects of these fields because it produces noticeable responses in the rod or in the pendulum.

Swedish science journalist Göran Brusewitz has done considerable research into the scientific merits of dowsing. He can show that there is sufficient validated evidence to prove that an experienced dowser can detect energy fields. However, dowsing is still a practice, not a science, and the discourse is dominated by non-scientists. Hence, considerable scepticism exists in scientific quarters and there is no accepted theory on why and how dowsing works. One can compare the circumstances for dowsing with the ancient Chinese practice of acupuncture. Scientists have still not validated the existence of subtle energy fields in the human body, which acupuncture is said to stimulate, but acupuncture has become an accepted practice in Western medicine.

The idea that energy fields or currents underlie many of the ancient monuments and sites is old and originates from the concept of 'ley lines' in the UK, 'snake lines' in India, 'dragon lines' in China and the 'Hartmann lines' and 'Curry lines' known from Germany. Research into sacred sites such as Stonehenge and the location of churches in England indicates that at least some sacred structures may have been built along lines of geomagnetic energy. Research in Sweden also confirms that ancient remains may have been constructed with energy fields in mind. Arne Groth, at the Swedish Defence Research Establishment FOA, established that the walls of old soldiers' homes from the 1700s are situated exactly where the Curry lines pass. This minimises the energy effect inside the house. Another researcher, Dan Mattsson, has found a strong connection between energy fields and archaeological remains in Sweden and published his findings in 2000 in *Jordstrålning: Hälsa och forntida vetande* (*Radiation in the Earth: Health and Ancient Science*).

The field of detecting subtle energies with the pendulum is also called radiesthesia. The use of pendulums grew after the First World War and several pendulum professionals became celebrities in the 1920s and 1930s due to their skills in finding lost property and missing persons and in solving archaeological problems. Even Einstein considered dowsing fascinating and believed the new field of electromagnetism would somehow give us some scientific answers to why and how radiesthesia works.

Today there is an active and serious dowsing profession in many countries including the Dowsers Society of New South Wales (Australia), the American Society of Dowsers and the British Society of Dowsers. They have accumulated a considerable number of results from controlled experiments, many of them accepted by independent scientists. The field has become quite lively in recent years and one can come across amateur archaeologists all over Europe walking the fields with pendulums and dowsing rods. Mainstream archaeologists, however, tend to avoid dowsing.

The established wisdom among dowsing professionals is that when the pendulum operator holds the pendulum over the earth, an object, or a person, they are measuring the interaction of the force field of the earth, the object or person with their own nervous system. There seems to be an agreement – also by sceptic scientists – that both the dowsing rod and the pendulum amplify the signals that our nervous system detects; this is also called the 'ideamotor' effect. The debate is primarily about what those signals mean and whether one is measuring anything except one's own wishful thinking. As I have established myself after considerable training: it is possible to get a pendulum to swing in any direction without moving the hand, just by 'thinking it to swing'. A crucial requirement for the pendulum practitioner is the ability to keep one's mind still – as in meditation – when using it.

The pendulum indications that I report in the book are of 'enthusiastic amateur quality' and they do not prove anything. Being the first dowsing ever reported on these Aboriginal sacred sites, the value of the measurements is primarily as hypotheses to be tested more carefully by professionals.

Sources: Gerber (2001) discusses medical evidence for the effect of energy fields on the body. Deveraux (2001) describes ley lines. Nielsen & Polansky (1987) is a handbook for pendulum practitioners. Mattsson (2000), only in Swedish, describes research on geomagnetic energies and archaeological sites. Brusewitz (1999), also unfortunately available only in Swedish, describes a wide range of scientifically validated tests on subtle energy fields and dowsing.

The journey of knowledge

Knowledge, especially sacred knowledge, had to be respected. In general, one must be initiated to be allowed access to sacred knowledge. Even if an initiated person had learned something regarded as sacred knowledge they did not necessarily have the right to teach others. One had to be the custodian to be allowed to teach knowledge and access was graded (Rose 1996: 32). Mary Tarran describes in Rose & Clarke (1997: 85–7) how knowledge was withheld from white people: 'In those days they weren't giving out that information about country. It was a communal thing and a thing for the families and people associated with that cultural experience. It was a gift to give at the right time. It was the biggest gift because you had this very special knowledge.'

Corroborees: learning by enjoyment

The description of the dance is from Curr (1968: 139–40).

5. KNOWLEDGE ECONOMY

Quotes are from Oxley (1828: 24, 33), Eyre (1845: 250–4), Curr (1968), Grey (1841: 261–2), Mitchell (1839: vol. 1: 223). Sahlins cites Hodgkinson's observation in 1845 from northeastern New South Wales, Smyth (1878) and Curr (1968). The quote is from Sahlins (1974: 17–20). Also Diamond (1997: 96).

A person needs to, on average, obtain some 2000 to 2500 kilocalories (8400 to 10,500 kilojoules) of energy per day to survive long term.

Quote from Butlin (1993: 68–86). Butlin uses the term *owner* of land – however, according to Aboriginal tradition, we have chosen the more appropriate term *custodian* of land.

Trade is trust

Sources: Mitchell (1839: vol. 1: 92, 207–8, 213, 237, 252) and McCarthy (1938: 83–7, 98, 99, 174, 409), Flood (1999: 271, 273) Braudel (1979: Ch. 7). The map is from McCarthy (1938: 191).

A red cloth bag of pituri is on display in the collections of the South Australian Museum. It was traded from Cooper Creek near the South Australian/Queensland border, ending up at Quorn in the Flinders Ranges, a distance of 700 kilometres.

The Nhunggabarra goods trade was always based on barter, but the exchange values in pre-European times were not set according to market principles, except around Cape York, which was under the influence of Indonesians. For instance, Sahlins (1974) cites a chain of trade that linked communities along a line running approximately 650 kilometres south from the Cape York coast. Each community was limited to contacts with its immediate neighbours, thus indirectly related to bands further along the line. The trade itself proceeded in the form of gift exchange between old people standing as kinship brothers.

Even trade agents have been recorded (Clarke 2003: 110–11). The trading according to market principles that early settlers and anthropologists observed was most likely influenced by European practices.

Trade in intangibles

Quotes from Reynolds (1981: 10), Mitchell (1839, vol. 1: 72, 75), Howitt (1904: 423). T.G.H. Strehlow (Hill 2002) did more than any other scholar to study and translate Aboriginal songs. He also studied how the songs travelled from community to community. His work became the inspiration of a much-cited travelogue, *Songlines* by Bruce Chatwin (1987).

Ecofarming

Quote from Mitchell (1839: vol. I: 237–8, 291), who saw the hay racks on 19 and 30 June 1835. Flood (1999: 259–61), Clarke (2003: 57, 146–7, 203) and Mulvaney & Kamminga (1999: 87) have provided information about Aboriginal farming methods and food production.

There exists a suspicion among many palaeontologists and archaeologists that the extinction of the so-called megafauna was caused by humans. This is because the extinction coincides with the estimated arrival of humans on several continents. Scientists know that giant animals such as the giant wombat, the giant tiger and the giant crocodile, existed on the Australian continent when the first humans arrived 40,000–60,000 years ago. They died out between 20,000 and 30,000 years ago, and the reason could have been that they were not able to adapt to the changes in habitats caused by Aboriginal hunting and fires.

With the disappearance of the megafauna went the only animals that were candidates for domestication on the Australian continent. Gifford Miller from the University of Colorado analysed some 1500 fragments of fossilised eggs, some as old as 140,000 years, from three regions in South Australia. The eggs belonged to the emu and another large flightless bird, which became extinct around 50,000 years ago. His team established that the diet of the emu changed from one high in grasses to one high in leaves from fire-adapted shrubs and trees, while the diet of the extinct bird remained the same. The emu, which was able to adapt to the shift in the environment, survived. The scientists believe that fires must have become more common around then and suggest that they were caused by hunter–gatherers (reported in *Science*, vol. 309, p, 287).

Flannery (1994: 208–41, 271–98) argues, based on work originally carried out by Dave Gibson and Ken Johnson, that the huge herbivores of the megafauna kept the land open and the soil fertilised, much like the savannas of Africa and America. When they disappeared, the land turned less nutritious. The Aborigines responded by finetuning 'fire-stick farming', maintaining suitable conditions for middle-sized mammals.

Sources on the megafauna: Palaeontologist Paul S. Martin (*Discover*, February 2005), Gifford Miller (*New Scientist*, 16 July 2005: 18), Flood (1999: 187–92). Mary Gilmore wrote about the abundance of fish and animals in her memoirs, *Old Days, Old Ways* (1986: 139–43, 187).

Remains of fish traps can be found in many rivers in the area, which suggests that fish traps may once have been constructed in all rivers. The extent of the Narran River fish traps can no longer be validated, but archaeological work at Victorian Lakes has revealed similar fish traps as in Brewarrina. Considerable effort must have gone into the construction, but only some twenty people were required to operate the whole system (Flood 1999: 242). The Ngemba story about how Baayami and his sons constructed the fish traps in Brewarrina was recorded by Peter Dargin and can be found in Isaacs (2005: 52).

Historical records show that fish traps could provide more than 1.5 kilograms of fish per person per day. Plenty of evidence from the southeast indicates that assemblies of several hundred people were supported in various places by seasonal abundance of millet grass, fish, bunya pine nuts and bogong moths (Mulvaney & Kamminga 1999: 34, 80).

The study of survival rates of big and small fish was reported in *New Scientist*, June 2005.

The live larder

Quote from Keen (2004: 23). Quote about the tree trunks is from Mitchell (1839: vol. I: 55). Information about storage methods is found in Butlin (1993:68-69), Gilmore (1986: 164), Flood (1999: 263), Langloh Parker (1905: Ch. XII, XIII). Flannery (1994: 289) describes a 'story place' in the Cooktown area – the last refuge for Bennett's tree kangaroo.

Why did the Aboriginal population not grow?

The archaeological records indicate a faster population growth around 4000 to 6000 years ago. How reliable this so-called 'intensification' is as an indication of a shift from 'simple' to more 'complex' social structures is debated among archaeologists. Flood (1999:137, 248–9) leans towards the view that population growth is the only reasonable explanation. But even if a faster population growth can be assumed, it was still very slow and well in balance with the resources, otherwise the continent would have shown signs of ecological crisis.

Several Aboriginal measures for keeping their population in balance have been reported by sources compiled by the historian Geoffrey Blainey (1997: 96–123) – among others, a survey of 350 pre-industrial societies, which concludes that abortion was 'an absolutely universal practice' in hunter–gatherer societies. Blainey also regards infanticide, particularly of deformed babies, as a common practice in hunter–gatherer societies. Blainey's sources do agree that infanticide did not seem to be practised in more fertile areas with a semi-sedentary population along the Murray River (this would also apply to the Nhunggabarra and their cultural bloc). Berndt & Berndt (1999: 154) and Broome (2005: 63–65) dismiss infanticide as exceptions in traditional society, and point out that the reported infanticides occurred only after European contact and in areas where Aborigines and Europeans relations were unhappy and filled with conflict.

Assertions about infanticide are controversial and they are absolutely denied by present-day Nhunggabarra, because infanticide would have been against the law.

Why did the Nhunggabarra not develop agriculture?

The first farmers on a continent could not have made a conscious choice to do so, because they would have had no other farmers to observe. However, once farming had arisen in one part of the continent, neighbouring hunter–gatherers could see the result and judge the benefits for themselves.

Broome (2005) cites several eyewitness reports from Victorian Aborigines' first encounters with European technology.

Sources: Clarke (2003); Flood (1999: 262, 265), who cites Allen (1974); Diamond (1997: 140–68).

6. LEADERSHIP: ALL HAVE A ROLE

Quote from Tench (1996: 40–1, 57). The explorer Eyre, quoted by Reynolds (1981: 28); Berndt & Berndt (1999: 490ff). The lack of chiefs in the European sense is confirmed by Howitt (1904), Berndt & Berndt (1999) and Reynolds (1981: 113–14).

The 'huge winged monster' is a description that comes from Swan River Aborigines on seeing the first ship approach the shore. One man ran 22 kilometres inland to spread the alarming news (Reynolds 1981: 5). the 'sacred place where Baayami lived' mentioned in the Black Swans story is Wubi-Wubi Mountain.

The law

Sources for the law, other than the Nhunggabarra stories, have been Berndt & Berndt (1999: 336–66) and Tonkinson (1978: 139–51).

The Nhunggabarra Ideal Person. Quotes from Gilmore (1986: 104) and K. Langloh Parker (1905: Ch. VII).

Sanctions. Gatherings or councils convened by old people have been reported from other Aboriginal areas, but are not confirmed by the Nhunggabarra stories. They seem to have sometimes been held on ad hoc bases for particularly complicated offences involving many communities.

A leader role for everyone

Mary Gilmore (1986: 169–70) tells about teamwork. Tonkinson (1978: 142–5) describes leader behaviours among the Mardu and confirms in his study that control exerted by senior men and women is a generalised one, not concentrated in the hands of a powerful few, and 'not only is ritual leadership context-specific and therefore highly variable, but there are many "bosses"'.

Gender roles

Phyllis Kaberry was the first female anthropologist to study the knowledge of Aboriginal women. Her 1939 thesis, *Aboriginal Women Sacred and Profane*, argued against the foremost European sociologist at the time, Emile Durkheim, who had claimed that Aboriginal men were 'sacred' while the women were 'profane'. She broke new ground in that she as a female was able to get access to Aboriginal female perspectives on their role in the society. She and later female anthropologists were able to show that the male-dominated field of anthropology had missed the importance of women in Aboriginal society.

The female anthropologists, who got access to Aboriginal women, could establish that there was no difference between women and men in their spiritual connections to the land; that the women had the economic power; that men were betrothed in accordance with customary laws; that women were frequently involved in conflict resolution; and that both men and that women had sustained rights and responsibilities within the customs of the law. The women held their own secret ceremonies and their own secret objects that men or younger women were never allowed to see. They were living in equal partnership; the rights, self-respect and dignity of members of both sexes were guaranteed. The Aborigines had a 'two-sex' model in the words of Catherine Berndt (quoted by Hamilton 1981: 73), with a horizontal rather than vertical power structure.

Annette Hamilton (1981: 69–85) argues that the Australian Aborigines had a fundamental form of sociality, which rendered each sex powerful to itself, but was premised on the ability of men to dominate by violence when their interests were in irreconcilable conflict. Both sexes, however, were subject to the law – ruthless behaviour was punished.

The Nhunggabarra law stories show that the law regulated only men's abuse of power; in this way the law acted as a balance against violence by men.

The most interesting 'white' interpretation of the Nhunggabarra stories I have come across is Johanna Lambert's work, *Wise Women of the Burruguu* (1993). She bases her work on the Nhunggabarra stories collected by Langloh Parker and, coming from a female perspective, she is able to show how female power permeates the stories.

In an exquisitely argued book, Margrit Eichler (1980: 20–8) shows how the choice of words in texts written by male anthropologists display their unreflected male bias and assume male-dominance in hunter–gatherer societies when there probably was none.

Caring for most everyday illnesses was the realm of the women. The Nhunggabarra woman's medicine kit included plant infusions and wrappings of ground and pounded leaves for pain, swelling and insomnia. The plants included aromatics such as pennyroyal, saltbush, pine and eucalyptus species. The fat of goanna, echidna, fish and emu was applied to help cure head pain and stiffness, dress the hair and skin, and prevent dry skin. A directory of the medicinal plants of the Northern Territory lists 167 plants used by the Aboriginal women of the area. It is likely that the Nhunggabarra woman's medicine kit would have included a similarly impressive number of medicinal plants.

The stories suggest that Nhunggabarra society, far from being dominated by men, was far more 'female' than any observers of the remaining society structures have been able to ascertain. The stories are a more reliable source than witnesses, because they describe the society before it collapsed. As Berndt & Berndt (1999: 296) say: 'Women were considered to be innately sacred and did not require the kind of ritualised enhancement, which was believed to be essential for male novices and for men in general.'

Sources: Clarke (2003: 47–50), Kaberry (2004: xxvii–xli, 10, 20–7, 36–8, 71–4), Hamilton (1981: 69–85), Berndt & Berndt (1999: 84, 119–20, 149, 296). Medicinal plants from Ungunmerr et al. (1993), Sturt (1983:55). Nhunggabarra medicine practices are found in Langloh Parker (1905: Chs IV and V), Lambert (1993).

Role planning and record keeping

Information about cylcons primarily comes from two sources kindly provided by the Melbourne Museum: Lindsay Black who constructed the first systematic cataloguing of the cylcons, published in 1942, *Cylcons: The Mystery Stones of the Darling River Valley*, and the archaeologist Giles Hamm, *Data Documentation of Cylindro-conical stones of Australia* (1988). Flood (1999: 192) describes a find of a 20,000-year-old cylcon at Cuddie Springs.

The primary area of discovery of cylcons is around the cultural bloc of the Nhunggabarra and their neighbours, along the Darling and Culgoa rivers, from 80 kilometres northeast of Brewarrina (i.e. Nhunggal country) to 80 kilometres south of Menindee. Only very few have been found elsewhere in Australia, which suggests that the cylcons may have been unique to this area. Sixty-one per cent of the 195 cylcons investigated by Hamm are made of sandstone, a soft material, which suggests they were designed for incisions.

Our hypothesis about the record-keeping purpose of the cylcons does not explain their whole mystery, however, because only 37 per cent of the cylcons investigated by Hamm have visible incisions. Some of the incisions may have been deliberately deleted in order not to reveal the sacred information and some of the cylcons may have been recently made when the epidemics hit and not incised yet. Still, it seems that record-keeping cannot have been the only purpose for the cylcons, given the large number of cylcons not incised.

Low risk of war

Many of the early settlers reported fights between Aborigines, and the early anthropologist Howitt (1904: 326–30) claimed that warfare between tribes was fairly common in the early days before European arrival. However, the cases he mentions are private quarrels that ended in fighting or death and feuds between two larger parties concerning eloped women and hunting ground infringements, and expeditions to punish criminal offences such as murders. The convict Buckley, who remained at large for three decades from 1802 to 1835 and lived among the Aborigines in Victoria, reminisces about many fierce fights between neighbouring Aboriginal communities (Blainey 1997: 106). However, this was in the days of rapid European settlement expansion, when the Aborigines lost their best land, which must have caused severe stress and disintegration of social structures. Philip Clarke believes that most pre-European conflict was over women; men and women obstructing marriage planning or men stealing a wife.

Anthropologists Berndt & Berndt (1999: 37, 223), Kaberry (2004: 139) and Elkin (1977: 28) agree: there were no European or Asian style wars deliberately designed to take over other countries or enemies before the Europeans arrived. Land hunger as a motive did not exist in pre-European Australia and the anthropologists concur that the reason for this was the spiritual connection with the land.

Society research source is Service (1971).

Low risk of disease

Source about health: John Pickrell, *National Geographic News*, 13 July 2004 and email conversation with Jared Diamond in 2004.

There is some evidence that at least smallpox may have existed on the Australian continent before European arrival. In his book *Aboriginal Victorians* (2005), the historian Richard Broome cites studies that smallpox was first introduced into the Aboriginal community by Malaccan fishermen from Indonesia who traded with Aboriginal communities in northern Australia. For our purpose it does not matter how and where smallpox was first introduced; from Charles Sturt's and Thomas Mitchell's journals it seems clear that the disease was raging simultaneously or just ahead of the first explorers in the area inhabited by the Nhunggabarra and their neighbours.

The Aboriginal tendency to explain disease in terms of 'black magic' is well-established among European observers (see Berndt & Berndt 1999: 304–31). This suggests that disease in pre-European Australia could have been an extraordinary event requiring an extraordinary explanation. If diseases were as common in

Aboriginal Australia as in Europe today, the consequences should have been that a) people would have been constantly in fear of sorcery – they would 'know' they would experience it themselves many times in a year; b) during the course of a year more or less every person in a community would be accused of conducting sorcery; c) the wiringins would have been doing little else but countering this type of sorcery with their own ceremonies and sorcery.

The economic effects of these consequences would have been a substantial withdrawal of male production capacity. This does not seem logical in societies as careful with their energy balance as the Aborigines. Is it not more likely that sorcery was regarded as the reason of disease, because disease was so rare before the Europeans introduced their viruses?

Sources for assessing the risk of diseases are: Diamond (1997, 2004). Mulvaney & Kamminga (1999: 67) provide the example of the Cadigal band. Archaeological evidence about diets of Palaeolithic hunter–gatherers is from *www.medicinenet. com/script/main/art.asp?articlekey=23820&page=3*, accessed 3/1/2005.

The safety net: tuckandee

Tuckandee might have been an institution unique to the Nhunggabarra and the other communities in their cultural bloc. It may have existed in other Aboriginal areas, but the only other reference to the concept and the word that I have been able to find is in Langloh Parker's (1905) *The Euahlayi Tribe*, where she lists a few Yuwaalaraay words and an explanation in the glossary: 'Tuckandee; a young man of the same totem, reckoned as a sort of brother.'

Build community

The American anthropologist Elman Service (1971) developed an evolutionary theory of society development, classifying societies according to gradually increasing levels of complexity.

Australian bands, before the arrival of the Europeans disrupted their social structure, were generally *patrilocal*, which means two things: marriage had to take place outside the band and, at the time of marriage, the daughters moved from their families to the family of her husband. The children therefore would grow up in a family group on the same land where the father grew up. The whole Australian continent contained bands of this type (Service 1971: 48–9).

The old people claimed that the Nhunggabarra did not move frequently, and when they moved, the whole community moved; this suggests that they were semi-sedentary. The 'villages' reported by Thomas Mitchell along the Barwon/Darling, close to or on Nhunggal country also point in this direction. He also rode through a village, from where the inhabitants had recently fled (1839: vol. 1: 76–7, 225, 240). Other observations suggest tribal societies in Aboriginal Australia; villages with dozens of huts have been excavated adjacent to the eel farms in Victoria, suggesting sedentary populations of several hundred people (this is outside Nhunggal country).

Since the Nhunggabarra had developed the 'band organisation' to a more complex level, their organisation may be closer to what Service calls a *dialectical tribe* (1971: 58): 'collections of bands that share language and culture to the extent that they have a felt unity as against others...[A dialectical tribe] seems to cluster around 500 [people]'.

There is no evidence of the next level of societal complexity, *chiefdoms*, having emerged in any part of Australia. A chiefdom would have been considerably larger than a tribe – ranging from several thousand to tens of thousands of people. The chief would have been a centralised authority and held a recognised office by hereditary right. He would have secured monopoly on force and on critical information. Unlike the tribe's 'big man' or wiringin he would have been distinguished by special dress and a larger hut and he would own some luxury items.

There are many examples where societies revert from being centralised organisation and disintegrate. Jared Diamond cites his own experience in New Guinea, where Fayu hunter–gatherers live in small family groups in constant war with each other. The Fayu lack conflict resolution mechanisms entirely, so blood feuds have reduced their numbers from around 2000 to today's number of around 400. Tim Flannery (1994: 245–6) cites the Maori in New Zealand, who began fighting each other when they had overexploited the resources.

When the British arrived in Australia they found no chiefdoms, only societies that lacked a warrior class and had no leaders with experience in organised warfare, and little in terms of weapons suited for war.

People in Aboriginal Australia apparently saw no reason to defend themselves against conquests from their neighbours. Mitchell (1839, vol. 1: 240) noted that the habitations he came across suggested the Aborigines must be living in peace, because if they were in war 'such habitations could neither be permanent nor safe'. No defence constructions, such as forts or even simple barricades, have ever been discovered on the Australian continent. Unlike the fiercely fighting Maori of New Zealand, who lived in chiefdoms and were experienced conquerors of the island populations nearby, the dispersed Australian Aborigines were an easy match for the British soldiers.

There are two theory schools about the formation of societies. The *conflict schools* (such as Elman Service's theory) argue that dissent and conflict are the fundamental features of social systems. According to them, states were originally formed from conflicts between groups of people, competing for the best land or for increasingly scarce resources. As population density increased and arable land came into short supply, competition over land ensued. Eventually, the best-governed society prevailed and conquered the others, following the Darwinian theory of natural selection. It sounds absurd, but Service cites 'lab tests' to confirm this theory: if two insect species compete for resources in a confined space, eventually one of the species will conquer the other. (The relevance for human societies of this lab experiment is however not discussed!) One picture emerging from history is that the formation of the earliest forms of states, chiefdoms, always involved war and conquest, either at the formation or at some later point. The close link between conquests and chiefdoms is also argued by Robert Carneiro in Cohen & Service (1978: 205–23).

The *integration theory schools* agree that state formation involves countless conflict. Their argument is that the state organisation is so clearly superior to the alternatives that the state, despite conflicts, eventually arises out of a widespread consensus of values. Both schools do agree, however, that conflict/consensus seem to co-exist. A successful conquest is eventually followed by integration.

Another reason why centralised organisation is inevitable according to Cohen & Service (1978) is the problem of how to resolve the inefficiency of goods exchange between two individuals when the values have to be reciprocally equal. The theory prescribes that large societies can function only if they have a redistributive economy, where one individual's needs are matched against another's by a centralised mechanism, such as a money system. The theory fails to explain, however, how the Nhunggabarra people, without a money system, could still be active in a decentralised system of trade that did not function according to market principles, yet in which goods and intangibles moved across the whole Australian continent.

A final reason mandating complex organisation for large societies has to do with population density. A very densely populated area can function only under central power and complex organisation. This makes sense, but the argument is circular and can just as well work the other way: the preventing of a society from developing into a more densely populated society by avoiding centralised power.

Preventing centralised power

In 594 BC, a series of poor wheat crops in the city state of Athens saw the peasants increasingly having to sell themselves to slavery in order to survive, and the ruling wealthy class progressively more in debt and threatened by violent gangs. In desperation, the wealthy class agreed to hand over all political power to a new *Archon* (the sole ruler), Solon, with a mission to reform government. Solon's constitution was the first to recognise equality of law for all classes of citizens. It also included institutions which balanced power between *demos*, the common people, and the wealthy and the noble. His constitution included the first version of an elected Lower House or House of Commons – the *Assembly* – and the first Supreme Court for interpretation the laws. *Source:* Rhodes (2004)

A community of communities

Australian-based anthropologists in the late 1800s tried to understand Australian Aborigines in the term that was fashionable at that time – that is, 'nation'. The term 'nation', however, does not fit at all the society organisation of Aboriginal Australia and it has become highly emotionally charged. Still, it has survived into our days and is even used in the *Encyclopaedia of Aboriginal Australia* and its accompanying map: 'Aboriginal nations of Australia' (Horton 2000). We regard the term unsuitable for our purpose and have chosen the term favoured by Berndt & Berndt (1999: 35), 'cultural bloc', which describes the reality of the community of communities much better that the word 'nation'.

We have also considered the term 'confederacy'. Berndt & Berndt (1999: 35) refer to the Narrinyeri society on the Lower River Murray in South Australia by this term. However, 'confederacy' is a Western concept and may infer a state-like agglomeration, such as the American Confederacy in the 1800s. It suggests a type of society organisation that did not exist in Aboriginal Australia.

Our best description of the Nhunggabarra and their neighbours, then, remains *communities, which formed a cultural bloc*. The only other possible alternative, Service's term 'dialectical tribe', is too academic for a book of our type.

Innovation: living at stone-age level

Quote is from Grey (1841: 341). The 'boomerang propeller' is mentioned by Flannery (1998: 171). The 'real' propeller was invented and patented by the Swede John Ericsson in 1836.

Throwing sticks were invented by Hopi Indians in Arizona, Eskimos and peoples of Egypt, India, Indonesia, Vanuatu, Denmark, Holland and Germany. It is not possible to say how many of them were independently invented. The oldest throwing stick on record is a mammoth tusk carved in the shape of a boomerang excavated in Poland, estimated to be 23,000 years old. The oldest wooden throwing stick is Australian, at least 10,000 years old, and it is also the oldest with a returning capacity. *Source:* Jones (1996)

Breakthrough innovation is random

The speed by which new technology is developed varies greatly in the industrialised world and no less than fourteen explanatory factors for this have been suggested by historians of technology. One is long life expectancy, which enhances an inventor's accumulation of knowledge and increases the chance that the same individual will come up with more inventions. Five factors have to do with organisation of a society; one of them is cheap slave labour that discouraged innovation. The remaining four factors are claimed to speed up innovation: 1) the existence of patents and property laws; 2) modern encouragement of technical training; 3) financial rewards provided by modern capitalism (USA); and 4) strong individualism (USA), which makes it socially acceptable for inventors to keep their fortunes instead of sharing them.

Another four factors are ideological: 1) risk-taking behaviour is more widespread in some societies; 2) the scientific approach is a unique feature of post-Renaissance Europe; 3) strong emphasis on traditions is said to have prevented the Chinese from utilising their relative competitive advantage in medieval times to grow into a world power; 4) some religions, such as Judaism, are said to be more open to innovation, while others (such as Islam and Hinduism) are said to be less compatible with innovation.

The remaining four factors appear to have inconsistent influences; sometimes they stimulate innovation, sometimes they stifle it. They are: 1) war; 2) centralised government; 3) climate; and 4) resource abundance.

The major source is Everett Rogers (1983). Other sources are Diamond (1997: 246, 252ff), Grey (1841: 341), Flood (1999: 16, 236, 257–8), Jones (1978) cited in Mulvaney & Kamminga (1991: 101), Clarke (2003: 81, 181). Reynolds (1981: 37) describes the adoption of dogs into the culture.

7. THE FOURTH LEVEL

Eyewitness accounts from Elkin (1977: 9–11, 46, 96) and Howitt (1904: 386ff).

Explorers Grey (1841: 341), Mitchell (1839, vol. 2: 338) and early anthropologists like Howitt (1904: 357–8) commented on the medicine men's use of crystals. Howitt witnessed an event in which a wiringin seemingly caused a quartz crystal to pass from his hand into his body.

Over the last 30 years, growing research is discovering the properties of crystals that may have been known to ancient cultures. Gerber (2001: 337–49) describes how quartz crystals have piezoelectric qualities – that is, when quartz crystals are subjected to mechanical pressure they produce a measurable electrical voltage. The crystalline structure has been found to respond in unique and precise ways to a wide spectrum of energies, including heat, light, pressure, sound, electricity, gamma rays and even the subtle energies of consciousness. Researchers at IBM and elsewhere have established that a properly cut crystal can release negative patterns in the energy flows in a person.

Quotes are from Elkin (1977: 6–7, 46, 58), Howitt (1904: 386ff), Mitchell (1839, vol. 1: 145) and Barker (1977: 71).

Dreams play an important role in Western societies as well as in Aboriginal spiritual life. A source for how dreams are used in communication, including tele-pathic dreams, is *Our Dreaming Mind* by R. van de Castle (1994).

The spirit of Wubi-Wubi: a touch of the fourth level

The Balima in the story is an area in the sky with no visible stars, also known as 'the Coalsack', in the generally bright background of the Southern Cross. The Nhunggabarra and some other Australian Aborigines saw the head of an emu whose body and neck stretched the whole length of the southern Milky Way, expanding its wings and feathers in Sagittarius and with spindly legs and splayed feet. The Coalsack cannot be seen from the city, and it is not visible in moonlight. On the best nights in the darkest places it appears as pure blackness (Malin 1993: 94).

Thomas Mitchell (1839, vol 2: 214) climbed Wubi-Wubi seven years after Charles Sturt, in 1835. He was also impressed by the view, but not by the name Sturt had invented, *'that strangely named hill, never seen by Oxley, and in fact, not a table-land'*, so he lobbied to have it changed and eventually succeeded. The mountain was renamed Mount Oxley, the name by which it is known today.

'Eaglehawk' is Australian English for the wedge-tailed eagle, Australia's largest bird of prey. Its wingspan can reach 2.3 metres.

The mystery of the 'rockpools' on Wubi-Wubi Mountain has fascinated explorers and geologists alike. They may have been formed by gas explosions, but no gas has been found in the area. A plausible, but unproven, geological explanation is that extreme heat followed by rapid cooling may have caused the exposed surface of the rock to burst. Indeed, unexplained sounds have been reported in the area by both Aborigines and settlers. Also, Sturt reports in his diary that he heard *'the report of a gun once'* at 3pm after a *'remarkably fine'* day, when he was travelling in the area on 7 January 1829 (Sturt 1983, vol. 2: 98).

8. THE SPIRIT OF DEATH ARRIVES . . .

Quote from Mitchell (1839, vol. 1: 45). The date for the Nhunggabarra's first encounter with white men is inferred by combining the written sources. It is not recorded in the oral tradition.

Nhunggal country today

Examples from Mulvaney & Kamminga (1999: 87), Flood (1999: 251), Jones (1969), Gilmore (1986: 163). Diamond (2005: ch 13) describes the unsustainable politics of Australian governments and even makes an estimate for a sustainable population: 8 million for the whole continent. The current population is 20 million.

Employment and income multipliers are used to assess impacts on the community of an industry or a farm. The employment multiplier reflects a change in the total number of people employed given a direct change in employment or output, such as a trucking firm hiring or firing drivers because there is an increase or decrease in wool production. Multipliers for agriculture tend to vary between 1.5 and 2.5. The Australian national employment multiplier for agriculture is a relatively low 1.23 (due to high petroleum import), meaning that on average an additional 0.23 people is employed indirectly for every farm worker employed. A fairly high multiplier of 1.5–2.0 is used for the calculation to be sure the effect is not underestimated. *Source: Yearbook Australia* 1998.

Cotton: Hi-tech, no-touch

Example from Gilmore (1986). Quotes from Mitchell (1846, vol. I: 216, 222, 293).

John Naisbitt (1982: 35–36) coined the concept 'high tech/high touch' to describe a technology-balancing long-term trend in society: whenever a new technology is introduced, there must be a counterbalancing human response or else the technology will be rejected by people. The cotton industry is an example of a technology not in touch with humanity; hence my phrase, 'high-tech, no-touch'.

The most common herbicides in Australia contain Atrazine as the active ingredient. It is used to control weeds in summer crops such as sorghum, maize, sugarcane, lucerne, grass seed, pasture and potatoes, and in pine and eucalypt plantations. Facts about Atrazine come from the Australian Pesticide and Veterinary Medicines Authority, *www.apvma.gov.au/chemrev/atrazine_draftfinal2.pdf*.

Information about Endosulfan and the cotton industry is from Mary White (1997, 1999) and the following websites (all accessed from 27–29/12/04):

www.cottonaustralia.com.au
www.pan-uk.org/pestnews/pn44/pn44p21.htm
www.panda.org/about_wwf/what_we_do/freshwater/news/news.cfm?uNewsID=9208
www.rense.com/health/aussiebeef.htm

Facts about soil erosion from Eisenberg (1998: 30).

9. THE NHUNGGABARRA 'RECIPE' FOR SUSTAINABILITY

Knowledge-based theory

Sources for knowledge-based theory are: Sveiby & Lloyd (1987), Sveiby (1997, 2001), Allee (2002) and Von Krogh, Ichijo & Nonaka (2000).

In 1987 I chose the term 'knowhow organisations' rather than 'knowledge organisations' because I wanted to emphasise the importance of action-orientation and practice in organisations, rather than theoretical knowledge. Today the term 'knowledge-based organisations' has become a more common concept.

How general is the model?

Diamond (2005) is the main source. Japan is the only society with top-down management that historically has avoided collapse. It is blessed with robust ecological conditions with high rainfall and good soil fertility and the land has been spared grazing goats and sheep. The Tokugawa family and the elite were able to avoid deforestation, by requiring active forest management including replantation in the 1600s (Diamond 2005: 300–6).

10. SUSTAIN OUR WORLD!

Sources for Karl Popper's philosophy is Luebke (1991) and conversations with Andreas Suchanek, professor in ethics and sustainability at Leipzig University.

Exploit or sustain?

Sources: The analysis of soil ecology is from Eisenberg (1998:23). Marine life outside USA's coastline is from marine palaeoecologist Jeremy Jackson in *Discover*, February 2005. Shell Oil in Diamond Louisiana – *Discover*, January 2005. Airborne mercury levels – *Scientific American*, January 2005.

Innovation: responsible or reckless?

Source about DDT in USA: Rogers (1983). Internet sources for chemical substances were accessed 12/12/2004: *news.bbc.co.uk/1/hi/health/1167962.stm*; *news.bbc.co.uk/1/hi/world/europe/3006419.stm*

Also Christensen (1997).

Western economies are becoming intangible

Leonard Nakamura (2004) applies an indirect method to estimate intangible investments from three perspectives: expenditures (how much users pay for investments), labour inputs (what workers' occupations are and how much they are being paid), and corporate operating margins (as viewed through tax accounts and public financial reports). He notes that: 'All these estimates suggest strongly, if imprecisely, that at least 6 percent to 10 percent of US GDP is spent annually on intangibles, and possibly substantially more.' He then uses the estimates to correlate the ratio of consumption

Composition of Australian GDP, 1788 and 2003

Hours spent on:	Min.	Max.	Average	Proportion (%)
Food	2	5	3.5	22
Tools	1	3	2	13
Sleep	8	8	8	50
Intangibles	13	8	10.5	66
Hours per day	24	24	24	100
Total production hrs	16	16	16	
Intangibles of total	81%	50%		

Composition of value added in GDP	Aboriginal Australia 1788 (%)	Australia 2003 (%)	OECD median 2003 (%)
Intangible services	66	70.9	68.5
Tangible goods	13	25.7	28.1
Food	22	3.4	3.3

Sources: OECD Basic Structural Statistics 2005, explorers' journals and own estimates.

to true gross domestic product, including both tangible and intangible investment. His assumption is that this ratio should be relatively stable.

Composition of the Aboriginal economy pre-1788 is an approximation based on estimates presented in Chapter 5.

Leadership: can all have a role?

The labels on organisations come from organisation theorist Gareth Morgan (1986).

A German study (Peneder et al. 2001) into the knowledge-based sector for the period 1970–95 concluded that the rise of the service economy has been primarily driven by the growth of knowledge-based services, out-performing manufacturing growth and other service categories. In many cases, the growth differential is quite substantial. Apart from minor exceptions, knowledge-based services have consistently been the fastest growing sector of all industries, with a mean annual growth of 3.34 per cent of real output (or 6.96 per cent if measured at current prices). In contrast, distributive services have only grown by 2.38 per cent (5.32 per cent), which is similar to the mean of 2.48 per cent per annum (5.01 per cent) in personal and social services.

Other sources: Semler (2004) and Sveiby & Lloyd (1987).

Freedom to choose: for excess or happiness

The paradox of declining happiness in market democracies has been studied by, among others, Kahneman & Tversky (1984) and Barry Schwartz (2002, 2004). Clive Hamilton cites a large number of papers in his 2003 book *Growth Fetish*.

Respect: balance and strength

Sources on stress-related problems in modern society are Victorian Government (2001), *www.betterhealth.vic.gov.au*, and HSE report, *www.hse.gov.uk/stress/index.htm* (accessed 20/8/05).

Sara Lawrence-Lightfoot is one of the few authors to address respect in society. Her book from 2000, *Respect*, describes respect in teacher–learner situations.

Community building the European way

Main source is Reid (2004).

Sustain our world

The quote from James Cook (1770) is his journal entry, cited in Reed (1969: 136).

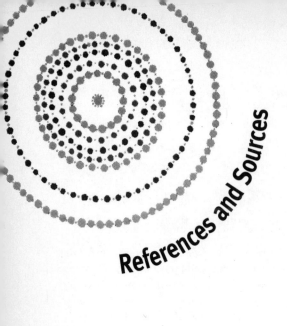

References and Sources

Allee, V. (2002). *The Future of Knowledge: Increasing Prosperity through Value Networks*. Butterworth-Heinemann, Boston.

Barker, J. (1977). *The Two Worlds of Jimmie Barker as Told to Janet Matthews*. Australian Institute of Aboriginal Studies, Canberra.

Berndt, R.M. & Berndt, C.H. (1999). *The World of the First Australians*. Fifth revised edition. Aboriginal Studies Press, Australia.

Black, L. (1942). *Cylcons: The Mystery Stones of the Darling River Valley*. Privately published. Accessed at Museum of Victoria.

Blainey, G. (1997). *Triumph of the Nomads*. Third edition. Pan Macmillan, Sydney.

Blake, B. (1981). *Australian Aboriginal Languages: A General Introduction*. Angus & Robertson, Sydney.

Book of Australia, The (1997). Watermark Press, Sydney.

Braudel, F. (1979). *Les Structures du Quotidien. Le Possible et L'Impossible*. Swedish translation 1982. Gidlunds, Stockholm.

Broome, R. (2005). *Aboriginal Victorians: A History Since 1800*. Allen & Unwin, Sydney.

Brusewitz, G. (1993). *En Ny Världsbild Växer Fram*. ICA Bokförlag, Västerås, Sweden.

Butlin, N.G. (1983). *Our Original Aggression: Aboriginal Population of South East Australia 1788–1850*. Allen & Unwin, Sydney.

Butlin, N.G. (1993). *Economics and the Dreamtime: A Hypothetical History*. Cambridge University Press, Cambridge, UK.

Carneiro, R.L. (1978). 'Expansion as an Expression of the Principle of Competitive Exclusion'. In Cohen, R. & Service, E., *Origins of the State: The Anthropology of Political Evolution*. Philadelphia Institute for Human Issues.

Castle, R.L. van de (1994). *Our Dreaming Mind*. Random House, New York.

Christensen, C.M. (1997). *The Innovator's Dilemma: When New Technologies Cause Great Firms to Fail*. Harvard Business School Press, Boston.

Clarke, P. (2003). *Where the Ancestors Walked: Australia as an Aboriginal Landscape*. Allen & Unwin, Sydney.

Cohen, R. & Service, E.R. (1978). *Origins of the State: The Anthropology of Political Evolution*. Institute for the Study of Human Issues, Philadelphia.

Curr, Edward M. (1968). *Recollections of Squatting in Victoria: Then Called the Port Phillip District (from 1841 to 1851)*. George Robertson, Melbourne. Facsimile of original 1883.

Deveraux, P. (2001). *Shamanism and the Mystery Lines*. Quantum, London.

Diamond, J. (1997). *Guns, Germs and Steel: The Fates of Human Societies*. Norton, New York.

Diamond, J. (2004). *The Impact of Epidemic Diseases*. Key note at Biology Conference in Helsinki 2004, and subsequent correspondence.

Diamond, J. (2005). *Collapse: How Societies Choose to Fail or Succeed*. Viking, New York.

Eichler, M. (1980). *The Double Standard: A Feminist Critique of Feminist Social Science*. Croom Helm, London.

Eisenberg, E. (1998). *The Ecology of Eden*. Vintage Books, New York.

Elkin, A.P. (1977). *Aboriginal Men of High Degree: Initiation and Sorcery in the World's Oldest Tradition*. University of Queensland Press, St Lucia.

Etheridge, R. (1918). *The Dendroglyphs or 'Carved Trees' of New South Wales*. Government Printer, Sydney.

Eyre, E.J. (1845). *Journals of Expeditions of Discovery into Central Australia, and Overland from Adelaide to King George's Sound, in the Years 1840–1*. Vols 1 & 2. Facsimile edition. Boone, London.

Flannery, T. (1994). *The Future Eaters: An Ecological History of the Australasian Lands and People*. New Holland, Sydney.

Flannery, T. (1998). *The Explorers: Stories of Discovery and Adventure from the Australian Frontier*. Text Publishing, Melbourne.

Flood, J. (1999). *Archaeology of the Dreamtime: The Story of Prehistoric Australia and its People*. Angus & Robertson, Sydney.

Gamilaraay/Yuwaalaraay/Yuwaalayaay Dictionary (2003). Compiled by Ash, A., Giacon, J., Lissarrague, A. and the Yuwaalaraay Language Program, Walgett. IAD Press, Alice Springs.

Gerber, R.G. (2001). *Vibrational Medicine. Handbook of Subtle Energy Therapies*. Bear and Company, Vermont, USA.

Gilmore, M. (1986). *Old Days, Old Ways*. Illustrations by Robert Avitable. Angus & Robertson, Sydney.

Grey, Sir G. (1841). *Journals of Two Expeditions of Discovery in NorthWest and Western Australia, During the Years 1837, 38 and 39 . . . with Observations on the Moral and Physical Condition of the Aboriginal Inhabitants*. Boone, London.

Hamilton, A. (1981). *A Complex Strategic Situation: Gender and Power in Aboriginal Australia*. In Grieve & Grimshaw (eds), *Australian Women: Feminist Perspectives*. Oxford University Press, Melbourne, pp. 69–85.

Hamilton, C. (2003). *Growth Fetish*. Allen & Unwin, Sydney.

Hamm, G. (1988). *Data Documentation of Cylindro-conical Stones of Australia*. Masters Thesis. Museum of Victoria.

Hawken, P., Lovins, A. & Lovins, H.L. (1999). *Natural Capitalism: Creating the Next Industrial Revolution*. Back Bay Books, Boston.

Hill, B. (2002). *Broken Song. T.G.H. Strehlow and Aboriginal Possession*. Vintage, Sydney.

Hodgkinson, C. (1845). *Australia, from Port Macquarie to Moreton Bay: With Descriptions of the Natives...* Boone, London.

Horton, D. (2000). *Aboriginal Australia*. Australian Institute of Aboriginal and Torres Strait Islanders, Canberra.

Howitt, A.W. (1904). *The Native Tribes of South-East Australia*. Reprinted 1996. Australian Studies Press, Canberra.

Isaacs, J. (ed.) (2005). *Aboriginal Dreaming: 40,000 Years of History by Aboriginal Story Tellers*. New Holland, Sydney.

Jones, P. (1996). *Boomerang: Behind an Australian Icon*. Wakefield Press, Adelaide.

Jones, R. (1969). *Fire-Stick Farming*. Australian Natural History, vol. 16, pp. 224–8.

Kaberry, P. (2004). *Aboriginal Women Sacred and Profane*. Facsimile edition of original 1939. Routledge, London.

Kahnemann, D. & Tversky, A. (1984). 'Choices, Values and Frames'. In *American Psychologist*, vol. 39, pp. 341–50.

Keen, I. (2004). *Aboriginal Economy & Society: Australia at the Threshold of Colonisation*. Oxford University Press, Melbourne.

Laine-Sveiby, K. (1991). *Företag i Kulturmöten*. Doctoral thesis. Stockholm University.

Lambert, J.(1993). *Wise Women of the Dreamtime*. (Commentary on the stories collected by K. Langloh Parker.) Inner Traditions International, Rochester, Vermont.

Langloh Parker, K. (1905). *The Euahlayi Tribe: A Study of Aboriginal Life in Australia*. www.sacred-texts.com/aus/tet/index.htm.

Langloh Parker, K. (1978). *Australian Legendary Tales*. Bodley Head and Angus & Robertson. Contains both her *Australian Legendary Tales: Folklore of the Nhunggahburrahs as told to the Piccaninnies* (1896) and *More Australian Legendary Tales* (1898).

Lawler, R. (1991). *Voices of the First Day. Awakening in the Aboriginal Dreamtime*. Inner Traditions International. Rochester, Vermont.

Lawrence-Lightfoot, S. (2000). *Respect: An Exploration*. Perseus Books, Cambridge, Massachusetts.

Levi Strauss, C. (1980). *The Savage Mind*. University of Chicago Press, Chicago.

Lourandos, H. (1997). *Continent of Hunter–Gatherers. New Perspectives in Australian Prehistory*. Cambridge University Press, Cambridge, UK.

Luebke, P. (ed.) (1991). *Vår tids Filosofi (Philosophy of our Time)*. Forum, Stockholm.

McCarthy, F.D. (1938–40). '"Trade" in Aboriginal Australia and "Trade" Relationships with Torres Strait, New Guinea and Malaya'. In *Oceania*, vol. 9, pp. 405–38; vol. 10, pp. 80–104, 171–95.

Malin, D. (1993). *A View of the Universe*. Sky Publishing, Cambridge University Press, Cambridge, USA.

Mattsson, D. (2000). *Jordstrålning. Hälsa och forntida vetande*. AWJ-Länstryckeriet, Nyköping, Sweden.

Mitchell, Sir T. (1839). *Three Expeditions into the Interior of Australia*. Vols 1 and 2. Limited facsimile edition. Boone, London.

Mitchell, Sir T. (1847). 'Account of the Exploring Expedition into the Interior of New South Wales'. In *Tasmanian Journal of Natural Science*, vol. 3, no. 3, pp. 165–82.

Morgan, G. (1986). *Images of Organization*. Sage, USA.

Mudrooroo (1995). *Us Mob*. Angus & Robertson, Sydney.

Mulvaney, D.J. & Kamminga, J. (1999). *Prehistory of Australia*. Allen & Unwin, Sydney.

Myers, F. (1986a). 'Always Ask: Resource Use and Land Ownership among Pintupi Aborigines of the Australian Western Desert'. In Williams, N.M. & Hunn, E.S. (1982 eds), *Resource Managers: North American and Australian Hunter-Gatherers*. AIAS. Canberra.

Myers, F. (1986b). *Pintupi Country, Pintupi Self*. Smithsonian Institution Press, Washington.

Naisbitt, J. (1982). *Megatrends: Ten New Directions Transforming Our Lives*. Warner Books, New York.

Nakamura, L. (2004). *The Rise in Gross Private Investment in Intangible Assets Since 1978*. Federal Reserve Bank, Philadelphia.

Nielsen, G. & Polansky, J. (1987). *Pendulum Power*. Destiny Books, Rochester, USA.

Oxley, J. (1828). *Journals of Two Expeditions into the Interior of New South Wales Undertaken by Order of The British Government in the Years 1817–18*. John Murray, London.

Peneder, M., Kaniovski, S. & Dachs, B. (2001). 'What Follows Tertiarisation? Structural Change and the Role of Knowledge-based Services'. In *The Services Industries Journal*, vol. 23, no. 2, pp. 47–66.

Radcliffe-Brown, A.R. (1930). 'Former Numbers and Distribution of the Australian Aborigines'. In *Australian Statistical Yearbook*. Government Printer, Canberra.

Reed, A.W. (1982). *Aboriginal Myths, Legends & Fables*. Reed New Holland, Sydney.

Reed, A.W. (1994). *Aboriginal Stories*. Reed New Holland, Sydney.

Reid, A.W. (1969). *Captain Cook in Australia: Extracts from the Journals of Captain James Cook Giving a Full Account in his Own Words of his Adventures and Discoveries in Australia*. A.H. & A.W. Reid, Wellington.

Reid, J.R. (2004). *The United States of Europe: The Superpower Nobody Talks About*. Penguin, London.

Reynolds, H. (1981). *The Other Side of the Frontier: An Interpretation of the Aboriginal Response to the Invasion and Settlement of Australia*. Penguin, Melbourne.

Rhodes, P.J. (ed.) (2004). *Athenian Democracy*. Edinburgh University Press, Edinburgh.

Rogers, E. (1983). *Diffusion of Innovations*. 3rd edition. Free Press, New York.

Rose, D.B. (1996). *Nourishing Terrains: Australian Aboriginal Views of Landscape and Wilderness*. Australian Heritage Commission, Canberra.

Rose, D.B. & Clarke, A. (eds) (1997). *Tracking Knowledge in North Australian Landscapes: Studies in Indigenous and Settler Ecological Knowledge Systems*. Australian National University, Northern Territory.

Ross et al. (1986). *Outback Heritage: Bygone Years*. Bewarrina Historical Society Development & Advisory Publications of NSW, Dubbo.

Sahlins, M. (1974). *Stone Age Economics: The Original Affluent Society*. Tavistock Publications, London.

Schwartz, B. (2004). 'The Tyranny of Choice'. In *Scientific American*, April.

Schwartz, B., Ward, A. & Monterosso, J. et al. (2002). 'Maximising Versus Satisficing: Happiness is a Matter of Choice'. In *Journal of Personality and Social Psychology*, vol. 83, pp. 1178–97.

Semler, R. (2004). *The Seven-Day Weekend: Changing the Way Work Works*. Portfolio, New York.

Service, E.R. (1971). *Primitive Social Organization*. 2nd edition. Random House, New York.

Sim, I. (1999). *Yuwaalayaay, The Language of the Narran River* (ed. John Giacon). Walgett High School, Walgett.

Smyth, R.B. (1878). *The Aborigines of Victoria*. Government Printer, Melbourne.

Sturt, C. (1983). *Journal of an Expedition into the Northwestern Interior of New South Wales 1828*. Facsimile edition. Sullivans Cove, Adelaide.

Sveiby, K-E (1997). *The New Organisational Wealth: Managing and Measuring Knowledge-based Assets*. Berrett-Koehler, San Fransisco.

Sveiby, K-E (2001). 'A Knowledge-based Theory of the Firm to Guide Strategy Formulation'. *Journal of Intellectual Capital*, vol. 2, no. 4.

Sveiby, K-E & Lloyd, T. (1987). *Managing Knowhow*. Bloomsbury, London.

Tench, W. (1996). *1788: A Narrative of the Expedition to Botany Bay and a Complete Account of the Settlement at Port Jackson*. Edited and introduced by Tim Flannery 1996. Text Publishing, Melbourne.

Tindale, N.B. (1940). *Distribution of Australian Aboriginal Tribes: A Field Survey*. Royal Society of South Australia, vol. 64, no. 1, pp. 140–231.

Tindale, N.B. (1974). *Aboriginal Tribes of Australia: Their Terrain, Environmental Controls, Distribution, Limits, and Proper Names*. University of California Press, Berkeley.

Tonkinson, R. (1978). *The Mardjudjara Aborigines: Living the Dream in Australia's Desert*. Rinehart & Winston, New York.

Ungunmerr, M-R. et al. (1993). *Traditional Aboriginal Medicines in the Northern Territory of Australia*. Conservation Commission, Palmerston, Northern Territory.

Victorian Government (2001). *Work-related stress*. *www.betterhealth.vic.gov.au/*, accessed 15 Oct 05.

Von Krogh, G., Ichijo, K. & Nonaka, I. (2000). *Enabling Knowledge Creation*. Oxford University Press, New York.

White, M. (1997). *Listen: Our Land is Crying. Australia's Environmental Problems and Solutions*. Simon & Schuster, Sydney.

White, M. (1999). *After the Greening*. Simon & Schuster, Sydney.

Williams, N.M. & Hunn, E.S. (eds) (1982). *Resource Managers: North American and Australian Hunter–Gatherers*. AIAS, Canberra.

Williams, N.M. & Mununggurr, D. (1989). 'Understanding Yolngu Signs of the Past'. In Layton (ed.) *Who Needs the Past?*, Unwin Hyman, London.

Worldwatch Institute (2004). *The State of the World 2004*. Norton, New York.

Yearbook Australia (1998). *The Impact of the 1995–96 Farm Season on Australian Production*. Special Article. Canberra.

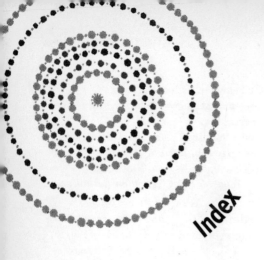

Index